Willia Purves

Revenue of the Scottish Crown

1681

Willia Purves

Revenue of the Scottish Crown
1681

ISBN/EAN: 9783337232863

Printed in Europe, USA, Canada, Australia, Japan

Cover: Foto ©Suzi / pixelio.de

More available books at **www.hansebooks.com**

REVENUE

OF

THE SCOTTISH CROWN, 1681

REVENUE

OF

THE SCOTTISH CROWN, 1681

BY

SIR WILLIAM PURVES

EDITED BY

D. MURRAY ROSE

WILLIAM BLACKWOOD AND SONS
EDINBURGH AND LONDON
MDCCCXCVII

An

Accompt of his Majesties Propper Rentes
arryseing from the few & blench duties
of the severall landes holden
few & blench of his
Majestie in his King-
dome of
Scotland

With

The Deductiones, Alterationes & Differences
betwixt the presentt rentall and the former,
preceeding King James of blissed
memory his goeing into
England in
Anno
1603

Extracted
out of the Rolles & Registers
be Sr. William Purves
his Majestis Sollicitor
in anno
1681

INTRODUCTION.

Sir William Purves of Woodhouselee, who became Solicitor-General for Scotland in the reign of Charles II., was directed to inquire into the condition of the King's revenue. In 1667 his researches in this connection resulted in a folio volume of 71 pages, entituled " Ane Abbreviat of his Majesties proper and constant rent peyit be several feuars for the respective lands, and be the sheriffs for the blench dewties, castlewairds and others out of the respective shires as the same compts in the present Rolls, with the deductions and differences betwixt the same and the former Rolls preceding King James of blissed memorie his goeing to England in anno 1603."

The question of the condition of the patrimony of the Crown possessed great interest for Sir William, and in 1681 he drew up a more elaborate account of the Revenue, which is now in the British Museum. The authorities of this great institution, with that courtesy for which they are distinguished, at once consented to the publication of the volume. The title is—" An Accompt of his Majesties Propper Rentes arryseing from the few blench duties of the severall landes holden few blench of his Majestie in his Kingdome of Scotland; with the Deductiones,

b

Alterationes & Differences betwixt the presentt rentall and the former, preceeding King James of blissed memory his goeing into England in anno 1603." There are four copies of this MS. in the Advocates' Library, Edinburgh, but they, with others elsewhere, are incomplete.

The volume has been drawn up in the usual canting and servile style of the period; and as there is always a certain curiosity to know something of the man, or of his forebears, who acted in an official character in the reign of the Stuarts, it is well, before entering upon details in regard to this work, to tell what is known of the career of Purves.

Sir William claimed to represent the family of Purves of Purveshauch, a race long settled in Berwickshire, of whom, through the loss of family papers, no connected genealogy can now be given. They appear to have been vassals of the great Earls of March, and originally had their seat at Ercildoune, now Earlston, on the banks of the Leader, "whose waves," sang the bard, "dance shimmering in the ray," ere it joins and becomes lost in the classic Tweed. An element of romance is attached to the cradle of the race; it is a place of eerie memories—the home of the prophetic bard, Thomas the Rhymer, the father of Scottish poetry. The weird story which circles round the grey ruin, still pointed out as the remains of his "high and ancient hall," even yet fascinates the people of the Borders, and one cannot gaze on the spot where stood the Eildon tree without recalling the scene depicted 'neath its shade when "True Thomas" gallantly kissed the lips of the Fairy Queen. The legend runs that seven years spent in Elfland was the penalty he paid for his rashness, being only permitted to revisit the earth on condition of returning to his mistress when called upon. It will be remembered in how strange a manner that call was given on the evening when, with knights of great renown, he held high revel in his ancestral hall, little dreaming that in so short a space he would be roused from slumber to bid

> "Farewell to Leader's silver tide,
> Farewell to Ercildoune,"

and never again be seen in the haunts of living man.

We have no knowledge of the lineage of Thomas, although a remarkable personage in his own day, and his surname has been given as Learmonth and Rhymer. In regard to the first, the charter of his son Thomas, to the Trinity House of Soltra, in 1299, as well as his own signature to a charter by Petrus de Haga to the monks of Melrose, show that if his name was Learmonth, he discarded it for the more popular designation of Rhymer or Rimor, by which he is now known. If any weight be attached to the traditionary name of Learmonth, and the circumstance that the armorial bearings of the Purveses and Learmonths were similar, it is an open question whether the Purveses of Earlston were not the immediate relatives or descendants of Thomas. It is vain to speculate as to how they became possessed of the lordship of Ercildoune. From the *Liber de Dryburgh* we know that before 1318 it was held by Alan Purves, whose daughter Margaret is said to have married Petrus de Haga of Bemersyde. One would expect to find (considering the family must have occupied the Rhymer's Tower at a time when the glamour he had thrown around it was still fresh) that they were not unknown to fame in the stirring days of the gallant Brus, when neighbouring lairds were earning undying honour; but they never were a leading family, and took no conspicuous part in the chivalrous exploits which have made the memories of the gay Gordons, Swintons, and others the theme of song and story. Three names only occur—that of Alexander, probably the son of Alan, who was member of a sanguinary band associated for the purpose of killing every Berwickshire man found across the Border; Roger, who, for his stout defence of Bolton Pele, was reckoned the greatest evil-doer on the Scottish March, and was sentenced, on the capture of the place, to be hanged and drawn for resisting the English in 1318; Ucthred, whose lands were confiscated and bestowed on his cousin John because he let a prisoner escape who had been intrusted to his care by Edward of England. These were ordinary everyday incidents in the life of the men of the Merse, and were beneath the notice of the historians and the ballad-mongers of the time.

Alan Purves of Ercildoune was succeeded by his son Alexander, who in 1333, for the salvation of his own soul, as well as that of his father and mother, his ancestors and his descendants, conveyed to the church of St Mary of Dryburgh a messuage of land in Ercildoune—a grant which was afterwards confirmed by Patrick, Earl of March, his superior. Having thus invoked the prayers of the saintly monks of Dryburgh, the family settled down to peaceful vocations, and we trace no further record of them until 1428, when a John Purves appears as witness in the process between the monks of Melrose and the Haliburtons relating to the neighbouring lands of Hassington and Pittlesheugh. Another interval elapses, and in 1466 we find the Abbot of Kelso convey to Alexander Purves and his brother Hugh certain rights in the lordship of Mellerstain and Fans. Two years later, on 21st June, David Purves appears as a witness along with lairds of high standing—Cockburns, Nisbets, and Ormistons—in a process as to the division of the lands of Crailing between the Homes, Rutherfords, and Kerrs. David died before 1479, when his children—William, John, Janet, and Margaret—were defendants in an action before the Lords of Council. In 1483 William Purves and his son William were witnesses to the sasine of the lordship of Earlston in favour of Archibald, Earl of Angus, and two years later William, evidently the elder, was obliged to pay the teinds of the lands of Fans, while in 1499 another William had sasine of Earlston. Five years later Oswald Purves had sasine of the same lands, and on 14th May 1537 he is designated "of Purveshauch " in a charter under the Great Seal of the lands of Huntshaw in Earlston, which he received along with his spouse, Elizabeth Kerr.

From 1539 to 1580 there is notice, as serving on retours of inquest, of Alexander Purves of that ilk, styled occasionally "Alexander Purves, portioner of Earlston," and "Alexander Laird Purves " in Earlston. Whether these were father and son has not been ascertained, but on 29th June 1580 Alexander Purves, portioner of Earlston, with consent of John his son and heir, sold to his third son Thomas in Earlston the four carucates, or sixteen husband-land, in Earlston, of which Thomas had charter of confirmation under the Great Seal on 25th February 1581.

John Purves, the son of this Thomas, was served heir to his father in the above carucates on 19th November 1612. He married Agnes, daughter of Thomas Redpath of that ilk, and on 30th November of the following year there is a charter under the Great Seal confirming the liferent disposition he had made in completion of his contract of marriage with said Agnes. He was a man addicted to violence, and possessing supreme contempt for law and order. On 21st July 1623 he, with consent of Agnes Redpath his spouse, Isobel Home his mother, and Charles Cairncross her spouse, sold his lands to his near kinsman, Hector Purves, eldest son of Andrew Purves, burgess of Edinburgh, who had charter under the Great Seal on 1st October 1623. The carucates thus disponed were Purveshauch, Whitfield, Earlston, and Huntshaw. This Andrew Purves possessed the "Temple lands" in Earlston, apparently by inheritance from Alexander Purves of Earlston. He married Marion Cramond, daughter of Mr John Cramond, Advocate, burgess of Edinburgh, in 1601, and was admitted a burgess in her right on 9th August 1603. On 22d March 1631 Andrew Purves resigned the "Temple lands" of Earlston into the hands of Thomas, Earl of Haddington, for new infeftment in favour of his son Hector of Purveshauch, who had charter from the Earl on same day.

Hector of Purveshauch married Isobel Adair, and had two sons — Andrew (baptised 5th February 1630) and Robert. Hector died soon afterwards, and his son Andrew was served heir before the Sheriff of Berwick on 21st February 1656. He married Marion Aikman, and, dying without issue, was succeeded by his brother Robert, who, on 24th February 1665, was charged to enter himself as heir in special, when Andrew Aikman, W.S., apprised the estate of Purveshauch from him for £5075, 7s. 5d. Scots. Aikman on same day received charter under the Great Seal; but the lands were acquired on 9th December 1671 by Sir William Purves of Woodhouselee from Marion Aikman, spouse of the "deceased Andrew Purves of that Ilk."

SIR WILLIAM PURVES.

The connection of Sir William with the family of Purves-hauch has not been traced. His father, Robert Purves, was probably nephew of Andrew of Edinburgh, the father of Hector of Purveshauch : it is, however, certain that neither the father nor grandfather of Sir William were designated " of Abbeyhill," as represented in the various pedigrees of the family. The above Robert was apprentice to John Hepburn, and was admitted a burgess of Edinburgh on 21st October 1616, through payment of £5, and appearing sufficiently well armed with hagbut and pistols. Robert's surety on this occasion was Patrick Douglas, baxter, Edinburgh, who afterwards became his father-in-law. It was usual in those days for the younger sons of gentle families to engage in mercantile pursuits, and through being tradesmen they did not lose their social status. Innumerable instances might be given where timely aid from burgess kinsfolk prevented the old acres from passing to other names, and through such means many historic families acquired a new lease of life. Three times this has been the fate of the house of Purves : first, in the person of Thomas in Earlston; secondly, when in 1623 Hector Purves purchased the family estate from John of Purveshauch; thirdly, when it was acquired by Sir William, the son of another Edinburgh merchant.

Robert Purves, on 4th February 1618, received sasine from Patrick Hepburn of Fineven of six acres of temple lands in Kemston, within the constabulary of Haddington, possessed by his late brother George, who had been admitted a burgess of Edinburgh on 12th April 1615. Robert had nine children, of whom William, the fifth but eldest surviving son, baptised 19th October 1623, was served his heir on 15th July 1630 at an unusually early age. On 17th November William had sasine, proceeding on a charter of same date granted by his grandfather, Patrick Douglas, his curator, of four acres of land in the barony of Restalrig, together with the lands of Craigchat and others; the liferent of Isabel Logan, the spouse of Patrick, being reserved, as well as the provision made for her daughters Isabel, Janet, and Catherine. Patrick Douglas, as curator, alienated the Kemston lands in favour of Francis Hepburn, a disposition which William Purves became bound to ratify on attaining his majority; undertaking at the same time to relieve the said ladies of all damage which might be sustained through the transaction. He was, on 12th November 1640, a party to the marriage-contract of his sister Sibilla, who married James Matheson of Broughton, to whom she brought as tocher the sum of 11,600 merks. The settlement provided that the sum of 15,000 merks should be set apart in case there might be daughters of the marriage, in which event the eldest was to receive 8000 merks, the remaining 7000 merks to form the portions of the others.

William Purves became a writer, and secured a lucrative practice. On 16th December 1642 he entered into a contract of marriage with Marjory Fleming, daughter of Thomas Fleming of Longherdmiston. Those acting on Marjory's behalf were Sara Miller, her mother, Thomas Fleming, her brother, and her uncle, Patrick Fleming of Cowburne. Sara Miller, with consent of her son Thomas, assigned to Purves, as his wife's tocher, the sum of 2300 merks, due by Sir William Dick of Braid by obligation to said Sara, dated 28th December 1639 ; also the sum of 5000 merks contained in an obligation by the late Sir James Sandilands, and Francis Wauchope of Niddry, his cautioner, to the late Alexander Miller, Master Tailor to the King, dated the last day of July, and registered 2d January 1610. She made him assignee to other sums, extending in all to 10,000 merks, of which 8000 were to be secured on heritable lands, with the advice of said Sara Miller, Thomas and Patrick Fleming, for behoof of Purves, his spouse, and their heirs. Purves, on the other hand, constituted Marjory his assignee to the annual rent of 10,000 merks, decerned as due to him by Sir William Gray of Pittendrum.

The marriage was celebrated on 12th January 1643, the contract being registered in the Books of Council and Session on 29th January 1644. Immediately after his marriage Purves took a lease of the mansion-house of Drumsheugh from John Aitchison, advocate, at a rental of £100 Scots per annum. There is little trace of him during the next few years, save through the payment of tradesmen's bills, and the baptism of his children—a ceremony gone through in those days with elaborate preparations and a profuse hospitality. It is noteworthy, as evidence of his social advancement, that while the witnesses to the baptism of the elder children were burgesses of the city, the baptism of his daughter Margaret, on 8th July 1649, was attended by the *élite* of Edinburgh society, lords and ladies of high rank — such as John, Lord Balmerino, James, Lord Coupar, Sir Archibald Johnstone of Warriston, Sir Alexander Belches of Tofts, and others. Charles, Earl of Loudoun, the Earl of Wigtown, Lord Ramsay, and Sir Henry

Nisbet, were prominent among the guests attending the baptism of the younger children.

Fickle fortune had, however, evil days in store for the ambitious writer, and he who in the full tide of prosperity turned his back on burgess friends was now obliged to seek protection from his enemies in many a "lowly land." He had embraced the Royalist cause, but the unhappy struggle between Charles I. and his subjects proved disastrous to the King's partisans, for Cromwell took possession of Edinburgh and became Master of Scotland. Purves designated himself "of Abbeyhill" in those days, and the houses he had erected there were destroyed by order of the Committee of Estates. He has been held by some to be the prototype of Sir William Worthy in Ramsay's pastoral, "The Gentle Shepherd," but, while the opening scene in the third act would certainly represent his condition at this time, there is no reason to conclude that Purves and Sir William Worthy are identical.

When Charles II. and his Parliament met at Stirling in 1651, Purves sent a humble supplication to the king representing what loss he sustained through the destruction of his property by command of the Committee then with the army. The Estates requested Lord Coupar and Lord Tofts to comprise the damage done, so that reparation might be given. They assessed the loss at 6178 merks, but of this money Purves received no part, save a few sheep which belonged to the Laird of Dundas. He therefore prayed that, seeing he is put from any kind of subsistence, all his "Lyffly-hood" being on the other side; also considering the extraordinary charges he has been put to, in attendance on the Committee of Grievances and provisions for the army, the King and Estates of

Parliament would consider his case, and take some effectual course for his further payment, by constituting the balance due as a public debt.

The Committee of Bills who dealt with the matter, on 28th March 1651 recommended that the 6178 merks should be regarded as a public debt—the sheep he had already received being apprised. In respect to attendance on the Committee, they thought the sum of 100 merks per month ought to be allowed to him out of the general Commissary or other public dues of the Burgh of Aberdeen. Three days later the King and Estates ordered steps to be taken for his satisfaction.

Purves in this time of trouble had good reason to bless his mother-in-law for her generous assistance : she advanced him considerable sums, so that shortly afterwards he purchased lands adjoining his property at Abbeyhill. He acquired in June 1652 seven acres in the Cannoflat from Finlay Taylor and Margaret Boswell, his spouse, a conveyance which on 16th June was confirmed by the Magistrates of Edinburgh, who, in consideration of the good service he had rendered to the city, passed a special Act discharging the Master of the Trinity Hospital from uplifting £120 due as composition for entry to the lands. About the same time he had a liferent disposition, from John Stirling of Orchardfield, of eight acres of land with bog and meadow, and four rigs described as lying on the north side of the bog, in the barony of Restalrig.

As there appeared but little prospect of the restoration of Charles during the life of Cromwell, Purves, remembering how his political leanings had brought him into trouble, determined to secure some appointment in the service of the Commonwealth, accepting in 1655 a clerkship in the Exchequer, with which he had some previous connection. He never took kindly to the Protector's rule, and in private gave vent to his feelings by endorsing various bonds as being registered in the "pretendit Court Books of Justice"!

Soon after his appointment it became necessary to issue a proclamation charging all possessed of any part of the Kirk lands, or King's property, to exhibit their titles before the Lords of Exchequer—an ordinance which gave rise to very great feeling, as well as to unjust reflections upon Purves. It was entirely due to the fact that, "through the great distractions and disturbances, many of the registers, rentals, and rolls of the revenue are lost—at least for the present cannot be found—whereby a true and perfect rental and condition of the revenue cannot now be known." The measures adopted were regarded as solely due to Purves's malevolent designs, for his signature was appended to the proclamation, and contemporary writers refer to these proceedings, known as "Purves's Production," as one of the twenty hardships under which the nation suffered. The exhibition of titles was especially obnoxious, for those who failed to produce their rights were dealt with in arbitrary fashion. Purves's influence was exerted in many instances on behalf of needy Royalist families; yet the ability he displayed in his difficult position won him the friendship of Cromwell, and led to his appointment in the following year as Head Clerk of the Exchequer.

The Executive in Scotland had protested in vain against the removal of the national muniments to London, but on this point Cromwell was as firmly resolved as Edward I. Great inconvenience was consequently felt, particularly in regard to fiscal matters, and in May 1658, when Purves was in London with proposals for the improvement of the revenue, the Master of the Rolls was ordered to appoint a fit person to aid him in the separation of the Records sent from Scotland, so far as related to the revenue, from others in the Tower.

During the years 1658 and 1659 there were signs of deep-rooted discontent, indications that the country would not much longer submit to the military despotism under which it groaned. There were expectations of a Royalist attempt, and a renewal of the terrible struggle between Cavalier and Roundhead; but the death of Cromwell, the feeble rule of his son, the dissensions between the heads of the English army, paved the way for Monck's master-stroke and the peaceful restoration of Charles II. The true proclivities of Purves now found vent in various ways: he hastened to London to await the issue, and through the friendship of Monck was among the first to congratulate Charles when he entered London. The King's reception of him was not encouraging, for he was ordered back to Scotland to be tried by the Scots Parliament. Fortunately he had good friends in Edinburgh, and the Estates on 21st June 1661, having considered the Report made to them by the Committee appointed to investigate his conduct during the troubles—

Find that he, being in charge before the incoming of the Usurper, hath public testimony from the King's Majesty and Committee of Estates at Stirling of his good service, and albeit, by the burning of his houses, destroying of his lands, and other losses, he was induced to serve in some employment under the Usurper, yet his service was rather an advantage than otherwise, for, by his kindness and care to the loyal subjects— whereof many persons of known honor and integrity have given many testimonies—promoted some public good for this country. And as to the matter of production of Evidents, they found after trial that he did not project the same, and when it fell in his hands to officiate, he did all the advantage he could to the subjects, without any considerable advantage to himself; and therefore the King's Majesty, with advice and consent of the Estates, do acquit him from all question of his services.

This public testimony to his integrity led to the sarcastic remarks of Lord Fountainhall.

He regained the royal favour through the friendly offices of Sir John Gilmour and the Earl of Lauderdale, and on 2d September 1662 a warrant was issued appointing him his Majesty's Solicitor for life : he also became Procurator of the Church of Scotland, being admitted advocate on 13th November of same year.   This advancement of a Cromwellian official proved annoying to such as had been more steadfast in their loyalty.   Attempts were made to prevent the warrants passing the seals ; and hearing of these intrigues, Purves wrote the following curious letter to his friend and patron, the Earl of Lauderdale :—

RICHT HONOURABLE AND MY MOST NOBILL LORD,

Seeing it is by yor lordeship's favor that I enjoy that place which yor lordeship obtenned from his Majestie to me, I presume the more when I apprehend prejudices to arryse to shelter myself under yor lordeship's patroncie.   I wes so happy at being with yor lo: that I do confedently rest upon yor favor.   Whenever yor lo: shall think me unworthye, ayther of his Majesties or yor lo: favor let me only esteme it my happiness to lay it at yor lo: feit, and to beg yor lo: continuance to preserve me from the malice of my enemies till then.

I am informed that Sir John Gilmour not yet satisfyed with what his Majestie hes done to me (by yor favor) in nominating me his Solicitor and not his brother-in-law.   Mr James Windred heath written to yor lo:, and som oythers, letteris to my prejudice.   If I knew what they were I could easily answer them. I do not apprehend any prejudice from them, if they do not robe me of yor lo: favor, but finding so much nobilitie and generosity from yor lo: I shal ever rest upon yor lo: favor and patroncie till yor lo: discharge me thereof.

May I most humbly entreat yor lo: to acquaint my brother if ther be anything of this nature—not so much out of any desyr to knowe the matter as out of ane feare of yor lo: alteracion to him who is no more his owne then he is,

Yor lo: most faithful, real and humble servant,

EDINBURGH,
5th February 1663.

Charles created him a knight baronet on 6th July; on 12th August he had a receipt for forty merks from the Macers of the Council and Session in full satisfaction of their dues "for the title and dignity conferred upon him, be his sacred Majesty, as Knight and Baronet most deservedlie." His residence at this time was the house of Sir John Henderson of Fordell, and here he gave a grand entertainment which was attended by many nobles. Fortune again smiled upon him; he received a joint gift with the Earl of Lauderdale of Wards and Marriages, amounting to upwards of £20,000 Scots per annum, besides large sums for "his pains and zeal." He was frequently intrusted with affairs of great delicacy, his conduct throughout inspiring implicit confidence. In the following year he drew up his first account of the Revenue, which forms the basis of the present work.

Between Purves and William, Earl Marischal, a warm friendship had long subsisted, and the Earl on 25th August 1668
appointed him, and, in the event of his death, his eldest son
Alexander, to subjoin and append the Privy Seal to all writs,
&c., as should be sealed thereby; to receive all fees, casualties,
and dues belonging to the Lord Privy Seal, and to employ said
fees and dues to their own proper use as freely as the said Earl
or his deputies might do. They were to enter upon these
duties at Martinmas, and Sir William and his son became bound
to be careful of, and become responsible for, the said seals, and
to relieve and skaithless keep the said noble Earl.

Hitherto we have been chiefly concerned with Purves's
official connections. His sole ambition seems to have been
family aggrandisement, and in recording the steps taken to this
end, we deal with one of those quiet, unobtrusive men whose
energy and industry enabled them gradually to lay the founda-
tion for the future greatness of their descendants. Had it not
been for the fortunate discovery of certain family papers, as
little would have been known of him as of the "dark grey" man,
reputed founder of the house of Douglas. Soon after accepting
office under Cromwell, he acquired the lands of Fulford and
others through the renunciation in his favour by Helen Belches,
sister of Alexander, Lord Tofts, spouse of John Hume of Man-
derston, and by Marjory Coupar, lawful daughter of deceased
Andrew Coupar, of Fenton, by his wife Janet Belches, sister of
Helen. Cromwell, who loved to style himself "The keeper
of the liberties of England," granted precept of sasine for his
infeftment in these lands on 13th May 1657; while a charter
under the Great Seal was expede on 17th August following,
settling the lands on himself in liferent, and conveying the fee

thereof to his son Alexander—reserving power of redemption, what time he pleased. Purves soon afterwards took up his residence at Woodhouselee, a beautiful and romantic place on the banks of the North Esk, of which he had charter under the Great Seal on 31st December 1658, proceeding on the resignation of Alexander Bothwell of Glencorse and his son. The lands had been impignorated by William, Earl of Roxburgh, for 20,000 merks, and although possessed of the property since 1658, Purves only received sasine on 31st August 1665. On 29th January 1667 he acquired the lands and barony of Thankerton, with the tower, fortalice, manor-place, and pertinents lying within the sheriffdom of Lanark, from John, Earl of Wigtown—a disposition confirmed by the King and Estates of Parliament two years later. He also received sundry lands from the Laird of Tofts as security for his advances, and took advantage of an opportunity which presented itself of getting a disposition of the estate of Purveshauch from Marion Aikman, relict of deceased Andrew Purves, now spouse to James M'Lurg, on 9th December 1671 : charter under the Great Seal being passed on 22d January thereafter. This purchase led to the prospect of his owning large estates in his native country, and apparently induced him to dispone the barony of Thankerton to James Carmichael of Bonnington. About the same time he got absolute title to the lands of Nether Tofts, Cruicklaw, Over Tofts, Plewlands, and others from Belches, which, with the lands of Lambden, purchased from Hume of Kaims, were afterwards erected into the barony of Purves; the mansion-house of Tofts henceforth to be called Purves-hall.

The transaction with Tofts involved Purves in much trouble, for creditors led a process against him for reduction of the

d

sale. Sir William in a curious memorial charges Tofts with concealment of the true rental, the deception going so far that, he alleged, the Laird actually advanced money to the tenants to make up the rental to the sum affirmed by him. For a time this ruse was successful, but the facts coming to Sir William's knowledge, he compelled Tofts to give bond "to furnish tenants to the said lands for the space of five years at the rental he had given up"—an unsatisfactory arrangement. Sir William bitterly complained of Belches' dilapidating the mansion of Tofts, "which was reduced to a shell of a house and would not hold out a drop of rain. But worst of all, the dovecot was so ruinous that although it was in his possession for a twelvemonth, not one pair of doves had he gotten out of it yet. Further, the dykes would not keep out a mouse!"

The Berwickshire estates of Purves comprised the lands he purchased from Belches, Pittlesheugh, Mersington, lands of Purveshauch, Whitfield, Earlston, and Huntshaw, lands of Lambden, Plewlands, and others. As he had to make provision for his younger children, he decided to sell Woodhouselee and Fulford, and his rights in these were bought up by his son-in-law, James Deans, only son of James Deans of Highrigs. Accordingly he resigned the lands in favour of the Lords of Exchequer for new infeftment to be granted to James Deans, dated 21st August 1674. James Deans had married Rosina Purves, and on 10th August 1675 he signed a discharge for her tocher of 8000 merks.

Sir William's ambition seems to have been satiated when at length he was able to designate himself, with doubtful propriety—"Purves of that Ilk." The infirmity of his eldest son was a bitter sorrow, which the King with kindly consideration tried to alleviate by substituting the name of his third son, John, as joint-Solicitor for life, an appointment specially included in the confirmation he had from Parliament, in 1681, erecting and consolidating his lands into the barony of Purves.

The Treasury authorities were very remiss in the audit of their intromissions with the Crown Revenue. Charles in October 1681 directed the Commissioners of the Treasury to audit the accounts, especially to call Purves "to accompt for such of the wards and other casualties as he has uplifted since Lammas 1674."

This communication no doubt led to the preparation of the volume now published. Although dated in 1681, it was not completed until the autumn of the following year. It is fuller in details than the account drawn up in 1667, but unfortunately the portion relating to the "Improvement of the Revenue" with the "Record of Concealment" has either been lost or was never completed. The following letter from the Duke of Queensberry shows that it was looked forward to with not a little interest :—

SANQUHAR, 30th August 1682.

SIR WILLIAM,

Since coming here I have read your book with very great satisfaction, and do wish the other pieces there mentioned may be readie again the winter. I hope ye will not forget towards November to have in readinesse a full information in write of what I recommend to you at parting relating to imbeuzelments and concealments of the Revenue, and the particular caises of all persons who have in possession lands and others belonging to the Crowne : this I do assure you will be acceptable both *above* and to me, but I desyr and expect non alive save yourself know it.

Take effective ways to discover the value of Douglas escheat lately execute, as also those convict for the Syce of Error, and be able at meeting to give me an account of all. Faile not to let me hear frequentlie from you, and inform what is fitt for me to know relating to Treasury business during my absence. So expecting you'll do everything effectually and closely, and write fully and frequently to me, which Wallace will get weekly conveyed.

The King's Advocate told me at parting he was to raise several reductions upon the King's account this vacation, and have them readie against November, whereof mynde him, and whats done, or designed therein, let your first bear. I desire among other things ye'll exactly mynde against meeting to have a list of Council and Justice Court where money is to be expected. This I am much concerned in, and do absolutely trust to your care. I am, your most reall and affectionate friend,   QUEENSBERRY.

Purves was no favourite with James, Duke of York, and it was probably due to the latter that on 10th April 1683 the Privy Council were desired to appoint Mr George Bannerman joint-Solicitor with Sir William. This naturally roused the old man's indignation : he stoutly declared he would "yield up his rights to none"; the Council sided with him, and he held his position successfully against the King. This opposition to the royal will brought about a situation of great delicacy, which was not improved when Veronica, Countess of Kincardine, made complaints against him. The disagreement between her and Sir William arose out of the settlement of accounts with the late Earl of Kincardine. In February 1671 Charles II. had granted to the Earl a gift of the Wards and Marriages which fell due between November 1666 and 1st August 1671, of the vassals holding of his Majesty as King, Prince, and Steward of Scotland, whether the said vassals were marriageable or not, with power to uplift the same from Purves. Similar grants in favour of Kincardine were dated from 1st August 1671 to August 1674.

Dame Veronica de Airsin Van Summersdyck, relict of the Earl, obtained a gift of her husband's escheat from the King, under Privy Seal, dated 9th March 1681, and brought an action of declarator against Alexander, Earl of Kincardine, Lady Mary Bruce, and William Cochrane, her spouse, Lady Ann and Elizabeth Bruce, lawful daughters of the late Earl. Sir Alexander Bruce of Broomhall had acted throughout for the Earl of Kincardine, and between him and Sir William there was so great a difference that they could come to no agreement. Lady Veronica was a woman with some pretensions to beauty, of vigorous character, and, however unwilling to harass the friend of her dear lord in any way, she "hated extremely the delays which are so common in Scotland." Writing to Purves on 16th June, she hinted that lately she "got very much kindness from above," which gave her ground to hope for all assistance from those who are in authority. The case was not settled for many years, and it would be foreign to the scope of this volume to trace it further. Suffice it to say, that perhaps the representations of the Countess led to the retirement of Sir William from the Solicitorship in the following July, for Charles, as is well known, was very susceptible to female influence.

The infirmities of age warned Sir William to give directions for settling his worldly affairs; and to this end the closing days of his life were occupied. In September he gave Purveshauch in wadset to his second son James; other dispositions of his property were also made, and on the 8th November 1684 he signed the following deed :—

Be it known to all men by their present letters me, Sir William Purves of that Ilk, knight and baronet, for the love and favour that I have and bear to William Purves my grandchyld, and other good causes and con-

siderations moving me, to have granted and delivered, as I do hereby give,
grant, and dispone, to the said William Purves and his heirs who shall
succeed to my Estate, all moveables, as well moveable airschip as other
moveables, horse, nolt, sheep, maills, ferms, profits and duties of land,
household plenishing outside and inside, coache, jewels, gold, silver coinged
and uncoinged, watches and other moveables of whatsomever name or
nature now pertaining, or that shall pertain, to me at my deceis, dispensing
with the generalities and admitting the same to be as valid as if every
particular were specially named and exprest; Reserving always to me my
liferent of the haill premiss, and power to alter and to dispone otherways
upon all, or any part thereof, as I shall think expedient.

The curators he appointed were : Dame Marjory Fleming, his
spouse ; Sir Roger Hog of Harrears, Senator of the College of
Justice ; Mr Charles Hume of Aytoun ; John Hume of Mander-
ston ; John Hume of Ninewells ; James Deans of Woodhouselee ;
Mr David Hume, Tutor of Blackadder ; Mr James Daes of
Coldingknows ; Mr John Purves, his son ; Thomas Fleming of
Dalquhain ; James Hay, W.S. ; Mr John Belches of Tofts. On
8th December he transacted his last piece of business. He
called to mind the many kindnesses and faithful services of his
dear friend Sir George Lockhart during a long period of years,
and, anxious to encourage him in looking after his legal business, he granted him an annuity of £100. Sir William died a
few days later, and was succeeded in the title by his son Alexander, the names of whose descendants will be found in the
annexed pedigree of the family.

THE REVENUE OF THE CROWN.

In this Introduction it is not intended to deal in any detail with the revenue of the Scottish Crown, for the lapse of time and the consequent loss and destruction of important papers have further increased the difficulties which Sir William Purves had to encounter. We can therefore only briefly refer to the financial position of the Scots sovereigns at various periods.

Sir William Purves gives the sources of Crown revenue in his remarks, pages 30-35, and from these it will be seen how admirably adapted the feudal system was as a means of oppression and extortion. The extraordinary financial state of James VI., to which Purves draws attention in so discreet a manner, was not new in the history of our kings. In the days of the Alexanders the estates of the Crown were large and valuable. We know from the Exchequer Rolls, as well as from other sources, that they were possessed of castles and manors in almost every county in Scotland, but it is impossible now to estimate the gross revenue of the time.

It is Brus who is primarily responsible for the chronic impecuniosity of his successors. His own princely possessions, as well as the Crown lands, he gifted in reckless manner to those who fought with him for national independence. He himself was the first to feel the evil fruits of his generosity, and was obliged in 1326 to apply for a grant of money because the Crown lands were diminished through the causes stated. The Parliament on 15th July of that year granted him for life

the tenth penny of their rents, according to the Old Extent
of lands in the time of Alexander III.,—a gift, they declared,
would be null if the King defeated its object by application
beforehand.   They further decreed that payment ceased on
the death of the King, and that it was not to be drawn into
a precedent.   David II., through his extravagance and evil
fortune, was also obliged in 1367 to ask for a grant; but
Parliament decided that "the King can and ought to live
on the revenues of the Crown," and all donations of the royal
property, since the time of Alexander III., were revoked.
Through David's ransom heavy burdens were placed upon the
people, and to a great extent the Crown revenues were dis-
located.   The Stuarts on their succession to the kingly
functions were possessed of considerable estates, and the addition of these to the patrimony would have placed the reign-
ing family in at least affluent circumstances.   A portion of
their property was, indeed, set apart for the maintenance of
the heir-apparent as Prince of Scotland; but extensive lands
were gifted to favourites, or divided among illegitimate
children.

James I., whether on account of poverty or not, retained
the wards of his subjects in his own hands, and adopted
measures for the recovery of his patrimony by directing the
sheriffs to make diligent inquiry into the property of the
Crown, requiring the vassals to exhibit their charters.   These
methods were regarded as oppressive.   The untimely death
of James and the youth of his successor tended to render
his proceedings abortive; but they were not without advantage,
for Parliament recognised the justice of the proceedings, and
in 1431 declared that the Governor had no power to give

away lands, so steps were taken to recover those alienated, and provide for the scantiness of income of James II. In 1449 there is a grant for dower to the Queen of James II. of the earldoms of Athol and Strathearn, the lordships of Linlithgow, Menteith, Doune, Strathgartney, Drummond, Duchray, Kinclevin, and others, extending in all to the sum of 10,000 crowns. Two years later there is another grant to the Queen of

£500, the earldom of Fife, with Castle of Falkland, the lands of Fife forfeited by the Earl of Athol ; the great customs of Coupar, the earldom of Stirling; great customs of Perth, Stirling, and Linlithgow, and £100 from Aberdeen, the sheriffdom of Stirling and Linlithgow, the barony of Tullicultry, with 20 merks out of Cragorth.

Parliament in 1455 declared the following lands to be Crown property, inalienable without consent of the Estates :—

The customs of Scotland, the lordships of Ettrick and Galloway, with the Castle of Thrieve, the Castle of Edinburgh, the lands of Ballincrieff and Gosford in Lothian, Castle of Stirling and King's lands there, the Castle of Dunbarton, the lands of Cardross, Roseneath, pension of Cadzow with the pension of ferm-meal of Kilpatrick, the earldom of Fife and Strathearn, lordships of Breichen, Inverness, and Urquhart, superiority of Cortachy ; lordship of Abernethy with water-mails of Inverness, baronies of Urquhart, Bonech, Bonacher, Annoch, Ardmanoch, Petty, Brachlie, Strathnairn, Redcastle, and the lordships of Ross.

These extensive appropriations might be held as making ample provision for maintaining the dignity of the Crown ; but while James III., his son, and grandson revoked all alienations which were to the detriment of their soul and conscience, or prejudicial to their rights, yet their prodigal expenditure and reckless gifting reached such a pitch that, although the earldom of March with the extensive baronies of Dunbar and Cockburns-

e

path, together with the lordship of Annandale, were subsequently included, the Comptroller in 1525 protested the expenses of the King's household "cannot be met out of the property, as it is greater than it can bear." He had often represented the state of things to the Lords of Council of Regency, and now intimated that he will not hold himself responsible for the consequences. James V. in 1524 annulled all gifts, on the ground that his whole estates were required for his household. James Colville of Ochiltree, the next Comptroller,—successor in that office to Robert Barton of Overbarton,—undertook to furnish the household if a sum of £3000 out of the casualty was made over to him besides the other revenues.

In 1540 the Crown acquired great estates, such as Cromar and Braemar, Henderland, the Isles, Kintyre, Orkney, and Shetland; the lordships of Douglas, Bolton, Prestoun, Tantallon, Dunsyre, Jedburgh, Kerrimure, and Bothwell; superiority of Angus, Avondale, Liddesdale, and others. But these annexations do not seem to have been of much advantage, for after King James's death the Comptroller stated that the revenue had diminished by want of the customs, extending to £5000; the kirk tax, amounting to £10,000; the Queen's dowry, £10,000; the lands of Lord Angus and Lord Glamis, the Coalheughs of Waliford and Prestoun, estimated at 1100 merks; besides the profits of the sheep and nolt, amounting to 2000 merks, and the revenue of Guienne in France, together with the casualties of St Andrews, Holyrood, and the fruits of the abbacies belonging to the King's sons given to sustain the royal house.

James V. is supposed to have been an opulent king, gifted with shrewd common-sense, and well able to manage his affairs; but the papers of his reign do not bear any great proof of shrewdness in regard to his own concerns. It is true that he endeavoured by a system of farming and stock-raising to augment his revenues; the forest of Ettrick and the parks of Holyrood, Stirling, and Torwood, as well as Falkland, were stocked to their utmost capacity, yet the returns were inconsiderable. Like his father, he was a strange mixture of saint and devil,—the latter, unfortunately, predominating,—and it is certainly due more to his mad pranks and gallantries than to his virtues that his memory has been cherished in Scotland.

The ill-fated Queen Mary revoked all alienations of the patrimony in 1555, and in 1556 the Lords Auditors of Exchequer calculated her rents at £15,522, 8s. They appraised the victual, capons, poultry, mutton, salmon, &c., at £2020, 13s. 10d.; the grassums and entry silver of the earldoms of Moray, Mar, and Strathearn being £1592, 17s. 4d., the whole extending to £17,515, 4s. 4d. Thus at a most critical time Mary of Guise, with diminished resources, entered on her determined struggle against the Lords of Congregation and the intrigues of England. When Queen Mary returned to Scotland she found an empty exchequer and her affairs in great confusion.

Mary Stuart was, without doubt, one of the ablest monarchs of her race; had she been brought up in the rough and brusque ways of the Scottish Court, productive of a more masculine temperament, her fate might have been different. She upheld her dignity by means of her dower as Queen of France, and for a time she baffled the schemes of her enemies in Scotland and England. In a curious Memorial drawn up in 1561 there are various proposals " whereby the rentes of the Queen's Grace Crown may be augmented without grudge, hurt, or feeling of

the people." The methods advocated in this Memorial proceed
on the principle that the "well that is meikle taken of will
go dry if there be no springs brought to it," and to prevent this
the Queen was advised to retain the great abbeys, wards, and
marriages in her own hands for a certain space; to prohibit the
exportation of goods unless for her own profit, and to reform the
mint, which was farmed out. It was especially impressed upon
her how advantageous it would be to work the mines at her
own expense, or at least to let them to the highest bidder.
Another thing was that her affairs were managed by a stranger
instead of a Scotsman. The coal-mines were fairly profitable;
but owing to the price, and the methods adopted, it was feared
that the supply would become exhausted in a few years unless
the Queen took the industry into her own hands, so as to provide labour and cheap fuel for the poor. Queen Mary was
strongly advised to get vessels built and manned for the
prosecution of fishing, then altogether in the hands of strangers
and foreigners.

There had been enactments passed at various times to prevent
the flow of Scots money to Rome (the people were sorely tried by
the demands made upon them by the Church), and Mary was told
she would "win the treasure of all princes—the hearts of her
subjects "—if she would solicit the Pope that Churchmen would
abandon claim to " the upmost clothes and corseprefands, which
the rich subjects of no other realm pay. This exaction amounts
to £20 in the year, if there were only five persons in a parish
who gave 40s. for both. The establishment of a legate would
result in a revenue of over £10,000." The kirkmen of all other
countries paid the tenth penny of their fruits to their prince,
besides the fifth penny which they pay as subsidies in time of

war; this matter if well handled would possibly result in the clergy being persuaded to give the twentieth penny for purposes of administration and national defence, which would bring in about £20,000 per annum. The Bishops should be deprived of the Registers of Commissariot, and the duties pertaining thereto, so that the revenue from this source might be devoted to the discharge of the Queen's debt, and in return she would discharge them of the £30,000 they promised to the late King at the Raid of Solway; this being equivalent to £10,000 per annum, if there die but five persons in each parish whose goods are worth £20. Another curious proposal was that to enable the clergy to know "all those who worship not the Sundays and saint days, they might be persuaded to grant all such offerings to the Queen for some years; and if every householder be made to offer for himself, his wife, bairns, and family, but a penny on the saint days, and the hired servants one halfpenny in the week, the Crown would possess a revenue of £146,000 per annum," which shows that the number of delinquents must have been considerable, even calculating upon "2000 parish churches and 120 householders in a parish."

The protection of property formed a heavy burden upon the landowners of the time, and it was therefore proposed that the heritors should be taxed 2d. every week to pay for all "quick goods" that are stolen. This tax would be no burden, for they already paid twice as much in blackmail and to watchers, and the result would be a revenue of £100,000 per annum, collected by the sheriffs, who would be held responsible for good rule. The value of lands would increase, and the lairds being secured against depredations, will give the twentieth penny of their rents for four years, this being at the rate of £20,000 yearly.

The Memorial concludes thus :—

That your Grace may the better understand this calculation : there are 2000 parish Kirks, and if they are worth £100 overhead, and the manses and glebes worth 40s., the sum-total will be £204,000 per year. But the profit of every parish Kirk should be worth double as much, seeing all the lords' lands in the parish are no better than the Kirks if the said lords play not the part of a ploughman or herd. There are 13 Bishops, a Lord of St John, 60 Abbots and Priors, and reckoning the living of all at £1000 overhead it will be £74,000 per annum; yet some say that five abbots have given as much in a year. Then there are Trinity Friars, Carmelites, and others which would bring £5000, while from Provostries and Deaneries there would be £10,000. So that the total to the Queen's Grace by this calculation would be £302,300 [sic] a year besides what they have by law, the confirmations, upmost clothes, herezelds, and offering.

The Memorial indicates the trend of public feeling, but various influences at work completely upset the calculations of the Reformers; hence Knox and his party could not secure such advantages to the country as they believed would accrue through the downfall of Roman Catholicism. Mary had unwillingly consented to the appropriation of the Thirds of Benefices to public purposes. Stipends were set apart for the maintenance of the clergy, but difficulties and disputes arose with those who possessed kirk lands by rights derived from the Bishops, and as these retained possession the ministers had generally the worst in the contest. It was this which led to Knox's remark, "Two parts are freely given to the devil, and the third must be divided between God and the devil." The advantage to the Crown was but small.[1]

---

[1] The curse of the Stuarts was their generosity; they indulged in princely munificence through feelings which do them credit, but they were surrounded by artful and greedy courtiers—people who, according to an Act of Privy Council in 1566, "mair

The troubles which marked the close of Mary's reign, and the administration of the property by successive regents, led to reckless alienation. No wonder, therefore, that in 1584 James VI., realising the enormous hurt and prejudice he had sustained through yielding to the importunity of his subjects during his minority, revoked the grants made of the property. Under these circumstances one need not be surprised that James accepted the subsidy of £4000 from Queen Elizabeth. In the following year his financial position was so precarious that he made revocation of all pensions and dispositions, and of everything done in his minority in "detriment of soul and conscience" or prejudicial to the privileges and patrimony of the Crown. Things were going from bad to worse with him, so that in 1590 he confesses he "was meikle fashit and troublit" with the difficulty of providing necessaries for his household. Being greatly indebted to the wine merchants, they resolutely refused to supply his wants until they got security for the sums already due. He felt his position very keenly, and to save himself further annoyance he entered into a contract with his Comptroller, who undertook to provide the household for three months to the King's satisfaction, and afterwards for the remaining nine mouths. Notwithstanding all he could do, "a great heap of debt was still growing upon him," and in June 1591 he determined to take advantage of the common law which permitted all manner of persons to revoke things done

regarded thair awin particular profit nor the honourable estait of her Majestie and commonweal of the realm." Nothing can be plainer than the words of an Act of Privy Council on 21st July of same year, wherein it is explained how Mary and Darnley were moved by the shameless and indiscreet asking of their subjects to make disposition of that "quhairon thair awin liviu consists as well in propertie as casualtie."

in their youth which heavily damaged their heritage; therefore seeing that he had attained his twenty-fifth year on the 19th instant, he determined to maintain the right and privileges of the Crown conform to the coronation oath he had sworn, and for the better observation of the oath he revoked all manner of dispositions and infeftments made by himself and his mother.

Although the difficulties which beset the Comptroller, David Seton of Parbroth, were great, yet he was "nawise mindit" to relinquish his post; for in October 1591 he agreed to provide the royal household as heretofore, but stipulated that the King would cause him to be obeyed and see that he was paid the assignation made out of the Isles. James was not to intromit with this, and became bound to see that the Session did justice in regard to its inbringing. The Queen was to receive £2000 of the tocher for the Martinmas term and £4000 at Whitsunday term from the Provost of Edinburgh. If these provisions were not observed, and especially the payment of the rents in due time, the King was to permit Seton to demit office at the end of three months. By the end of October it became apparent that there were no rents available for the subsistence of the household during the next two months, and orders had to be given for the immediate sale of the fermes of Ross. James, as he might well be, was thoroughly alarmed at the straits in which he found himself. On 7th December he sent a Memorial to the Lords of Exchequer in relation to his affairs. On the following day the lords replied that the whole case must be taken into consideration. They thought the revenue could be greatly saved by a reduction of the feus and questionable rights by which the royal parks were held by subjects. It is monstrous, they declared, that the King should have to purchase hay and straw for his forty horses, and the parks must supply all that is necessary. Falkland could support 140 fed slaughter marts, besides kye, as it did in the Queen Regent's time; Holyrood was in possession of the Laird of Balvaird, who must be evicted and the place plenished with sheep bought, or *borrowed*, from well-affected barons, or taken use of by escheat—just penalties for breach of the laws.

In regard to the household the matter was of a very delicate nature, yet, as they were determined to do all in their power to further the royal affairs, they resolved to visit Holyrood House on the following Monday at 8 A.M. for the purpose of hearing Sunday's accounts. King James's Lords of Exchequer were as easy-going individuals as himself. They had again and again remonstrated with him about his prodigal extravagance, and whether it was that they could not be "fashed" with his private affairs, or forgot all about the appointment, certain it is none of them appeared at Holyrood. Such insulting treatment —of frequent occurrence apparently—roused his wrath, and he sent the following passionate letter to the Clerk Register :—

CLERK OF REGISTER,

Becaus the Chancellor is occupied in his dispatches I mauu drese my complent to you. I heve been Fryday, Setterday, and this day waithing upon the directioun of my affairs, and nevir man comand. Thame of the Chekker that wes ordainit to tak the compts nevir one. The turns of the hous sould have bene endit this day, na man comes down. I sent for the advocat baith Fryday and Setterday — nather met nor answer. Siclyk efter the bailies of this toun for the matter of the tocher—the lyk answer. I ordainit as ye hard a certane number to mak ane writing for reforming of the Session—na sic thing meditat. 1 ordainit the Thesaurer

f

to gar mak chargis about the Sorneris—I hav hard nathing of that as yit. In schort na trayst or dayet is keeped. Quhat is spokin this nicht is forgot the morne. In the morninge I see nathing menid but to gurne. Na mair of this work beholding of als lang as I am earnestlic vaiting on, and quhen I am compelled to rest myself then to [illegible] abon gek; [sic] nan cannot be always *vené*. Therefore let this writ be a witness for my part. Quhen evir it beis called in question I protest I may do na mair nor I may, gif I war thaim vaiting on als lang I cannot be vayted. Fairweill—shaw this lettre to the Chancellor and als mony of our folkis as ye meit with.

We cannot deal here with the ludicrous scenes which were witnessed in Edinburgh when King James hunted up the bailies of the town to compel them either to lend him money or borrow from him at extortionate interest. His Lords of Exchequer, though they did not imitate the bailies by escaping through the West Port, yet treated his peremptory summons with so little respect that it was not until Monday the 3d January following they appeared at Holyrood. They investigated the state of affairs in a spirit that was thorough if not commendable, and were determined to ply the pruning-knife with a vengeance. Their retrenchments so flustered and grieved the soul of honest Andrew Melville, the Master of the Household, that the shock of prospective parsimony caused him to forget many things. They actually cut down the supply of wild-fowl to five pair daily, "and it will be disagreeable to any order unless there be six pair." But worst of all was their neglect to note the proper amount of his Majesty's wine allowance. It savours of a species of revenge to read that they did "not allow him a quart to his afternoon, and one pint after collation," which was necessary.

From this account we learn that there was prepared and set

on the King's table on Sunday "six cunings, five partridges, four plovers, two wild ducks, one muir-fowl, one dozen laverocks, one goose, one groys (? grise), two quarters cow-beef, one great veal, and nine muttons." The provision for the Queen's table was similar to the above, but had in addition "two woodcocks, two capons, and four poultry." The prices charged are of interest, the "cunings" or rabbits cost 12s. each, partridges 10s., plovers and wild ducks 6s. 8d. each; the dozen laverocks cost 3s., the goose 10s., and the woodcocks 8s. each. The money set apart for the expenses of the household was about £40,000 per annum, being—Property, £10,000; fees, £10,000; import, £13,000; of the tocher (besides the £6000 given to the Queen), £3800; sold victual, £2200; while the expenditure was as follows: "The King's table, £3870; Master of Household's table, £3627, and others connected therewith, £765; officers of his hienes, £1256; the porters, £772; the Duke of Lennox' table, £3074; in satisfaction of same ordinaries, £4033, 6s. 8d.; in place of meat and fees, £4906; fees to certain having ordinar in the house, £3100; the King's stables, £1851, 7s. 5d.: total, £27,254, 14s. 1d." The expenses of the "Queen's table, £5418; the . . . £1886, 13s.; the beer, £543; her Master of Household's table, £980; ditto, £116; the second table for the Danish, £1440; maidens of Queen's chamber, £767; her hienes master cook, £576; the ladies' table, £2682, 10s.; for meat and fees, £584; for fees in the house, £2844; the Queen's stables, £835, 10s.: total, £18,672, 3s. The total expenditure as above was £45,926, 17s. 1d.," besides which there were a great deal of miscellaneous expenses for coals, candles, &c., the napery account alone being £666, 12s.

From the foregoing a good idea may be had of the state of

affairs. The Lords in their report declared that all amendment must depend upon the skill, care, and goodwill of the officers, and they recommended James to look to the state of his living "before it com to ower instant necessitie." They saw that the present revenue was inadequate to maintain the establishment, and thought the King ought to intromit with the property of the Crown which had been disponed to his own use, according to the 43d Act of James II., "and not to seke the supply of that quhilk wants fra your other gude subjects that hes not offendit." James seemingly had a project to "squeeze" the Islesmen, but the Lords scouted the idea of visiting the Isles, "because he had the principals and the pledges and let them loose without suretie, and to bring them in agane would be most difficult, most paneful, and costly to the country and him."

They next proceeded to reprove him for the extravagance of his own and the Queen's dress, declaring in plain language "we see na possibilitie how yor Majestie's and the Queen's cleithing, in the state the same is, and hes bene sen yor return fra Denmark, can be sustenit upon ony rent that is to be found in Scotland, and theirfore we traist that baith yor Majesties being weel and discreetly informit shall allow that this matter be reformit according to the loveable examples of yor guidsir and hir moder." James, who had some pretensions to be a "dandy," was wroth at this "meikle reproche"; but they paid little attention to the royal feelings, and next declared that the system of permitting persons who had been rebels to possess royal property and houses "was a plane illusion of justice, defrauding his Majesty, and should not be permitted in time coming."

The next to come "under their scorpion-sting" was Andrew

Melville, the Master of the Household. They proposed to cut down his salary and allowances to a minimum, and he wrote them indignantly : " We haif guid experience of the commoditie we haif of our office alreadie, quhilk is grite pane and continual querrelling and flyting, and everie day subject to fal in his Majestie's displeasaur for the faultis that other men comittis. Swa that to consent to serve his Majestie any langer therein, and sustene all thir panes, danger and inconvenence, and want our fee we will na ways consent thereto." Indeed from this report it would appear that Melville's office was no sinecure, and the Lords animadverted on the prodigal consumption and confusion in the maintenance of the house. According to late regulations, those dining at the Master of the Household's table " had neither bread nor drink allowed to them, and insufficient meat which must be augmented ; and besides, the maid-servants and porters of the kitchen could not live on bread and drink only." In times past they had an allowance of mutton, and must either have meat or silver. The consequences attending recent reforms were such as are almost beyond belief. Free fights for food were of daily occurrence, and sometimes these disturbances assumed proportions which required the presence of the guard to quell, and frequently terminated in not a few of the King's servants being placed *hors de combat*. James, who was anything but a hero, lived in constant dread of treachery, and in a state of nervous apprehension. The Lords therefore took the matter into consideration, and in order to put an end to the " schameful and unhonest reving of meat betwixt the kitchen and the tables," proposed that Melville should have authority to punish " the makaris of querrells and tumults as he will answer to his hienes."

They tried in vain to soothe the Master's ruffled feelings; he indignantly repelled their advances, and declared they meant to leave him without food and fees, "for your wisdomes can veill consydder rysing in symmer at our accustomat hour we cannot attend our service without our *dischone* till that time of day"— 2 P.M., the dinner-hour. He was not the only one to complain : the Lairds of Melgund and Carraldston were in the same plight, and remonstrating against their treatment, signified their willingness to relinquish his Majesty's employ because of their evil luck after nine years' service, without fees, they received no reward. The servants were not paid with any regularity, and in consequence the King's French footman, and another who was deeply in debt, took possession of some of the Queen's jewels. The poverty of James is all the more bewildering when it is taken into consideration that between 1586 and 1594 he received £33,000 sterling from Queen Elizabeth, besides the taxation levied in January 1593 of 30s. per pound-land of old extent, together with a large sum as surplus of Thirds or Benefices. Yet in December of the latter year, after receiving £2000 in November, he was obliged to borrow other £2000 from the lawyers of Edinburgh with which to entertain a noble of Almaine, a near kinsman of his Queen.

It is perhaps undesirable to further draw aside the veil which shrouds the private affairs and life of the monarch who for so many years held the destinies of Britain in his grasp, and it is hoped that the brief glimpse we have given of the management of his revenues sufficiently explains the reasons which led to the appointment of the Octavian Commission in 1595. The story, as told in Tytler's 'History of Scotland,' is that "on New Year's day 1595 the Queen's Commissioners presented her with a thousand pieces of gold, and coming playfully to the King, she shook a purse of gold in his face and bade him accept it as a gift. He asked her where she got it. 'From my Counsellors,' she replied, 'who have but now given me a thousand pieces in a purse. When will yours do the like?' 'Never!' said the King, and calling instantly for his Collector and Comptroller, he dismissed them on the spot, and chose those who afterwards became known as the Octavians." These Commissioners were well acquainted with the character of their Sovereign, so they took care that he became bound neither to "menace or boast" them to do things tending to his own detriment or against the terms of their oath. Yet with all their precautions they carried out their duties but indifferently, their proceedings rousing so much popular indignation that the life of James was endangered, at one of their meetings, on 17th December 1596, which led to his famous threat to transfer the seat of Government from Edinburgh—a politic resolution, no doubt, adopted for the purpose of filling his coffers in view of the fine of 20,000 merks levied on the city.

It was difficult for any commission to carry out recommendations for putting the revenue into a proper condition, because James was of so easy and facile a temperament that through the medium of favourites gifts could be extorted from him at any time. After his accession to the English throne the material increase of wealth was of little advantage to him, and he was so annoyed by his Scottish creditors demanding payment in person at Whitehall, that he got the Privy Council to issue an Ordinance prohibiting such impertinent people from resorting to him, as it was "derogatory to the honour and credit of his ancient kingdom."

Although he had promised in St Giles' to visit Scotland every third year, financial difficulties prevented his doing so; but when in 1617 he could no longer restrain his "salmon-like instinct and his vehement and unchangeable desyre to revisit his native land (which troubled not onlie his waking hours but often his sleep)," he was obliged to borrow 80,000 merks from William Dick, burgess of Edinburgh, and other 20,000 merks from Alexander Morrison. As he was ashamed to appear as the borrower, and thus expose his poverty, he got his Treasurer and others to borrow in their own names, and these sums were ordered to be repaid out of the taxation of £200,000 raised in 1616. Before he started on his journey he endeavoured to lessen his expenses by writing curious letters to North Country lairds, desiring them to forward him all sorts of game "be way of present, ye ken." He was never out of pecuniary difficulties, and at his death his debts, amounting to £400,000, were paid by a special taxation of 30s. on every pound-land of old extent.

The accession of Charles was marked, so far as Scotland was concerned, by the requisition of a like sum to defray the expenses of his visit. It was on this occasion that he took the first steps towards the establishment of Episcopacy. For the purpose of endowing a bishopric in Edinburgh, he induced the Lords of Exchequer to consent to his purchase of the barony of Broughton from the Earl of Roxburghe, to whom the King granted a bond on 4th August 1630 for 100,000 merks as part payment of 120,000 merks, the price of the lands.

An account for the years 1628, 1629, is interesting as showing the amount of revenue at this time. "Ferms, victuals, &c., amounted to £24,581; compositions, £12,580; property and casualty, £24,860; extra rents, £821; excise of wine,

£74,666, 13s.; great customs, £59,000; or a total revenue of £196,608, 13s." This proves how effectual were the measures adopted by James VI. The ferm or victual rent would certainly amount to over £50,000 had it not been for recent pensions, but the expenditure for public business became vastly increased through gratuities to servants for their pains and zeal.

Thus in June 1633 there was another taxation levied of 30s. Scots out of every pound-land of old extent. The Duke of Hamilton having paid the sum of 300,000 merks to Sir William Dick, and 52,000 merks to the Earl of Morton so long as he was debarred from the rents of Orkney and Zetland, was appointed collector of this taxation, with instructions to repay himself a sum equivalent to the amount of the debt due by the King.

A Commission was issued in the following May for investigating the state of the revenue in Scotland. It was found that the decrease in the rents, through assignations, conversions, and erections, assumed the most serious proportions. How extensive were the burdens may be gathered from the following statement as contained in the original MS.:—

The pensions paid yearly amounted to £169,130, 5s. 4d.; the fees and ordinary allowances out of Exchequer annually, £44,490; the gifts and precepts and other debts and burdens yet unrelieved extended to the sum of £922,087, of which precepts and debts there is that pays annual rents £786,487, the interest thereof being £78,648, which being added to the foresaid sums of pensions and fees extends to £292,279. The pensions paid in victual extends yearly to 148 chalders, but by and attour the foresaid burdens there is paid and allowed yearly out of the royal rents in pensions for maintaining the royal household the sum £10,562, 9s. 8d., besides 127 chalders of victual. The whole foresaid sums extend in money to £302,859, whereof there is assigned in money £9631, 13s. 4d. The

g

whole victual being 275 chalders is by assignation, which being converted at Exchequer prices is yearly £32,300. Of the foresaid sums there is ratified in Parliament £33,333, and renewed under the King's hand the sum of £109,973.

This extract shows at once the state of the royal finances; and besides the above heavy burdens there were allowances for transaction of business, the affairs of Council and Exchequer, with the maintenance of prisoners—a great annual expense in itself. Such, then, was the condition of Charles's exchequer at a time when he schemed for the establishment, by force, of Episcopacy in Scotland. He fell back on the usual method of rendering null and void all pensions and unnecessary offices, and curtailing the fees all round. These retrenchments were not carried out to any great extent, but certain it is they were highly unpopular, and, together with religious questions, fostered a feeling of resentment which found expression in 1638 when the Earl of Traquair had to meet "Twenty-two articles of Grievances." It was thus with an empty treasury, and much in debt, that Charles entered into the contest with his subjects which proved so disastrous to himself and his country.

In 1643 an attempt was made to raise £800,000 by way of loan. The proceedings were, however, of so arbitrary a nature as to provoke great feeling, inasmuch as the names of those declining to lend were to be publicly read over in Parliament, their goods escheat, and their persons imprisoned. These things caused general disaffection, and ended in the delivery of Charles to the English, who dealt with him in so summary a fashion.

Scotsmen under the iron grip of Cromwell were, if anything, in even a worse condition; they were ordered in 1652 to raise

£10,000 sterling per month, a burden against which they energetically protested. From a return made to Parliament in 1658 we can form an idea of the revenue at this time. The property and constant rent amounted to £5324 ; casualties and uncertain rent, £576 ; compositions on signature, £929 ; customs, £12,500 ; customs of sea-coal, £2216 ; excise, &c., £1674 ; excise of beer, ale, &c., £47,444 ; forfeitures, £600 ; interest on money set apart for judges' salaries, £390.

Parliament after the Restoration granted Charles II. an annuity of £40,000 for life, to be raised by an excise on beer and ale. On 19th January 1661 Charles appointed the Earl of Crawford his Treasurer at a salary of £4000 yearly, on account of the faithful service he had rendered when the royal revenues and income from the kingdom of England were withdrawn by the "insolency of the prevalent power of the army." Sir William Bellenden was made Depute Treasurer, and a few days later Charles issued a commission to William, Earl of Glencairn ; John, Earl of Rothes ; John, Earl of Lauderdale ; John, Earl of Middleton ; Lord Halkerston, and others, desiring them to assist the Earl of Crawford and his depute in all matters concerning the royal revenues. On 16th January 1664 another Commission was issued for auditing the Treasurer's accounts, because of the great prejudice it has been to the King's affairs that the Treasurer's accounts had not been audited since 1626, whereby "not onlie the rare fidelitie and faithfulness of his Majestie's servants employed therein, but also how the same has been expended, might appear to his Majestie." Owing to great confusion in the accounts the Commission had to be renewed two years later. It was also at this time discovered that the taxation of 1633 had not been paid, and that the King was due the representatives of the Duke of Hamilton the sum of £124,181, so on 20th January 1664 instructions were issued for uplifting the balance.

By Act of Convention of Estates there was an additional supply granted to Charles of £2 on each pound-land of old extent, for the space of five years, which came to £133,000, and two years later another supply was granted of £72,000 monthly for a year, so that Scotland paid in taxes in 1667 a total of £1,477,000 Scots, or £123,083, 6s. 8d. sterling. In 1672 the Scots Parliament voluntarily offered twelve months' cess, amounting to £72,000 sterling, to aid the King in his war with the States-General; so that, according to *Scrope and Clerke*, "Scotland paid a land tax of eight months' cess yearly for the King's life, which in all amounted to £88,000 sterling."

The Convention of 1678 granted a new supply to the King of £150,000 sterling, to be raised in the space of five years, and in this Act the whole supply is called twenty-five months' cess : thus five months' cess, or £30,000 sterling, was to be raised for each of these five years, besides the £40,000 sterling before-mentioned ; while in 1681 a supply of same amount was offered to James VII., the total sums levied in Scotland between 1670 and 1681 amounting to £5,688,000, or £474,000 sterling. At the Union the revenue was estimated as follows : Customs and excise, £100,000 ; Crown rents and casualties, £8500 ; post-office, £2000 ; coinage, £1500 ; land tax, £48,000.

An examination of this volume shows that the gross revenue of the Crown from blenches, property, and casualty amounted to £89,821, 4s. 9d. Scots in 1681. Of this sum there was, as usual, a large amount retained as pensions and fees, so that the free money only amounted to £47,445. It is thus apparent that during the reign of James I., his son and grandson, there had been considerable improvements effected, and the *Register of Exchequer* shows that to Sir William Purves was due no small share of credit. His zeal is attested by the many processes pursued against holders of the patrimony by questionable titles.

There is one feature which, while peculiarly interesting, is yet disappointing. Stories of curious blenches and tenures abound. There are none such recorded by Purves, yet it is certainly strange that, in a country where archery was so unpopular as to necessitate the intervention of Parliament, the duties should include so great a number of arrows and arrow-heads. It is evident that many duties had lapsed, or the holdings changed to ward during the reigns of James I. and Charles I. There is charter evidence to prove that "six horse shoes" were paid from the smithy lands in Auldearn, while a "falcon" was due from neighbouring lands in Ardclach. There were also the chaplets of white roses from Gask and Balvenie, while there is no mention of the two pair of shoes given to the fleetest of foot in the barony of Carnwath, nor of the mirrors for flushing larks due from lands in Stirling and Perth shires. There are two redden-dos which were as common at one time as they were acceptable to the sovereign—"the Leopars" or greyhounds from lands near Jedburgh and Perth. The Stuarts when engaging in sport were frequently obliged to borrow hounds from their nobles, and the famous breeds possessed by the Earls of Home and Huntly were especially in request, while to own a falcon of any repute and not to present it to the king was a sure way to lose the royal favour. James VI. did not hesitate to ask either hounds or falcons from his subjects, and his letters on such occasions conclude with the hint—"Seeing thay is but gifting geir and na otherwise to be accompted betwixt us and you."

In comparing the rental of 1683 with the earlier rentals, the greatest difference appears in that relating to Ross and Ardmanoch. The earldom of Ross and lordship of Ardmanoch were dissolved from the Crown for feuing purposes in 1587, and it was from this district that the chief supply of wood and fuel seems to have come. For instance, the lands of Ardville and others were charged as follows:—

Ardville—60 girthstings; 60 loads fir and 100 draughts of fuel; Kynhard —4 loads fir, 100 girthstings, 100 loads of fuel; Halton of Tarradale—60 loads of peats; Garguston—8 loads of fuel; Hilton—8 loads of fuel; Drumquidrin—80 loads of fuel; Wester half Davoch—40 loads of fuel; Drynie— 80 loads of fuel; Drumderfit—80 loads of fuel; Wester Kessock—100 loads of fuel; Snarden (*sic*)—200 loads of fuel; Acrow (*sic*)—2 loads of fir, 60 girthstings, 160 loads of peats, 100 draughts of fuel; Pitconnich—80 loads of fuel, &c.

These items do not appear in this rental, and it is interesting to note them as throwing some light on the condition of the district in early times.

To most of the copies of Purves's work there is added a manuscript entitled "The Retoured duties of the Haill Shyres," which is given in Appendix I., and forms an interesting addition as showing the old extent and value of lands throughout Scotland. The value of the lands in the sheriffdom of Inverness and Ross was the subject of a special inquiry at

Inverness in 1555 by the lairds of the district, while the rolls of the other Shires seem to have been made up at later periods —Aberdeenshire for instance in 1579.

Among the *Letters of the Reign of James VI.*, published by the Abbotsford Club, there is one dated 6th October 1614, from Sir Alexander Hay, which proves how great was the prejudice the King sustained especially in regard to the "Retoured duties." In Appendix II. will be found the "General Tax Roll of 1633," which forms a fitting conclusion to this volume, which it is hoped will prove of some advantage to those engaged in antiquarian and topographical research. It may be remarked that while the example of the *Record Office* has been followed in extending contractions, care has been taken to preserve the old spelling of place-names. In this connection it will be seen that the names of many farms and estates have become obsolete, and are not now to be found in maps, or surveys. This is due to the absorption of the smaller holdings through the extinction of minor lairdships, so prominent a feature in the territorial history of our country during the last two centuries.

In concluding these notes, the Editor cannot but express grateful acknowledgment to the authorities of the *British Museum*—especially to the Librarian, Sir E. Maunde Thompson, and to Messrs Scott and Bickley of the Department of MSS.— for the courtesy with which at all times they so willingly gave information and assistance. Sir Stair Agnew and Dr Dickson of *H.M. Register House* gave access to Records under their charge, thus enabling the Editor to give an account of the family of Purves, with a pedigree constructed from the Sasine and other Registers of Edinburgh and Eccles. Thanks are also due to the

Faculty of Advocates and their Curator—Mr Clarke—for the kind way in which facilities were afforded for collating *Purves's Revenue* with copies in their possession, and for permitting the publication of the General Tax Roll of 1633. Mr John Ferguson, Duns, when he heard of the printing of this volume, generously sent a Manuscript relating to the Tax Rolls, which had belonged to Boswell of Auchinleck.

D. M. R.

EDINBURGH, ALBANY STREET, 13*th March* 1896.

=MARJ
Th
of L
m.

|
VID.

b. 31s

; of
ge

ober
cher
rks.

Jan
m. A

barone
739 ;
ber

|
GRAC relict
b. 16 Hall ;
May 1 ch 181
d. 4
June

1s
ELL =

|
HEL
m. 1
July 1
d. 1

THE REVENEW OR PATRIMONY OF THE CROUN.

PATRIMONIUM principis aliud est publicum seu annexum Coronæ : aliud est privatum, seu non annexum.

Publicum est quod ex toto regno ad regiam dignitatem et regni onera sustinenda sepositum et separatum est, quod patrimonium Coronæ nuncupatur, quod alienari omnino ex jure prohibetur.

Privatum vel non annexum habetur, aliud quod ratione private vel jure successionis, vel per forisfacturam, bastardias et alias casualitates rationæ Eschetæ obveniunt, et in his habet liberam administrationem rex.

The patrimonie of the Croun being such as is before discribed; first, consisting in Landes & Rentes once annexed to the Croun which cannot be taken away therfrae, to the prejudice of the succeeding King. 2do Off such casualities as fall in to the King casuallie, which may be disposed by the King for gratifying any of his loyall subjects.

These two being the naturall branches of the revenew the first wherof is intended be the following rules to be cleired ; the 2d with conveniencie shall follow. It shall be necessar then for

A

cleiring of the first, not only in the generall, that these landes which are annexed to the Croun, for support of the dignitie therof, may not be given away, but also being given away may be brought back againe to the first condition by severall Acts of Parliament, Acts of Counsell & practiques of the session.

The annexed patrimonie of the Croun is that which by speciall Acts of Parliament is annexed to the same, therewith to remaine perpetuallie as is befor exprest. *Craig* sayes, that the King hes only the ryght of administratione of these landes, and may not dispone therupon in fee & heretage, without advyce and decret of the Parliament, for the great sein good & reasonable causes of the Kingdome; whilk if uthir wayes, it shall be lawfull for the King for the tyme to enter to the possession of the samyne landes without any proces of law; and the possessores to make payment of the profitt of the samyne dureing their intromission, as the 41 Act of the 11th parliament James 3ᵈ, and uthir Acts of Parliament made for that effect bears. So this annexed proppertie may not be given away from the Croun. And albeit the Kings, ether throw the importunitie of some, or for rewairding of, or encourageing of uthirs in thair faithfull services to them, have been induced to dispone part of the said patrimonie to severall persones, & therupon given grantes therof, confirmatione & dissolutione of the samyne; yet such wes the loyall caire of these Royall Ancestors, for the tyme to uphold the revenew for support & dignitie of the Croun, & for preventing the prejudices that might aryse therto, that no dissolutione made be any King continued longer than the lyfetyme of the King dissolver. Ffor *Skein*, in his *Verborum de Significatione*, sayes that the dissolutione endureing the lyfetyme of the King ceases, & att his death the annexatione revives and begines to quiken, as is decyded in ane action betwixt the King and the Earle of Crawfurd. So that it is cleir the revenew cannot be disposed to the prejudice of the Croun, both be the forsaides Acts of Parliament and be the 41 Act King James 2^d Parl. 11, and James 3^d Parl. 14 Act 112, and be the 84 Act Parl. 16 James 5th, and by the 115 & 116 Acts of the 7th Parl. James 5th. By which Acts not only the said first act is ratified & approven, bot also the landes therin annexed are declaired to remaine with the Croun, and cannot be disponed therfrae, except in few for augmentatione of the rentall. And the very nixt Act, which is the 116 Act of the said Parl. it is statute and ordained that it shall be lawfull for the King to sett the landes in few with this provisione : that the samyne be in augmentatione of the rentall. As also by the 176 Act & 203 Act of the 13 & 14 Parliaments James 6, and be the 234 Act Parl. 15 James 6, it is so cleire the King cannot dispose any of his landes in whole, or diminish the rentall ether by conversione, allocatione, dischairge, or any uthir maner of way, but that the samyne are null & of no effect, and the Thesaurer may intromett with the rent therof without any proces of law. And the intromettors with the rentes shall be comptable for thair intromissione, which is cleir by the Law and Acts of Parliament aforesaid ; so by these severall practiques viz.—

In the action of Reduction att the Kings Advocats instance against Wm. Scott of Tushielawes the Lordes, upon the 9th Junij 1612, fand the infeftment null, being within the Stewartrie of Annandaill as a pairt of his Majestis proppertie. And sicklyke, be ane uthir decret of the Lordes, ane infeftment granted be the King wes reduced att his oun instance. As also ane uthir infeftment of the proppertie wes reduced becaused made with a diminutione of the rentall, as the Acts of Sederunt in anno 1541 page 5, 8, 13, 14, 15, 22, & 26 bears, notwithstanding that the same wes twise ratifyed in parliament, because no ratificatione of parliament is sufficient to make up ane ryght of the annexed proppertie. Ffor, by the 293 Act Parl. 15th James 6, it is provyded that whatsomever generall lawes shall be made of dissolutiones, or ratificationes of the proppertie, or annexed temporallitie, in favoures of any persone shall be null, notwithstanding of the ratificatione & new dispensatione : except the said ratificatione & dispensatione be made with express & specialle dispensatione of the generall lawes, & by the advice of the States to be mentioned therin, ordaining the Lords to judge according to the generall lawes without respect therto. Albeit these former Acts and practiques be sufficient to cleir his Majestis interest concerning the dilapidat revenew, or that which is converted to small pryces, or uthir wayes disponed be his Majestis Ancestors to the prejudice of the revenew. Yet, for the further cleiring of his Majestis interest, and the caire his Majestis Royall father, of ever blissed memory, had for reduceing of his revenew to its ancient integritie, it will be necessar to sett doune what was then ordered be his Majestie in pursewance therof.

FIRST, in anno 1629 his Majestie by his instructiones to his Theasaurer and Advocat for the tyme ordained them to persew ane reduction of his annexed proppertie, which was accordingly done in ane action, 24th March 1631, persewed be the Kings Advocat against severall of the Kings vassalls and fewers (whose names might be heir insert whilk for brevitie is forborne) upon the forsaids Acts of Parliament for reduction of the infeftment of the annexed proppertie therin contained; and the unannexed proppertie wherof compt had bein made in Exchequer since anno 1455, which hath been taken in few with diminutione of the rentall, & omission of thair marriages contained in thair former infeftments. In which actiones the Lords reduced conforme to the Acts of Parliament as to the annexed proppertie; but as to unannexed they continued the same, & ordained the Advocat to condescend in speciall on the landes wherof compt had been made in Exchequer. And sicklyke be severall instructiones given be his Majestie to his Theasaurer and Advocat for the tyme being, in anno 1610, and the 19th day of November 1630, and 15th February 1635 (all which might be heir insert if it were not too prolix) whereby his Majestis care to have the revenew of the Croun brought in to its wonted conditione is most clear.

Haveing thus farr cleired the nature of his Majesties Revenew, and that the samyne cannot be taken away from the Croun, it shall be necessar in the first place to point att the Judicatorie who have the managment of the revenew which is called the Court of Exchequer.

Exchequer vel Scacarium.

Exchequer cometh of the French word Exchequir, which signifieth the court or place in which the Kings rents & patrimonie are brought in & compted for. Some take the name so in respect that, in ancient tymes, the Accomptants in that office used such tables as Arithmeticans in old used for thair calculationes. *Skein*, in his *Verborum de Significatione*, gives severall reasons of the name whilk shall not be necessar heir to sett doune; it being patent to every one seeing in the generall he condescends that it is a court used in Scotland for receaveing of the Kings Rents, and compting for the same. Whilk compts are made after the forme that *Tabulæ acceptæ* is esteemed to be the chairge, and *Tabulæ Expensæ* to be the discharge, which being made & the charge and discharge equall, either by giveing out as much as the charge, or otherwayes by presentt payment to the Receavers, such sommes as doeth ballance the same, wherupon the Treasaurer or Receaver subscrybs the syde of the Exchequer thus—Resp. Thesaurarius; or if the same be receaved by the Receavers they subscribe the same, wherupon the Exchequer is closed with *eqz eqz eqz* sic; wherof more particularlie it shall be spoken to in its oun place.

In England the Court of Exchequer is taken from the Normands, which was called ane assembly of Justiciaries to whom it pertained to correct & amend that which under-Baillies and Shiriffs had committed in receaveing of, or compting for the revenew. *Ockham*, in his *Lucubrationes*, doeth defyne it to have two parts wherof the one is conversand in the Judiciall hearing & determining of all causes whatsoever pertaining to the King's annext revenew. The other is called the recept of Exchequer, which is propperly imployed in the recept & payment of money. *Cromptum*, in his *Jurisdictiones* folio 105th, defyneth it to be a court of Record wherin all causes touching the revenews of the croun are handled, and *Polidor Virgill* lib. 9 histo. Anglo. sayeth that the trew word in Latine is scatarium, and by abuse is only called Scacarium. And some say it is taken from the German word SCAEZ, signifieing as much as Thesaurarius or fiscus, but the comone name now used is Exchequer, the Judges wherof are called Barrons of Exchequer wherof there are four. The Lord cheif barron, called *capitalis baro*, hath the prime determining of causes betwixt the King and his subjects in relatione to the revenew & the uthir three his assistants.

Haveing thus deduced the etimologie of the name befor wee speake to the constitutione of the Exchequer as it hath been of laite, it is to be remembered that in old the King's Secret Counsell exerced the dewties therof, as the Acts of Counsell in anno 1571 Parl. 23d and 27 & uther acts made theranent will cleir. But the Jurisdiction of Exchequer, as it hath been constitute in Scotland, *Skein* sayes, was ane Court certaine, stable, & not deambulatorie as the Session was befor King Ja. 5th, and had the determinating of all actiones concerning the Kings Majesties proppertie, & discussing of suspensiones & letters conforme ; breaking of arriestments, deforcments off officiers, as is more fully sett downe in the not printed Act of Parl. the 22 of May 1584 pa. 90 & ratified by King Charles of blissed memorie in his Parliament holden in anno 1633. This Act is wherby the Exchequer was constitute ane Court for decyding his Majestis whole effaires as well of the proppertie as of the casualitie. And sicklyke by ane statute of the Session 5th Junij 1538.

Haveing thus farr in generall insisted on the name & Jurisdictione of the Exchequer, forbearing to speak to the duty therof as it was discharged be the Lords of the Secret Counsell preceeding the year 1599, wee shall proceed as the samyne hath been constitute by Parliament & Commissiones, which wee find to have been in anno 1595, att which tyme the abuses of the Exchequer, the urgent necessities of the King's familie, did force a more particular & exact care of improveing the revenew then before. Wherupon ther was a Commissione granted to 8

persones, called the Octavians, with particular instructiones for
the manageing therof, & an oath requyred for the faithfull
discharge of the same, which for informatione is heir sett doune
as followes :—

"Our Soveraigne Lord ordaines ane Commissione to be
made under the testimoniall of the Great Seall, makeing mention that his Grace understanding perfytly the decay of his
Majestis rents by unprofitable dispositiones out of the Proppertie
& Collectorie, & be neglecting of the commoditie of the casualities ; togither with the non plenishing of his Majesties parks
& steids. The increase of all fies & pensiones for keeping of
castles & uthirs, with diminishing of his Majesties customes
notwithstanding the increase of ships & sailers, the interest of
all ; the dearth of all merchants & ventiners with the decay
of his rents, spilling of the coynzie ; the decay & ruine of his
policies, castles, and munitiones, with the daily spending and
wearing away of his Majesties moveables, without anie helping
or repairing therof. As also that the estate, order or spending
within his heines house is nowayes comptrolled, nor keeped
according to the ordinance of his Counsell and Exchequer,
swa that all things is come to such confusion that, efter tryall
taken, it is found that ther is not wheatt, bear, silver nor other
rent to serve his highnes sufficiently in bread & drink nor utherwayes. Ffor remeading of the whilk disorder his Highnes gives
grants & dispones, appoints & destinats to the holding of his
Majestis house the haill rents, maills, dewties, fermes, caynes,
customes, fishings, coall - heughs, casualities, and profeitts of
somever of his proppertie, collectorie, of the superplus of the
benefices & third therof & new Augmentationes be the annexatione of the temporallitie of the Kirk to the Croun. And his

Highnes haveing presenttlie all the saids offices of Comptrollerie, Collectorie & new augmentatione freely resigned, demitted & overgiven by the former officers, possessors therof in his hands to be disponed att his pleasure. And, haveing good prooff of the good quality of the persones following, has *nominat, elected, & chosen* Alex^r. Lord Vrquhart president of the Colledge of Justice, Walter, Commendator of Blantyre, Lord Privie Seall, Mr David Carneagie of Colluthie, Mr John Lindsay parson of Minimuire, Mr James Elphingstonne of Innerneathie, Mr Tho. Hamiltonne of Drumcairnie, Mr John Skein Clerk of Registers, Senators of the Colledge of Justice, & Mr Peter Young of Seatoune : Giveand, grantand, & committand to them the full and free administratione of the forsaid haill rents & dewties pertaining to the forsaids offices, in sic ample forme & maner and with alse great power auctoritie & jurisdiction, as was granted of befor to a part of them by an Act of Parliament, & articles of Instructiones adjoyned therto, anent the Administratione of the rents of the croun & recompensatione therof to his Majestis dereast Queen & bedfellow promittit. And lykas our Soveraign Lord be the tenor heirof promitts, in *verbo principis*, that, for eschewing of confusion & disorder which commonly follows the overgreat multitude of Counsellors, his Majestie will not appoint any more Counsellors or obtrud any more to be insert or adjoyned to this presentt commission att any tyme heirefter. And also that in case of any vacant place by decease of any of the presentt ordinar commissionars, or utherwayes, in that case his Majestie shall presentt no uther Comissionars to be received & admitted be the saids Lords of Exchequer except with their oun advice & consent. With pouer to them to depute & dischairge all inferiour Chamberlaines,

B

under-Collectors, Customers, Searchers, Officiers & Intromettors
whatsomever with any of the saids rents of the Proppertie,
Collectorie, or Augmentatione. And sicklyke deprive all inferiour clerks of the said offices & to appoint new Clerks,
Receavers, and Intrometors with all the forsaids rents belonging to the forsaids offices for whom they shall be answerable
to his Highnes & to the estaites of this realme. Excepting
alwayes the Clerk of Registers his office, fies, priviledges & uther
commodities whatsoever, pertaining or belonging to any of his
predicessors. With power also to hear the Compts of Shirriffs,
Stewarts, Bailliès, Provosts, Eldermen & baillies of burrowes
Customers, Clerks of conquests, Searchers, Chamberlaines,
Receavers, Fewers, & Intromettors with the fermes, maills
profeitts, and dewties, kaynes, customes, fishings, coallheughs,
parks, steidings, orchards, & uther rents of the proppertie,
or order of new augmentatione annexed, or unannexed, belonging in any wayes to the Patrimonie of the Croun : And also to
hear all the Theasaurers & Comptrollers compts of the Theasaurer and his deputts, of the generall & wardane of the Coynzie,
of the taxmen, labourers of the mines, mettalls, & mineralls,
of the Master of work, of invention & plenishing of castles,
of the Monks portions, of the payment of the guairds & men
of warr, of the rents of colledges, hospitalls, & schools, of
the common good of the burrowes & of his Majestis tocher.
And of his highnes haill money whatsomever, as weell within
the realme as comeing from uther countryes, & to allow or
refuise allowance therof. With power also to appoint & sett
fynes & penallties for offences, and to make & sett doune the
pryces of wynes yearly, & of his Majestis victuall & uthers,
kaynes, customes. And to make & performe the order of his

Majestis Equirie & stable, & provision of the sayme with the
fees & wages to be payed to whatsoever persons.   To consider
& repair the decayed customes, and appoint the order of the
uptakeing therof; & to sett and roup the samyne.   To consider
the profeitt & skaith by the presentt coynzie to his grace &
commonweall, & to direct theranent as they shall think most
requisit; with power also and express Commission to the saids
Lords, or anys of them, to be assessors to the Theasaurer &
Commissioners in all signators concerning the Theasaurer without whose advyce nothing shall pass.   The dilligence of Shirriffs
or other inferiour Judges, to enquire & examine thair offences
& negligences, togither with states of officiers of armes; to
cause correct & punish.   With power also to intromett, uptake,
compone, transact, & agree be sic as they shall agree, or
sic as they shall appoint to his Majestis behoof & utilitie, all
escheats of such persones as shall be denunced to the horne by
thair oun decrets, acts & letters; & to consider doe & performe all things committed of befor to the Exchequer with
sic place in Counsell & Parliament as the saids officiers had
of befor.   And with all jurisdiction, power, & priviledges, honors
& immunities belonging to the Exchequer of old be Acts
of Parliament or consuetud of this realme.   Declarand & pro-
mittand, in *verbo principis*, that his Grace shall not subscribe
any letters or signators concerning the dispositione of any
of his rents of proppertie, collectorie, or new augmentationes
forsaids; renewings or ratificationes in any forme, as gifts,
dispositiones, pensiones or infeftments therof, or of any uther
part of the same; or Letters & signators shall not be valid,
nor admitted in any Judgement, or to be ane warrand to any
Register or signett or sealls without the samyne be first read,

heard, allowed & subscribed be the saids Lords Auditors of
the Exchequer or anys of them sittand in Counsell, & then
presentit to his Highnes be them, or any of them haveing power
from the rest, & now succeeding in the place of the ordinarie
officiers to whom the said presentting & subscribing of the
signators pertained of befor; or in case any signators or Letters
pass otherwayes it shall be null be way of action, exception or
reply albeit the scall be appended therto. Dischargeing the
keepers of the Registers Signet, Privie Seall, or Great Seall
of all urgeing of the saids letters & signators, & of all affixing
or appending of seall, or signet, therunto. Except the samyne
be first subscribed be the number of the Lords & in maner
rehearst, under the paines of the tinsell of thair offices, by &
attour the nullitie of the letters wrongouslie past, & registrat
be them, otherwayes then is heir exprest. And farder our
So. Lo. declares that no suspensione of any charges, for in
gathering of any pairt of the saids patrimonies, shall pass
Exchequer or Session sittand & 3 of the saids Lords Auditors
subscribeing the same as said is. And for the mair securitie
Our So. Lo. hes ordained this presentt Comissione to be acted
& registrat in the books of Secret Counsell & Session in token
of all thair consents therunto & approbatione of this presentt
Commission. In contrair & to the derogatione therof the
saids Lords shall nothing doe nor discerne, but shall proceed
conforme therunto in all points till the nixt parliament att
the whilk tyme Our So. Lo. promitts, in *verbo principis*, to
cause ratifie the same by the estates & ordaine that in the
mean tyme Letters of publicatione therof, att the mercat cross
of Edinburgh, *tanquam communis partis*, pass hereupon that
non of the leidges pretend ignorance heirof. And that the

said Lords of Exchequer shall have power to direct Letters
of horning, poynding, wairding & also captione upon thair oun
decrets, acts & ordinances in sic ample forme as any Lords
Auditors of Exchequer had of befor, firme & stable, holding
& to hold all & whatsoever his highnes Commissionars in
maner & in number forsaid sitting togither shall think expedient to be done or necessar. And this said Letter to be
extended in most ample forme with all clauses, neidfull. Subscribt by our S. L. att Hallyroodhouse the 19th January 1595."

If the Commission & the cause of the granting therof be
considered, which doeth more particularlie hold out the causes
of the decay of the revenew. And the courses intended for
the improveing of the same, with the present condition of the
revenew, may incite a new prosecutione of these wayes & rules
then laid doune, especiallie when both his Majestis effairs, & the
conditione of the revenew requyreth the same. As it is my in-
tention to give the best discoverie for the improveing of the
revenew, so doe I conceave no probable means so advantagious
therto than to hold out first that which hath been formerly
practized and ordered therin ; wherfor I must creave leave
further, for informatione, to beg the consideratione of Instructiones following, viz.—

First—that the saids Lords shall convein for putting order
to his Majestis affaires in some speciall place appointed for that
effect as oft as occasion shall requyre, att least [blank] tymes in
the week, dureing the tyme of the sitting of the Lords of Session.

2°. Item, they shall take exact tryall of the presentt number
& qualities of the persones who has the present chairge of the
intromission and inbringing of his Majesties rents & patrimonie ;
and sett doune such a convenient number as may commodiously

bring in the same to his Majestis use; swa that a great pairt
therof be not exhausted by a superfluous number of unprofitable
officers. And for that effect they shall erect & choise the meet-
est & most qualified persons, and shall appoint such reasonable
fies & allowances wherby his Majestie may be weell and profit-
ablie served.

3°. Item, they shall retrinch the superfluous number of servants in his Majestis house, as weell of gentlemen as of officiers
and servants of all degrees, dischairgand their fees & allowances.
And shall reduce his household to the estate of the tyme of such
of his noble progenitors as it has been governed. And if the
presentt officiers be honest & cairefull they shall continue swa
many of them as shall be thought fitt & necessar, they finding
sufficient cautione for thair honest service. And shall discharge
the supernumerarie & under-servants that are not necessarie, &
shall modifie to them honest fies and allowances & shall take such
order anent those premises which they shall cause to be keeped
& observed in tyme comeing.

4°. Item, they shall see & provyd that his Majestis house be
stoked & served with his caine, victuall, wheatt, bear, meall &
corne, hay, mairts, muttons, conneys, capons, poultrie, butter,
cheese, salmond, herring, & uther caynes & customes, swa farr
as the samyne may extend; that non of them be sold nor utherwayes disponed till his Majestis house be first sufficiently served.
And the superplus, if any be, resting of victuall & uthers forsaids shall be sold to the utter availl & for such pryces as the
like stuff shall give in the Shirriffdomes wher they lye. And
the saids Auditors of Exchequer shall doe thair exact dilligence
that all sort of provision requisit that his Majestis house may
be weell & easily staiked.

5°. Item, for the more easie intertainment of the house they shall consider how his Majestis parks and forrests may be plenished, with all kind of store convenient for them, befor beltyme next.

6°. Item, that his Majestis Brewsters & uther officiers accustomed to furnish his Majestis house, shall give as much bread drink & furnishing of his wheatt, bear & uther stuff wherof they have the furnishing as uther provident subjects within the realme accustomed to receave, the stuff being of equall goodness.

7°. Item, that weekly, once or twise, one of the saids Lords shall sitt upon the saids accompts of the house, & dyett books; shall mark & comptroll the expenses, & shall repair the abuses as shall be found contrair to the order sett doune anent the house holding.

8°. Item, that all pensiones, rewards, fees, & gratuities, proceeding from his Majestis liberallitie to any of his servants or uthers his subjects, be no otherwayes admitted or allowed in Exchequer except they be reduced and allowed to a speciall liqudat soume of usuall money of this realme. And if they be excessive to be reduced to such mediocritie as his Majestis liberallitie be not hurtfull to his estate.

9. Item, that the saids Lords shall no wayes consent to any Licences for transporting of forbidden goods untill first tryall be taken if the inhabitants of the Countrie being weell staked may spare the same. And, they being well served, next regaird shall be had to his Majestis commodities in compounding of the saids Licences as the weightines of the cause shall requyre.

10. Item, that nothing shall pass the Thesaurers Register without consent of the saids Lords, att the least 5 of them conveined in Exchequer, & that they shall be Compositors with the

Thesaurer in all things concerning his office, & that non of the Compositiones be disponed without his advyce. And that they shall assist & concurr with his Majestis Thesaurer & his deputts in all things of his office which may redound to his Majestis Commodities.

11. Item, all compts of his Majestis rents, proppertie, causualitie, collectorie, & uthers they being ordinarie officiers conforme to the Comission given to them, they shall take dilligent heid that no just chairge be omitted, nor unjust admitted, but such as shall be necessarie, lawfull & instantly verified with presentt accquittances swa that his Majestie be not prejudged with wrong compt or unreasonable allowance.

12. Item, that no obligators, gifts, or dispositions whatsover be granted or given, but conforme to the ordinance of the Lords of the Counsell and Exchequer, subscribt by his Majestie & publicklie proclaimed att the mercat cross of Edinburgh 25th of Mertch last by past.

These aforesaid Instructiones being exhibited to the Comissioners, togither with an oath for the faithfull performance of the Comission and Instructiones, whilk they conceaveing themselves not able to dischairge that dewty, which either the trust his Majestie was pleased to gyve them, nor the necessity his affaires requyred, unlesse his Majeste would condescend in some measure for the utilitie of his decayed revenew to some proposall proposed be them for the enableing them to performe the duty. Wherfore befor accepting of the said Comission or giveing oath, haveing humbly represented the proposalls following, to which his Majestie condescending, for informatione & the more cleiring of what shall be heirefter spoken, wee shall heir insert togither with the oath wherby wee may perceave not only the bonds & tyes which the King himselfe was pleased to condescend to, but also the strait oath by which they were bound to dischairge thair duty in that Comission. All which being afterward compared with our presentt conditione & managment of the revenew, will make way in some measure to discover from whence the decay of the revenew doeth proceed; which, tho in some things are not very necessarie to our presentt conditione yet will in uthers serve for informatione.

Articles craved be his Majestis .Counsell, whom he burdined with the Comission of Exchequer, to be promised & performed, in verbo principis.

" For the first it is desired be the saids Lords Auditors that his Majestie for the better furtherance of his affairs will promise never to sollicit, nor request, boast nor menace, directly nor indirectly any of the saids Lords to doe any thing contrair to the tenor of the Comission granted to them, or the forme of oath made be them, in favours of any persone to his oun hurt & prejudice.

" Item, that his Majeste will promise faithfully to subscrive nothing concerning the Collectorie, Comptrollerie, nor Thesaurie of Augmentationes untill the same be first sein & found reasonable by the saids Lords sitting in Exchequer in ordinarie number. Att least by the Thesaurer & therefter presented to his Majeste be him.

" Item, his Majeste denuds himselfe att this tyme of the choyceing and electing any persone to be his Highnes Advocat, but shall give pouer to the saids Lords to elect & choyce a qualified man to be his Advocat in case of death, or depriva-

c

tione, or dimission, of any of them who presenttlie serves in
tho said office.

"Item, his Majeste shall approve and allow the order
which shall be sett doune anent the House & Equirie, number
of porsones, & necessar expenss, hearing, comptrolling of the
dyett book, & weekly accompts; and shall not for the importunitie of any person desyre the same to be broken. And
that his Majeste will cause my Lord Duke of Lennox as Cham-
berlaine of Scotland to hold hand to the keeping of good order
in the house, & punishing of transgressors therof as his Lo/ may
goodly doe the same & shall be requisit for that effect.

"Item, seing the proppertie when it was in the best estate
was not sufficient to sustaine the chairges of his Majestis
house, but that ther was yearly great soumes of money taken
furth of the Thesaurie for the entertainment therof, as the
profitt of the Cunzie thir 2 year bygone, to the soume of 50,000
merks yearly."

The oath taken by the Comissioners of Exchequer.

"Wee under subscrivers Comissioners, Auditors of his
Majestis Exchequer: Alexr. Lord Vrquart president of the
Colledge of Justice, Walter Commendator of Blantyre Lord
Privie seall, Mr David Carneagie of Colluthie, Mr John Lind-
say parson of Minnimuire, Mr Ja. Elphingstoune of Inner-
neathie, Mr Tho. Hamiltoune of Drumcairnie, Mr John Skein
Clerk of Register, Senators of the Colledge of Justice, & Mr
Peter Young of Seatoun, Elimosinar, faithfullie promises, and
in the most faithfull & sure forme, & maner of oath obligdes
& binds us & every one of us, as wee shall answere to the great

God our Maker & Creator, that wee shall have no respect in the administratione of our offices as Comissioners and Auditors of his Majestis Exchequer, by Comission given & granted to us the day and date of thir presentts, to do nothing nixt God & good conscience but for the advancement of his Highnes Majestis estate & weell allenarlie; and shall procure in all things in us lyes cairfully that belongs therto by reduceing his Majestis patrimony, pertaining to the Comptrollerie, Collectorie annexed temporallitie of Kirk Landes, to the greatest profitt they may be putt to, or hes been in any tyme of any his predecessors of worthy memory conforme to the lawes of this realme. And shall not give our consent ether for tennandrie or friendship, or particular profitt of any persone or commoditie to ourselves for feir of any respect of any persone, to the alien-atione or dispositione of any of his Majestis rents, landes, superplus of thirds of benefices, customes, caynes, casualities, whatsomever in few, reall rentall, tack long or short, or under whatsomever precept wherby his Highnes rentall may be any wayes diminished, untill his house be first provyded, and furnished effeirand to his Majestis estate & honor. And for the better executione of all and haill the articles and tenor of the old Comissione of Exchequer granted to us : Wee, & every one of us, shall dilligently and lawfullie dischairge our dewties as trew & honest Counsellors to his Majestes great weill & honour, so far as wee know & understand. And shall not give consent, nor subscriptiones severallie, nor out of counsell, in any thing that may tend to his Majestis hurt or prejudice, but shall pass subscrive & allow all things necessar & expedient anent the premisses in counsell sittand conveined for that effect, att least 5 in number. With no less consideratione of his Majestis

profitt in all respects, nor gife it were our oun particular
wherof wee shall have no particular consideratione, bot only to
doe honorable & profitable service to his Majestie as it becomes
obedient subjects & faithfull Counsellors.

"Provyding allwayes that this our presentt obligatione &
oath made for the causes forsaids to his Majeste, shall be no
declinator, exceptione, against us, or any of us, anent our office or
jurisdiction in the Session or Colledge of Justice in any actione
or cause wherin his Majeste hes or shall have interest in any
tyme heirefter, seing that non of us hes [*blank*] or intromissione
with his Majestis rents, bot only being his Majestis naturall
subjects and bound to serve him efter our full power allenarlie.
The oversight and directione of the intrometors with the saids
rents of the patrimony, who shall be comptrollers therfor to the
effect they may be imployed to the weell of his Majestis realme
and croun; which all & sundrie the premises befor God Al-
mighty to performe fullfull and underly efter our power and
knowledge be thir presentts subscribt with our hands att Hallyroodhouse the 19th January 1595."

Haveing from the Comissione & instructiones aforsaid
holden out what wes intended for improveing of the revenew,
which from thir groundes ther may be some consideratiores
that may move a prosecuting of the same. So the Comissioners in this Comissione seemed to lay doune att the begin- .
ing such grounds. Yet they were soon blasted, and thair caire
throw the multitude of the Comissioners, each of them acting
for their interest & friendes. The samyne Comissione had no
endurance, but for about 2 yeirs, ffor, in December 1597, ther is
a new Comissione granted to the Thesaurer & uther Comis-

sioners of the Exchequer & so it came to its own channell.
And in the yeir 1603 att King James his goeing to England
ther is also a new Comissione granted to the Thesaurer &
Comissioners of the Exchequer. And in absence of the
Thesaurer, because he wes to goe with the King, to John
Arnot burges of Edinburgh, Thesaurer depute nominat be the
Thesaurer. All these Comissiones may be heir particularlie
sett doune if it were not too tedious. Therefore it shall only
be our work, as wee intend, to branch out the revenew in its
severall particular branches & so to prosecute the same, according as they fall in the way. Bot as wee have sett doune ane
discriptione of the Exchequer of Scotland which is a court
wherin the affaires of the revenew are treated and handled;
and altho wee have a resolutione in its dew & propper place to
speake to the severall offices & officers, nature, aryse, and
dewtyes of the same imployed in the managment therof, which
in its propper place wee resolve to prosecute. Yet in respect
that the two great offices of the Exchequer were the Thesaurer
and Thesaurer Depute, who are employed in the management
of the revenew in its severall branches, wee humbly offer to
sett doune the arryse, dewtie, and dignitie of these respective
offices, and doe forbear the remainder offices att presentt
which will, from the dewty of thair place, the more illustrat
what the revenew is. And for the better cleiring therof it
would be considered that in old tyme the revenew wes managed by these offices: Thesaurie, Collectorie, & Comptrollerie,
so by cleiring these will give the greater dignitie of the office
of the Thesaurer. The one being joyned for the uther and the
power of both consolidate in the persone of the Thesaurer.

And (1°) to the name Comptroller quasi *Contra Rotulator*

which of old wes used for him as Budeus sayes, in his *Annota-tiones de officio*, Questoris cui id muneris conjunctum erat et observaret pecuniam quam in usum principis vel Civitatis Collegerunt exactores; there are severall distinct offices under this name used in England as Comptroller of the Kings house, Comptroller of the Navie & Comptroller of the Customes, Comptroller of the Mint & uther offices.   In Scotland wee have no mentione of any but Comptroller, whose office wes to dischairge the dewtie of all these particular offices, he wes esteemed in greater accompt then the Thesaurer, he haveing the management of the whole proppertie, the placeing of all Receavers, Challmerlaines, & uther officers, the takeing of a cautione for thair fidelitie, the censureing & punishing them for abuses & disposeing them of thair offices, passing of all infeftments of the proppertie, & the managing of the haill affaires pertaining & belonging therto.   And the Thesaurer haveing only the managment of the casualitie aryseing out of Kirk landes, & blench dewties.

To speake further of this office, than to cleir what wes the distinctione betwixt the Comptroller & the Thesaurer, is not our purpose, nether shall wee digress so farr to presume what hath been the cause of this alteratione; it being wholly att his Majestis disposall, save only this farr that it hath been for preventing of divisione.   And therefore haveing cleired what the Comptrollers office wes, wee shall speake to the office of Thesaurie.

1° to the name; Thesaurer or Thesaurarius cometh from ane French word Thesairier: Id est questor Prefectus Fisci, and signifieth ane officer to whom the Thesaurie of any uther is comitted to be keeped.   To speake to this office as it is established now, haveing both the office of Comptrollerie, Thesaurie & Collectorie, would prove a large extent.

Wee shall only touch the office in generall, to whom the managment of all the wealth and revenewes belonging to the King under whatsoever name is comitted, who haveing not only all the priviledges which formerly belonged to the Comptroller & Collector but also to the Thesaurer doeth evidence so much the more greatnes dignitie & auctoritie of him who is Thesaurer. Haveing thus farr touched the former constitutione & distinction betwixt the Thesaurer & Comptroller wee shall now speak to them as they are joyned in one. And (1°) As it is his propper dewtie, as said is, to have the managment of the whole proppertie, casuallitie, & revenew of the King, so to nominat & appoint all under officers, and to make acts for the better management & improvement therof. He is President in Exchequer tho' of old the Kings Majestie did nominat & appoint ane President, as in the comissione 1608 (13th Junij) did nominat the Archbishop of Glasgow to be President, and in uther commissiones of that nature, but with that provisione that the Thesaurer & Thesaurer depute *sine quibus non.* And that of late the Chancellor as claiming the priviledge to be President in all courtes did challenge this ; yet his Majeste be his letter the 24th January 1635, and one uther of the 5th Mertch 1635, wherby in the first he did ordaine the said Thesaurer & depute Thesaurer to be President in Exchequer in absence of the Archbishop of St Andrews. Bot in the uther more particularlie ordaining them to be President in Exchequer in all tyme comeing. From both which, and from the nature of the judicatorie being the Kings oun particular court concerning the managment of his revenew to whose care the same is comitted & to

whom a negative voyce in the regulating therof is granted, &
that the members of that court are but Assessors to him in the
managment therof; it will appeare that the same seemeth to
be most consonant with, & agreeable to, his Majestis service that
the Thesaurer be President seing without him they cannot
meet nor act.

As he hath not only the whole pouer of regulating and manageing the revenew as said is, the stoping all signaturs that is,
or may be, past in that Court of Exchequer so hath he been
allowed by the Kings Majeste to stop any signature which
shall come from his Majestis handes, which he apprehends to
have been obtained upon a misrepresentatione to the prejudice of
the revenew, wherof many instances may be given as well wherin
his Majestis predecessors for the profitt and utilitie of the
croun have oblidged themselves, *de verbo principis*, not to passe
any gift, nor grant without the trew condition of the same be
represented by his Thesaurer to him, as by severall Acts made
declairing the same to be null in case the samyne sould be so
granted. But seing this priviledge cannot so much be granted
as a priviledge dew to that office, but as ane act of favour flow-
ing from the Kings wise consideratione of his oun affaires so
shall wee forbear to speak to them, & only for informatione
shall touch what wes the practice of his Majestis father of
blissed memory, which is evidenced in that conference betwixt
his Majeste & the E. of Dunfermling then Chancellor & the E.
of Dunbar Thesaurer att Royston, the 12th of October 1610,
wherin amongst uther particulars concerning the revenew then
offered and approven by his Majeste this is expressed in thir
wordes viz. " That your Majeste give no gift nor grant of any
casualitie which may ether fall to the croun, or may prejudge

the revenew, bot by the speciall advyce of the Lord Thesaurer to whose chairge the same pertaineth." To which his Majeste graciously condescendes in these wordes : "That in case through the importunity of any persone wee give any such gifts of that nature wee doe allow thee our Thesaurer to stop the same till wee be informed therof."

And, sicklyke, the same prejudice being represented to his Majeste, in anno 1638 & 1635, by this Thesaurer his Majeste by his particular instructiones in May 1633 and July & December 1635, by which instructiones they are not only allowed, bot positively comanded the Thesaurer as a dewty to stop these signatures. And seing the stoping of such may very much conduce to the advantage of the revenew, as wee have cleired the allowance & comand of the samyne wee shall only represent how gracious & acceptable such office wes esteemed as the letter following evidences :—

"C. R.

"Right trustie & well beloved Cousin & Counsellor and trustie & well beloved Counsellors Wee greit yow well. Wee receaved your letter touching the stoping of that signature of the Abbacy of Lyndores till our pleasure should be known in that purpose, wherin wee approve your proceeding, & give yow thanks for the same. And still it is our pleasure (as of late wee did signifie to yow our Treasaurer depute) that no signatur pass unlesse yee receve a speciall warrand from us for expeding therof. And in the meanetyme that yee fayle not to call for the signature & keepe it in your custody, ffor all which these presentts shall be your warrand."

D

As he is not only allowed to stop the signaturs passing his Majestis oun handes as said is, bot also *natura officij* hes the priviledge to stop all signaturs and process wherin his Majeste is, or may be, concerned befor the Lordes of Session, which being questioned in some measure by the Lordes in a particular of the E. of Murrayes anent the Lordschip of Doune. His Majeste haveing wrytten to them challenging it as his prerogative, the saides Lordes did by thair Act of Sederunt, in January 1637, make ane Act that whensoever any action or busines whatsoever occurs wherin his Majeste in his propperty, customes, impost, or casuallitie or any uther part of his rentes or revenew be concerned that the Thesaurer, or in his absence the Thesaurer depute, shall be aquainted & that the proces shall sist till they give order theranent.

As he hath the priviledge of stoping all proces befor the Lordes of Session, wherin his Majestis revenew may be concerned, so hath he the power to raise & intent actiones against all persones detainers of his Majestis revenew. As also reductiones of his Majestis proppertie, or any uther landes wherin his Majeste hes ryght as may appeare (1°) be the severall Acts that have been granted of old be the Comptroller wherof one of the 12 Junij 1593, the Comptroller wes ordained by the Kings Majeste to presentt his Majestis revocatione to executione, & to cause raise reduction theron as he would answere with the priviledges of his office. And sicklyke by ane uther Act the Kings Majeste, on the 7th December therefter, being in Exchequer did ordaine the Comptroller to informe himselfe of all pensiones, wodsettes, of the proppertie, and to give order to persew & reduce the same, but more particularlie in these latter tymes by speciall instructiones given to the Thesaurer to cause raise reductione agaynst severall particular landes as of the Lordschips of Torphichen, Abercorne, Doune, Scoon, Blantyre, Kintyr, Jura & uthers of that nature which accordingly hath been raised, tho through the distraction of the tymes small progres made.

(2°) By the severall orders given by his Majeste to his Advocat, not only comanding him to consult with his Thesaurer in all things concerning his affaires, bot also that he shall receave orders from him from tyme to tyme theranent. And that before he shall docquet any Signatures to be presented or passed by his Majeste, he shall comunicate the same to the Thesaurer.

(3°) By a more particular instructione the Thesaurer is impowered in case of matter of difficulty, or in case of neglect, to make use of ane uther Advocat. In which instructione Sir Lewes Stewart is particularlie named.

Thesaurer Depute.

Haveing spoken something too large, tho not according to the Eminencie of the place, nor so full as ether it ought, or should be, wee shall only say as to the priviledges therof that the Thesaurer Depute may challenge in absence of the Thesaurer principall the same, bot tho it be sufficient that wee endeavoured to branch out the Thesaurers office which consequently in his absence as said is, is the Thesaurer Deputes, yet least wee may be adjudged short in dewtie, if wee shall alltogither passe it, wee shall therfor crave leave to speake a litle to the aryse of the same & how it came to be a distinct office.

Wee find in non of the old records any mentione made of

the Thesaurer Deputes office, ther seeming to be no necessity
of any such office, in respect that the revenew being divided,
in a Comptrollerie, Thesaurie & Collectorie the officers therof were sufficient to dischairge the dewty & manage the
severall parts of the revenew belonging to thair chairge.
The first Thesaurer depute that is named is in Novr. 1583
wherin Robert Melvell of Cairnes is nominat Thesaurer Depute
& Thesaurer Clerk wherby it semes this place hes not been
of such power & account as now. Bot in more late tymes
wher through the absence of the Thesaurer or Comptroller,
or upon what uther occasione wee find ether of them have
Deputes viz Sr James Hay of Kinglassie then Comptroller
did in anno 1589 nominate Sr John Arnot Depute-Comptroller,
who efterwards wes nominate Thesaurer Depute; bot passeing
this wee shall come to the office now in hand, which is the
Thesaurer Deputes office. Both by the frequent altering &
nominating sometyme one, and sometyme another, the samyne
hath not been any setled office as may appeare by the nominating of the persones following viz: Wee find, on the 28
December 1597, Tho. Foules, Goldsmith burges of Edinburgh
to be nominate by Walter Comendator of Blantyre then
Thesaurer, to be Thesaurer Depute wherof the wordes of his
Comissione & nominatione bears as followes viz: Giveing him
full power to receave all Compositiones of Signatures & haill
casuallities of the Thesaurie: to indorse the recept on the
back; deburse & furnish unto his Majeste & his affaires such
things as are necessarie as shall be commanded from tyme
to tyme by the Thesaurer Principall. Lykwayes wee find,
in Mertch 1598, Mr George Young to be nominate by the
said Walter Comendator of Blantyre bearing in his Comissione

the forsaides express wordes. As also, in anno 1599, wee
find John Arnot, therefter designed Sir John Arnot, to be
nominat Thesaurer Depute be the Kings Majeste and Exchequer per expressum only in absence of the Thesaurer
principall pro tempore, with this provisione that the Thesaurer
shall relieve him of any sommes of money that he shall depurse
in his absence, in case he shall happen to receave non. And
lastly in anno 1603 be Comissione to the Exchequer, whilk
is particularlie befor insert, he is nominat John Arnot burges
of Edinburgh Thesaurer depute in absence of the Thesaurer
with consent of the Thesaurer. And also wee find that the
E. of Dunbar being Thesaurer & residing much att Court
doeth (least his Majestis affaires should be prejudged by his
absence) obtaine commissione to Sir John Arnot as Thesaurer
Depute, with power to him to dischairdge the dewtyes of
the said office as fully as he might doe if he were presentt.
And also wee find that, efter the death of the E. of Dunbar,
the E. of Somerset haveing obtained ane gift of the Thesaurer
principall office, in respect that he constantly remained att
Court & did not come to Scottland, to exerce the dewtyes of
the same, he obtained ane comissione of the Thesaurer Deputes
place to Sir Gideon Murray which both from his oun knowledge
of the dewtyes therof & the Thesaurer principall, his constant
absence not only gave the first luster to that office but the
aryse therof in honor & estate.

Haveing, from the comissione, instructiones & oath forsaid,
given some informatione of what wes done in these tymes I
shall forbear to proceed to the severall Acts made be them.
Thair caire towardes the improvement and managment of
the revenew is fully evidenced, rather choyceing as the oc-

casione shall offer in the severall particulars to speake therto. Haveing already spoken in generall to the jurisdiction of Exchequer for managment of the King's revenew, it will be necessar to give ane more particular accompt therof, in its severall branches. But seeing it is ane subject of ane large extent we shall lay doune for methodes sake these following generall heides, which wee resolve to follow so farr as wee can in this litle informatione viz.—

1. What is to be agitate in Exchequer.
2. What offices are to be imployed therin,
   And the aryse, nature, & dewty therof.
3°. The reasone of the decay of the Revenew.
4°. Articles & propossalls for the improvement of the same.

For the first what is, or ought to be, agitate in Exchequer. Haveing befor in generall cleired what the Exchequer is, and that it is ane court wherin all thinges concerning the Kinges revenew were to be agitate, it will therefore be necesar for informatione to cleir wherin this revenew consistes to the effect wee may take aryse therefrom particularlie to speake therof.

Which consistes in
$\begin{cases} \text{Proppertie.} \\ \text{Casuallitie.} \\ \text{Gratuitie.} \end{cases}$

Proppertie may be called two fold; the old proppertie, & the annexed proppertie. The old Proppertie is also twofold viz: *ffirst* such landes as did propperly of old belong to the King, and were his propper heretage and sett to tennents for payment of the full value therof. 2° Such landes as are only for payment of yeirly few dewties; the rent of which landes and the few dewties payable furth therof, consisting in few dewtyes victuall, caynes, and uthers are yeirly payed: att least ought & should be payed to the Comptroller.

The annexed Proppertie is also threefold.

First, Customes.

Secondly, Kirk landes.

Thirdly, Forfaulted landes.

First, Customes are, and ever have been, either formed for Tackdewtyes, or gathered in by commissione. Which Tackes and Commissiones so granted are, immediatly befor they be delyvered to the parties, registrat in the Bookes of Exchequer, which doeth become a chairge to the partie for payment of the soumes contained in the Tack or Commissione. The parties haveing so compted and enrolled in the roll called· the Custome Roll, the Thesaurer, Comptroller, and others are chairged thereby, wherein also the bullzion is compted for.

Kirklandes whither paying few or blench dewties are yeirly chairged as uthers of the Proppertie, and compted for in the roll called the Proppertie Roll, which is ane chairge to the Thesaurer of the new augmentationes.

Casuallitie may be said to be \{ First, Propper Casuallitie.
twofold. \{ Secondly, Casuall.

Propper Casuallitie may be adjudged to be blench dewtyes of all temporall landes, and which are yeirly compted for in Exchequer, be the severall Shirriffes Baillies, and Stewartes, and so ingrossed in the roll called the Shirriff Roll, which is a chairge to the Thesaurer and others.

Casuall may be said to be of sundrie sorts. First wairdes and Mariages which are of two sorts viz taxed and untaxed.

Taxed, are chairged by the Register of the Thesaurie or Comptrollerie or Thesaurie of new augmentationes. *Untaxed*, are either compounded for in the Exchequer or not, if compounded for then the compositiones therof are ingrossed in the Thesaurers Register by which the Register Thesaurer is chairged. Those not compounded for, the Thesaurer may intromett with the haill rents of the lands dureing the tyme of the waird, and doeth compt for the same in the Proppertie Roll which is a chairge to him, or the intromettors therwith. But this hes not been these many years prosecute.

Escheatts, compositiones of infeftments, Tutories, Bastardies, & uthers of that nature which passeth be way of signatur & compounded for in Exchequer which compositiones are to be ingrossed in the Thesaurers Register which is a chairge to the Thesaurer or Receaver therof.

Nonentries are of 3 sorts: (1°) either such as are be way of Signatur passed & compounded in Exchequer which is chairged in the Thesaurers Register as in uther signaturs; (2do) are such as are entered in the Exchequer by the Responde books which are a chairge to the respective Sheriffs who compting therfor in the Shirriff Roll which is ane chairge to the Thesaurer or Recevars; (3°) such as are conceilled which ought to be tryed for & uplifted.

Fynes which are of sundrie sorts (1°) Those which are befor the Counsell chairged by the Clerk of Counsells Register. (2°) Those befor the Justice called the Justice aire, circuit Court be Comissione, or uther wayes ought to be compted for in the Exchequer & chairged by the Register of the court. (3°) Those befor the hie Comissione are chairged be the Register of the Judgment seatt.

Licences are granted in two maner of wayes as the meritts of the cause requyres. (1°) Great matters are passed by signatur & so compounded for in Exchequer, and so registrat & chairged be the Thesaurers Register. (2do) Small causes by delyverance upon Supplicationes, Acts of Counsell & Exchequer.

Unlawes which are of 2 sorts (1°) Those that are of a certaine cause to a definit tyme; such as are unlawed before the Justice may be befor the Counsell Exchequer, & uther Judges. These are chairged be the Roll of the judicatorie. (2do) Indefinit must abyde ane declarator of the Advocats instance wherein all paines & unlawes of laborrows are included whither decerned or not.

Gratuitie is that which is imposed by King & Parliament upon the Leidges as Taxationes which are not of ane constant revenew or appropriat to the Croun.

The Revenew being thus branched out & divyded in its severall heids & articles, it would be a prolix work to begine & compose a rentall for these branches from the first anexatione of the patrimony of the Croun, & would therin occasion a confusion of the rentall. Tho something of this nature may be done heirefter, as is intended both as to the old patrimony of the Croun, the blench landes, & of waird landes taxed, ether or converted to few blench. Yet at presentt the following rentall is only to cleir what the presentt fewers of the propperty in the old landes yeirly payes; and how farr the same is altered diminished or converted from the old rentalls preceeding 1603, which was the tyme of King James his goeing into England.

E

The subject matter of this rentall is only the constant rent which consisteth of these dewtyes which are yeirly compted for be the Shirriffs, baillies, & stewarts, and is called the propper casuallitie, aryseing from the blench dewtyes of all temporall landes, which is particularlie befor mentioned in that heid called Propper Casuallitie & which is compted in the shiriff Roll. The 2^d is the fewers of the proppertie compted in the Proppertie Roll. The 3^d is the burrow maills & fewes which is also proppertie. The 4th is the custome, all which is called the annexed proppertie.

As for the first the Shirriffs charges themselves with these three which is a constant rent not differing, nor altering, yeirly viz. :

1. With the blench dewtyes of the Blench landes in every shyre.
2. With the Castlewairds in every shyre.
3. With the book.

First as to the blenches. It is so unconsiderable a dewty that it would be ane great prejudice to the vassalls to come in to the Exchequer & pay the same yeirly, for preventing wherof it was ordained that ilk shirriff should uplift the said blenches within thair respective shyres, & for that effect ther was ane List given of them to the said Shirriffe by which they did compt *ratione officij* yeirly whither they got payment or not.

CASTLEWAIRDS is a dewty or taxatione very old, neir 300 yeirs since the samyne was first imposed on waird landes for the provyding & mentaining of Castles in tyme of warr viz.: the Castle of Edinburgh, Dumbar, Berwick, Blaikness, Roxburgh, & Lanrik. Ffor the mentainance of which castles this small taxatione or imposition was imposed & ordained to be collected by the respective Shirriffs & paid in be them to the saids severall castles and so called castlewards, or rather castle guardes, which is also charged on the Shirriff & compted be him yeirly *ratione ut supra.*

THE BOOK.—The shirriff did yeirly compt for the fynes of the courts, and produced thair book of the ffynes & gave thair oath on the trew extract of the samyne. Bot the King, with advyce of the Lordes of Exchequer, did indulge that favour to the shirriffs to compone for the saids fynes for ane modified soume yeirly to be payed in place of the said Book.

· The uther two being the propper fewes of his Majestis rents doeth compt yeirly, ether by themselves or uther wayes by Chalmerlaines. These being the subject of the following rentall are sett doune as followes viz: first what it paid yeirly by the Shirriff. And nixt, what is paid be the proppertie ether by the Fewars themselves, Challmerlaines, or Burrowes: the soumes therfrae aryseing being sett doune as they pay be the presentt rentall. Nixt is sett doune what deductiones is deduced to the compters & upon what grounds; and then is sett doune the free money paid; and the last is the differences & alterationes aryseing betwixt the old rentall & the presentt rentall.

This method being prescribed is essayed to be prosecute throw the severall Shyres as follows :—

BERWICK SHYRE.

Payed be the Shirriff for book blenches and Castellwairdes as followes:

Money	.	.	17 01 01
Argents	.	.	01 12 00
Gilt spurres 2 p[r]	.		16 00 00
Broad Arrowes 4	.		00 08 00
Pepper one pund	.		01 10 00
Cumin seed one pund	.		00 06 00
Gloves one pair	.		03 00 00
Castlewairds	.	.	22 00 00
Book	.	.	40 00 00

101 17 01

Of the which soume of 101[lb.] 17s. 01[d.] there wes to be deduced 12[lb.] 14s. 11[d.] out of Edringtoun; 42 shilling out of Shirreff-bigging, Reid-pleugh Land, & Bonetoune. And 20s. of Castlewairds because these landes are bounded within England & estimate waist; extending in all to the soume of 015 16 11

The Shirriff of Berwick doeth only compt yeirly for 81[lb.] which is 4[lb.] 19s. 1[d.] less, for which he ether must compt or instruct how the same is taken away

BAILLIARIE OF LAUDERDALE.

For book & blenches viz:

Money	.	.	00 00 11
Argents 3[d.] in scotts money		00 03 00
Peper 2 pund	.		03 00 00
1 Leopar	.	.	05 06 08

008 10 07

Proppertie.

Earledome of March	.	.	. 153 00 00
Coldinghame Lordschip	.		. 066 13 04
Couldstreame { of blench dewtie		. 040 00 00
{ of few dewtie	.		. 159 10 00
Cranshawes	.	.	. 021 00 00

Fewar of Theripland . . .	026 00 00	
Graden	010 13 04	
Graystonrig	002 00 00	
Colbrandispeth . . .	020 00 00	
Item of wheat 8 chall. att 100lb.	800 00 00	
Item of beir 8 chall. att 100lb.	800 00 00	
Husband landes of Colbrandispeth .	001 06 06	
Teyndes of Lauder . . .	003 00 00	
Fascastell by the E. of Home . .	003 00 00	
Flemingtoune	004 00 00	
Bot now the samyne hold blench & so is deduced		04 00 00
Farnisyde	010 13 04	
Burgh of Lauder . . .	005 09 00	

Suma of the haill chairge of the shyre . . .	2236 07 02	
Suma of the deductiones extend to .		19 16 11
Which being deduced from the charge ther remaines of free money . . .		2216 10 3

Differences betwixt the old & present rentalls.

The Earldome of March wes annexed to the Croun be K. Ja. 3ᵈ par. 14 act 112 "And did compt in the proppertie roll ac- " cording to the rentall efter sett doune in anno 1502 bearing " particularlie as followes :

RENTALL OF THE PARTICULAR FEWARS OF THE EARLDOME OF MARCH.

Earlestoune & Phillipstoune	19 00 00
Greinlaw & millne thorof Greinlaw-den & Greinlawhamo .	46 13 04
Annuitie of Whitsyde	00 02 03
22 husband landes of Dunce	22 00 00
Anuitie of the mylne of Dunce	04 00 00
Coattages of Dunce	12 00 00
Plenderleuch	05 00 00
Annuitie of the toune of Dunce	00 10 05
Dunce park	04 00 00

BERWICK. Calshell		05 06 08
Cockburne		20 00 00
Tochrig		15 00 00
Thornesyde		32 00 00
Mylne therof		04 00 00
2 part of the dominicall landes of Thornsyd		04 08 00
Novæ terræ in Chirnisyde		01 13 04
Lethame		73 00 00
Minsingtoune		20 00 00
Mylne therof		03 00 00
Hirsell		26 13 04
Lochbrighame & Brighame-Sheills		40 00 00
Meikle Brighame		50 00 00
Colbrandispeth		51 12 00
Landes of Dunce which belonged to the E. Tweddell		01 06 08
Upsadleingtoune		10 00 00
Forrest of Dunce & Handaxwood		10 00 00
Peccox		20 00 00
Meikle & Litle Pincartoun		50 00 00
Milne of Eist Barnes		05 06 08
Milne of West Barnes		08 00 00
Mylne of Whitinghame		05 06 08
Burgh of Dumbar		04 00 00
Annuitie of Lambden		01 06 08
Rigg & Flures		03 00 00
Annuitie of Wm· Eduardsons tenements in Dumbar		00 08 00
Ge. Aikens aikers in Dumbar		00 04 00
Annuitie of the assyse of Watsland in Pinkartoun		00 06 08
Annuitie of the assyse of Bincarton in Pincartoun		00 04 00
Woodsland in Budslie		00 01 00
Annuitie of Popill		00 04 00
Annuitie of Hallyburtoune		00 10 00
Hairlaw		00 03 04
Annuitie of the tennendries of Ja. Ingles in Greinlaw		00 06 08
Ja. Glintlawe's land payes		00 01 00
Popill by vendition of 2 pair gilt spurs payes		00 13 04
Hoprig		01 00 00
Auguland in Hoprigg		00 03 00
Five husband lands in Birgham		00 03 00
Larrinks in Ballheaven of blench ferme		00 01 06
Graden by venditione of one pund cumin		00 01 00
Annuitie of Stanipeth		00 08 00
Lowsheill one pund pepper		01 00 00

Goldingstaine 1 pund pepper	01	00	00 BERWICK.
Fishing of Brighame 72 salmond att 10s. the peice . .	36	00	00 —
Grainge, eister & wester of Barrings & Oxans den & Newtoune			
Leyes payes, viz. :—			
of wheat 30 chall. att 100^lb. is . . .	3000	00	00
of beir 15 chall. att 100^lb. is . . .	1500	00	00
Suma of the Earledome of March according to the abonewritten rentall is . .	5121	06	00
The Earledome of March according to the preceiding old rentall payes	5121	00	00
But according to the presentt rentall payes only . .	153	00	00
So the rentalls differ be the soume of .	4968	00	00

Observations.

It is found in anno 1582 that the Earle of Home did compt for the Earledome of March att 174^lb. yeirly which doeth differ from the presentt rentall be 20^lb. Nether hes the one, nor the uther compted these 60 yeirs, except Graden & the burgh of Dumbar. The cause of the not compting for some of these yeirs being conceived to be because a part of these few dewties wer allocat to Archbald Hay his Majestis Chirurgion who is dead long since. As to the particular rentall befor sett doune, contained in the rentall 1582, it is conceaved that the Earle of Home hes no ryght now to these few dewties, but any ryght he had to the same wes be way of lease which is expyred long since. And which wes sett for payment of the forsaid few dewtie of 174^lb. as the tacke dewty therof & which tacke dewtyes were assigned to the said Archbald Hay.

Coldinghame of old ane Priorie of the order of the Black fryers founded be Edgar K. of Scotland falling in his Majestis handes be the Act of Annexatione of Kirk Landes, and was sett out to Francis Stewart who paid 200 merks of few dewtie.

DERWICK. In anno 1634, there wes ane action of Reduction & Improbatione raised att the Kings Instance agaynst the vassalls of the said Priorie & agaynst the said Francis Stewart his ryght.

The 28 Novr. 1636 there is ane contract past betwixt the King and the said Francis Stewart, be the whilk contract the said Priorie is wodsett, and disponed to the said Francis ay & whill the King should make payment to him of the soume of 5000^{lb} ster. And did assign him to the benefit of the reduction & improbatione agaynst the vassalls; & dispones the haill casualities of the superiorities & the compositiones of all the infeftments to be past in the Exchequer with his consent & the compositiones paid in to him. The blench dewtie therof wes formerly 200 merks, bot by the forsaid contract it was reduced to 100 merks which hes not been paid these mony yeirs.

Cauldstreame of old ane Cloister Ordinis Cistertiensis founded be the Countes of Merch paying of blench dewtie 40^{lb} & of few dewtie 159^{lb} 5s., which is in all 199^{lb} 10s. as is before charged.

Cranshawes payes monete sterlingor. There hes been great debate what this monete sterlingorum wes, some alleadgeing that the Kings dews should be paid in white money, in respect of the great plentie of copper coyne then used. Uthers say that it should be paid in Sterling pennyes which wes decyded, the last of Febry. 1600, to be according to the intrinsick value of the money att 10^{lb} scotts for each 20s. ster. as in ane action persewed be Da. Murray of Gospertie, knight, comptroller agaynst William Barckley burges of Montrose. In the which action the comptroller persewes the said burgh for payment of their few dewtie in Sterling money att 12^{lb}

scotts for each 20s. ster., but the Lords decerned att 10^{lb.} as is BERWICK.
befor exprest.

Fascastell belonged to the Laird of Restalrig and was
disponed to the E. of Home, as a part of the fforfaulter of
Restalrig, who disponed the same to the Laird of Wauch-
toun. Of old it was compted as a fyft part of the Abbacy
of Coldinghame, bot the house of Fascastell & some aikers
besyde it holds few of the King for payment of 3^{lb.} yeirly, which
hes not been compted nor paid thir many yeirs.

Fairnisyde hes not compted thir many yeirs, bot should
be compted for & paid be Alexr. Home of Hunwood & [? John]
Kerr of Morisone.

Flemingtoun is a part of the Lordschip of Coldinghame
which belongs now to the Lord Rentoun, who by ane new
Chartour hes gotten these & uther landes holden blench so
that the forsaid soume of 4^{lb.} of few dewtie is now to be deduced
in maner forsaid.

SELKIRK SHYRE.

Paid be the Shirriff for book & blenches viz.:

Argentes 10^{d.} in scotts money . .	00 10 00
Money	00 00 03
Gilt spurres one pair . . .	08 00 00
1 broad arrow . . .	00 10 00
1 broad arrow heid . . .	00 02 00
Book	10 00 00

019 02 03

Proppertie.

Dumfedling by a charter to the E. of Buccleuch dated 7th April 1607 (sic) . .	26 13 04
Longshaw	03 10 00

F

SELKIRK. Hassinden & Kingwood feild . . .	52 00 00
— Burgh of Selkirk . . .	06 00 00

Challmerlanrie of Etrick Forrest conforme to
the rentall following—

Wester Montbenge	70 10 00
Eister Montbenge & Eastlacknow [?] . .	70 10 00
Eastlackburne [?] & Shutting Leyes . .	70 03 04
Black graine	70 10 00
Laidhop	31 00 00
Wester Dolorian & Wordihop . .	26 00 00
Mylne of Nework	06 00 00
Whythillbrac	32 00 00
Auldwork	24 00 00
Carterhauch	36 00 00
Glengath	08 00 00
Softheugh [? Eastheugh] . . .	30 00 00
Fawsyde	26 13 04
Tynnes	50 00 00
Whythop	24 00 00
Augmentatione of the said haill landes .	01 00 00
Hirtherne	30 00 00
Auldishop	14 00 00
Elibank	30 00 00
Glenport	24 00 00
Priesthop . . . ; .	05 10 00
Eister Dollorian	20 00 00
Eldinghop	59 00 00
Kirkhop	40 02 00
Deiphop	10 03 04
Inner Huntlie	11 00 00
Hellvellan	13 06 08
Eltrieff	50 00 00
Gamascleuch	15 00 00
Corsileuch [Corscleuch] . . .	12 00 00
Burehop	20 06 08
St Marie Loch in the Lewes . . .	01 00 00
Hangit shaw	50 00 00
Levinghop	50 00 00
Howhard	50 00 00
Augmentatione of thir landes . .	01 00 00
Hayning	25 06 08
Midlesteid & Black Middings . . .	30 06 08
Hartwood burne	26 00 00

Langhop	18	15	00
Utter Huntly	11	00	00
Hartwood myres	28	03	04
Hyndhop	15	13	04
Aikwood	28	00	00
Southbowhill .	14	00	00
Westsyd landes of Karhop	12	05	00
Hetrieburne .	16	03	04
Whythauchbrae	17	10	00
Howfurd	25	03	04
Helen burne & shawes	44	02	00
Bairlielie	24	06	08
Earnheuch	28	00	00
Singlie	28	00	00
Augmentatione of the said 2 landes	00	06	08
Dodhead alias Dodbank	18	05	00
Gilminscleuch	20	10	00
Fawoodsydhill 3 part of	16	03	04
Barterburgh .	21	06	08
Fawood Grange	12	03	04
Fawoodhill 2 part	33	06	08
Tuschelaw & Cumblaw	32	00	00
Cackrabank	18	00	00
Augmentatione of the said 2 landes	00	13	04
Dryhop & Farniehop .	52	03	04
Kirksteid	14	03	04
Glensax	24	00	00
Soundhop	24	00	00
Halfe landes of Keishop	06	02	06
The uther halfe therof	06	03	04
Deuchar	46	00	00
Breadmeadowes	33	06	08
William hop .	26	00	00
Northbow hill	13	06	08
Reidfurd grein	15	13	04
Drycleuch sheill	15	13	04
Gallowsheills & Mossey leyes .	90	05	00
Blindley	50	00	00
Cadenheid	50	00	00
Byrhop	08	00	00
Augmentatione of the said 3 landes	00	06	08
Corslie	21	04	00
Whytbank	27	06	08

SELKIRK. Knowes	12 00 00		
— Torwoodley	30 00 00		
Cardonley	30 00 00		
Nowhall alias Craigloith . . .	15 13 04		
Windiedures	26 13 04		
Blaikhauch	32 00 00		
Cauldknowes	24 00 00		
Holiclic & Thornilio	52 06 08		
Fairnilio	50 06 08		
Yair	40 06 08		
Eschestoil	27 00 00		
Eister Plora	13 00 00		
Gaithop	44 00 00		
Scoithop	50 00 00		
Garlaclouch & Blackhouse . . .	50 00 00		
Douglas Craig	50 00 00		
Wester Plora	13 00 00		
Berribus	12 00 00		
Eister & Wester Fauldhops . . .	31 00 00		
Augmentatione of thir landes . .	01 00 00		
It. the augmentatione of S^r· Wm Scotts land be his last Infeftment	02 07 04		
of the which Challmerlanrie ther is deduced viz.:			
For Challmerlane fee		100 00 00	
For the Landes of Hyndhop because ther is no such landes in Etrick Forrest		015 13 04	
Suma of the presentt rent of the Shyre as the samyne compts in the burrow Shirriff & Proppertie Rolls .	2886 10 11		
Suma of the deductions		115 13 04	
So ther rests of free money . . .		2770 17 07	

Observations & differences
betwixt the presentt preceeding rentall & the old rentalls
of Ettrick Forrest in 1502 & uthers.

Montbenge eister & wester be the old
    rentalls paid . . . 266 13 04
And be the presentt rentall payes only .   211 00 00
    So the rentalls differ be . . . 055 13 04
Deuchar be the old rentall . . 66 13 04
Be the presentt 046 00 00
    So the rentalls differ be 020 13 04
Garlacleuch alias Blackhouse be the old
    rentall . . . 066 13 04
And be the presentt rentall . . 050 00 00
    So the rentalls differ be 016 13 04
With 160 muttones wherof the one halfe wedders att 40/ . 320 00 00
Tynnes be the old rentall . . 066 13 04
And by the presentt rentall . . 050 00 00
    So the rentalls differ be 016 13 04
Levinghop be the old rentall . . 66 13 04
And be the presentt rentall . . 050 00 00
    So the rentalls differ be 016 13 04
Hangit shaw be the old rentalls . 66 13 04
By the presentt rentall . . . 050 00 00
    So the rentalls differ be 016 13 04
Yair by the old rentalls . . 47 00 00
And by the presentt rentall . . 040 06 08
    So the rentalls differ be 006 13 04
Place of *Gaithop* be the old rentalls . 66 13 04
And be the presentt rentall . . 044 00 00
    So the rentalls differ be 022 13 04
Hemlet of Gaithop be the old rentals . 05 06 08
Bot it is not in the presentt rentall . . 005 06 08
Middsyde of Windiedures be the old
    rentall . . . 26 13 04
And be the presentt rentall tenet
Westsyde of Windiedures by the old rentall 44 10 00
Bot it is not in the presentt rentall . . 44 10 00
Cadenhead be the old rentalls . . 66 13 04
Be the presentt rentall . . . 050 00 00
    So the rentalls differ be 016 13 04

SELKIRK. *Benlessen of Cadenheid* bo tho old rentall   05 06 08
　　　Bot it is not in tho presentt rentall   .   .   005 06 08
Craigleith bo tho old rentall   .   .   23 00 00
　　　Bot bo tho presentt it is called Newhall alias
　　　Craigleith 015 03 04
　　　　So tho rentalls differ bo 007 16 08
Reidheid bo tho old rentalls payes   .   23 00 00
　　　Bot it is not in tho presentt rentall   .   23 00 00
Gallowsheills bo tho old rentall   66 13 04
Blindley & Moseyley bo the
　　　old rentall   .   133 06 08   200 00 00
　　　Bot bo tho presentt rentalls Gallow-
　　　sheills & Moseley payes   .   090 00 00 }
　　　And Blindley   .   .   .   030 00 00 } 140
　　　　So tho rentalls differ bo   .   .   .   060 00 00
Howhard bo tho old rentalls   .   .   66 13 04
　　　Bo tho presentt rentall   .   .   050 00 00
　　　　So tho rentalls differ bo   .   .   .   016 13 04
Warnewood bo tho old rentalls   .   14 00 00
　　　Bot it is not in tho presentt rentall   .   .   .   014 00 00
Eister Langhop bo the old
　　　rentall   .   16 00 00 ⎫
Midle Langhop bo tho said
　　　rentall   .   20 00 00 ⎬ 52 00 00
West Langhop bo tho said
　　　rentall   .   16 00 00 ⎭
　　　Bot bo tho presentt rentall ther is only mentione
　　　made of Langhop which payes .   .   018 05 00
　　　　So tho rest are supprest & tho difference is   .   .   033 15 00
Gildhouse called *Bairlielic* bo
　　　tho old rentalls   20 00 00 ⎫
Midle part therof bo tho said
　　　rentall   .   16 00 00 ⎬ 53 00 00
West place therof   .   17 00 00 ⎭
　　　And bo tho presentt rentall ther is only mentione
　　　made of Bairlilie which payes .   .   024 06 08
　　　　So tho rest being supprest tho difference is   .   .   028 13 04
Reidfurd, 3 places of, bo tho old rentall is   44 00 00
　　　Bot tho presentt rentall ther is no mentione
　　　made therof except it be Reidfurdgrein which
　　　payes 015 13 04
　　　　So tho difference is 028 06 08

Fawoodsheill & Grange be the old rentall	75 13 04			
Bot be the presentt rentall 2 part				
Fawoodsheill . . .	33 06 08 ⎫			
Item, 3ᵈ part therof . .	16 13 04 ⎬ 062 03 04			
Item, *Fawood Grange* . .	12 03 04 ⎭			
So the rentalls differ be . . .			013 10 00	
Edinghop & ½ therof be the old rent .	75 11 04			
Be the presentt rentall Edinghop is .		059 00 00		
So the rentalls differ be . . .			016 11 04	
Eltreiff be the old rentalls . .	66 13 04			
Be the presentt rentall . . .		050 00 00		
So the rentalls differ be . . .			016 13 04	

Suma of the haill differences betwixt the old and presentt rentalls of Etrick Forrest extends to **822 18 08**

ROXBURGH SHYRE.

Payed be the Shirriff for book, blenches, & Castellwairdes viz. :

Money	04 18 09 ⎫	
Argentes 24ᵈ· in scotts money . .	01 04 00 ⎪	
Gilt spures one pair . . .	08 00 00 ⎪	
Pepper one pund . . .	01 10 00 ⎪	
Cumin seed one pund . . .	00 13 04 ⎬ 92 16 00	
One broad arrow . . .	00 10 00 ⎪	
One pʳ gloves	03 00 00 ⎪	
For Yetton & Wauchop . .	23 16 02 ⎪	
Castellwairdes . . .	39 03 09 ⎪	
Book	10 00 00 ⎭	

Proppertie.

Jedburgh Lordschip ⎰ of blench dewtie .	133 06 08		
⎱ and of few dewtie .	375 16 08		
Kelso Lordschip ⎰ of few dewtie . 118 12 02 ⎱ 385 05 06			
⎱ of blench dewtie . 266 13 04 ⎰			
of the which blench dewtie of 400 merks ther is			
to be deduced for the causes contained in the			
following observationes 300 merks . .		200 00 00	

ROXBURGH. *Cardross Lordschip*, including Dryburgh, Cambus-
kennoth, & Inchmachamach .   .   200 00 00

Melross Lordschip { of few .   1148 07 02 } 1213 13 10
{ of blench .   0065 06 08 }

Hassingden & Reignewood feild   .   .   0052 00 00

Burgh of Jedburgh 0003 00 00

Suma of the haill Chairge of this shyre aryseing
from the Shirriff, burrow and proppertie rolls
extends to 2455 18 08

Suma of the deductiones is   .   .   .   200 00 00

Which being deduced from the Chairge ther remaines of free money the soume of   .   2255 18 08

Observationes.

Jedburgh or uther wayes Jedward of old ane Monastrie of
the order of St Augustine founded be David I. King of Scotland
comprehending the priorie of Coldinghame and Camnabie; all
which were erected in ane Lordschip, to Alexr. Earle of Home
in anno 1610 for payment of the blench dewtie of 266$^{lb.}$ 13s. 4$^{d.}$
wherof Jedburghes is 133$^{lb.}$ 6s. 8$^{d.}$, which hes not been paid thir
40 yeirs.

There is also few dewties which have been of old the proppertie befor the Erection & which were compted for be the Earle
of Haddingtoune in anno 1635, 37, & 1638 att the said soume
of 375$^{lb.}$ 16s. 8$^{d.}$ befor charged, which ought yet to be compted
for whereof the particulare followes & hath not bein compted
since 1638.

Imprimis for the Landes of Ulstoun, Over maynes of Ulstoun,
of the Great hill; Meadow of the prior; of Chapmansyd with
the woods of the same; landes of Spittlestaines; the 3 husband
landes is Nether Crailling with the halfe of one husband land in
Over-Nisbet; the landes of Plewlandes; the landes of Swyne-

lawes called Newhall; the landes of Hauchheid, Cesfurdburne; ROXBURGH.
Justiceley with the teyndes of the samyne; the landes of Old
Jedburgh, Rowcastell, & peice land in Langnewtoune ; the landes
of Abbotsrewell, Bowatsyde, Grange with the mylne ; the landes
of Fodderley, Over Bonchester Nether Bonchester ; the landes
of Makisyde, Gaithousetake with the woodes ; the landes of
Hartishauch, Langraw with the teyndes therof ; the landes of
Rapperlaw ; the landes of Firth with the teynds & woodes therof ; the landes of Westbyres with the teyndes ; the landes called
Brewlandes in Rapperlaw ; the landes of Bellshes with the mylne ;
the lands of Over Ancrum with the mylne and Cottages of the
same ; landes of Hyndhouse, Castellwood with the aikers of land
lyand att Glencos ; the Friers of Jedburgh & tenements back
and foir with the Taill of the samyne lyand in the burgh of Jedburgh & Monastrie therof, adjacent to the eist part the soume of
220^{lb.} 13s. 4^{d.}

Item, for the landes of Widingtounhall, mylne therof & mylne-
landes &c. : the landes of Pearchead, Hosley ; the landes of
Turneacknow, Widdingtonrig, Over & Nether Swynstead ; the
landes of Dedburne, Over & Nether Kirkwood, Brandisydbrae,
Newbiging, and Sycks with the mylne &c. The landes of Ox-
noue, Castellhill, Crooks and Harcas ; 2 husband landes & ane
halfe & Oxnautoune-heid ; 3 & ane quarter land in Langtoune ;
the landes called Abbotishauch & Lampland in Over Crailling ;
the 3 mylnes of Jedburgh with the waulk mylne ; the peice land
called the Virgin yairds, Orchyairds of the Conventus called
Seilrawyairds et Virgine with the barneyaird, & Friers-yaird of
the landes called Elschauch ; the 2 husband landes of Harden ;
the landes in the village of Plenderleith viz : Priestfeild-Knock
& Hennysfeild, Putton land with 2 aikers called Linthauch in the

G

ROXBURGH. barronie of Delphingstoune. The landes of Over & Nether Wells of the one husband land in Scraisburgh with the teynd barnes & yaird of Ormistaine, Cavertoun, and .Cesford. The landes of Baxtounleyes, Cleisthope, Over & Nether Whytkirk, Allulland, Ormeistcluch, Abbotsyde, & Abbotishawes the soume of 155$^{lb.}$ 3s. 4$^d.$

The Forrest of Jedburgh did compt in anno 1538 & uther yeirs att 300$^{lb.}$ yeirly, bot the reason & cause of the not compting now, & the maner how the samyne shall be brought in againe to his Majeste shall be sett doune in the discoveries & improvements of the revenew.

Kelso, or Kellkoa, of old ane Monastrie Ordinis Cistertiensis founded be K. David the first and was erected in ane Lordschip to Robert Earle of Roxburgh, the 10th day of December 1607 for payment of the forsaid blench dewtie of 400 merks.

In anno 1634 ther wes ane Contract betwixt the King & the Earle of Roxburgh bearing relatione to the said Earle his infeftments not only befor his erectione of Kellso, both temporallitie and spirituallitie therof, bot also befor the annexatione therof except the landes of Over & Nether Howdens, Humby, Eist & Wester Duddingstounes & certaine uther parcells of kirklands, and tenements pertaining thereto ; and the landes & teyndes of the Cell of Lesmahago. And bearing relatione of the payment of 8000 merks to Francis Stewart be the Kings Majeste decret arbitrall betwixt his Majeste & the said Earle for his pretended ryght to the said Abbacy. And also bearing that the said Earle had made ane offer to accept of ane new infeftment of the said haill temporall landes, both property & superioritie, pertaining some tyme to the said Abbacy : to be holden in few ferme for payment of the old dewties con-

tained in the infeftments granted be the Abbotts of Kellso
to the said Earles Authors (except the Cell of Lesmahago)
& to accept of ane infeftment of the teyndes, kirks, & spirituallitie of the said Abbacy, for the yeirly payment of 400 merks,
be the whilk the Kings Majeste is only prejudged in the
superioritie of the said landes of Howdens, Humby & Duddingstounes ; & for quyting therof the said Earle doeth intaill
to his Majeste & his successores, faylzieing of aires maill of
his oun body & Henry Lord Kerr his sone, the haill Lordschip
temporallitie & spirituallitie therof (except Lesmahago) & the
halfe landes of Sproustoun which wes his proppertie & pertained to the Chartourhouse of befor. Whilk offer his Majeste
with consent of his Thesaurers did accept, & the said Earle
for performing of his part oblidged himselfe & his aiers
to resigne the haill temporall landes, teyndes & kirks, pertaining to the said Abbacy with the offices, pertaining to the
same, & uther landes abone specifeit. Lykeas he makes ane
procuratorie to resigne the same for new infeftment to be
given therof to himselfe, and his aires maill ; & faylling
therof to returne *pleno jure* to the Croun. And for the
Kings securitie hes purchesed resignatione be the airs of
umquhile [blank] Mr of Roxburgh. Therefor, the King
ratified the said Earles authores ryghts of the said Abbacy
& promitts, in *verbo principis*, to passe ane infeftment under
the Great Seall gratis to the said Earle & his airs maill, whilk
faylzieing to return to the King of the haill landes proppertie
& superioritie, Kirks & teindes with the offices of Justiciarie
& Bailliarie of all the said landes, with ane new gift erecting
Kellso in ane burgh of barronie, uniting the saids landes in
ane free Lordschip & barronie to be called the Lordschip of

ROXBURGH. Haleyden : paying therfor yeirly the few fermes & uther dewties
contained in the old infeftments, granted to the said Earle
& his authores befor the said act of annexatione, & for the
personage & viccarage teyndes of the kirkes therof the soume
of 400 merks in name of blench ferme with the ministers
stipends.   And for the said offices ane reid rose ; but prejudice
of his Majestis annuities furth of the teyndes.   And containes
ane obliesment of the said Earle to doe no deid in prejudice
of the said taillie ; Reserveand power to the said Earle &
his forsaids to few the saids lands & sett the same in tacke
& rentall, provyding it be not in diminutione of the presentt
rentall given in, & subscribt be him & the Kings Thesaurer
& registrat in the books of Exchequer.   And also reserveand
power to the said Earle to dispone the teyndes of uther mens
landes according to the Act of Parliament, with ane promise be
the Kings Majeste to ratifie the same in the nixt parliament.
This contract is dated at Theobalds & Edinburgh the 18 &
17 dayes of September & November 1634 yeirs.   Conforme
to the whilk contract, & infeftment following theron, the said
Earl of Roxburgh compeired befor the Lordes of Exchequer,
& exhibite and produced the true rentall of the said Lordschip of Kellso which wes registrat accordingly ; and if necesar
should be heir insert.   Bot since his Majestis gratious restauratione the said Earle of Roxburgh hes obtained ane new
Chartour from the King in favoures of himselfe, his aires maill,
or taillie containing ane de Novodamus.

There is ane uther contract betwixt the King & the said
Earle of Roxburgh & Henry Lord Kerr his sone, dated the 10th
July 1637, in which contract they did surrender in favoures
of the King the teyndes of 20 Kirks viz. : Lauchtoune, Sym-

prem, Fogo, Gordon, Hame, Newthorne, Calder Cler, Muirtoune,
Dunsyrs, Todslait, Closeburne, Robertoune, Henstoune, Earl-
noch, Killmares, Dumfries, Symingtoune, Drungrie, Steplegor-
toun, Piterculter, for which the King restricts the blench
dewtie of Kellso to 100 merks. Which teynds of the saids
Kirks should be looked efter; and both as to the number valew
& quantitie shall be more fully exprest amongst the improvements of the rentall. So the forsaid soume of 200 merks ought
to be deduced.

Melross Lordschip of old ane Monastrie Ordinis Cistertiensis
founded be David I. King of Scottes in anno 1136, & erected in
ane Lordschip to the Earle of Hadingtoune, 29 Augt. 1609, for
payment of the forsaid blench dewtie, and the few dewties
being as is befor chairged, which are made up partly of the
Lordschip of Melross & partly of the Lordschip of Tunnighame
added to the same, & which is particularlie mentioned & sett
doune in the rentall 1611, extending in the haill, the said few
& blench dewties, to the soume of 1213^lb. 13s. 10^d. befor chairged,
which shall be more fully spoken to in the improvements &
rentall of Kirklandes.

Cardross Lordschip containing Dryburgh, Cambyskenneth
& Inchmachamach wes erected [27 March 1604] in ane Lord-
schip to the Earle of Marr for payment of the blench dewtie of
200^lb. Cambyskenneth of old wes ane Monastrie of the order
of St Augustine founded be K. David the first in anno 1140.
Dryburgh ane Monastrie Ordinis Premonstratensis founded be
Heugh Morvell [Moreville] one of the four slayers of Tho.
Bacquet Archbishop of Canterburie.

This few dewtie is payable partlie be the relict of the Earle
of Marr, as lyferentrix of a part of the saids landes, & partly be

ROXDURGU. the Lord Cardross, & some uthers, of the Earle of Marr who hes ryght to severall parcells of the same landes as is particularlie divyded in the severall Infeftments.

PEEBLES.   PEEBLES SHYRE.

Paid yeirly be the Shirriff for book and blenches viz.:

Money	02 04 04	
Argentes 14^d in scotts money . . .	00 14 00	
3 broad arrowes	01 10 00	034 16 04
4 broad arrow heids	00 08 00	
Book	30 00 00	

Proppertie.

Cross Kirk of Peibles	. .	03 06 08
Stanehop be Sr David Murray . .	29 10 00	37 00 00
with 5 carriages att 30s. the peice .	07 10 00	
Kingledoores	. .	09 01 00
Lethinhop & Morphingstoune of blench dewtie	66 13 04	234 00 00
And of few dewtie . . .	167 06 08	
Burgh of Peebles	. .	09 10 00

Suma of this shyre as it compts in the Shirriff burrow & Proppertie Rolls extends to . 327 14 00

Which is all free money ther being no deductions.

Difference betwixt the old & presentt Rentalls.

The Monastrie of Peibles, or Croce Kirk therof, wes formerly assigned to Walter Hendersone and his sone in pension, who are both dead long since, and be the old rentall did pay of Victuall viz.:

of wheat 8 bolls ⎫ 2 chall. 1 boll at 100$^{lb.}$ p^r chall. is in money
of beir 17 bolls ⎬ 206$^{lb.}$ 5s. by which soume it differs from the
of Ry 8 bolls ⎭ presentt rentall 206 05 00

Suma of the differences patet.

DUMFRIES SHYRE.

Payed yeirly to the Shirriff for book & blenches viz.:

Money	00 04 04	⎫
Argentes 4s. 7$^{d.}$ in scotts money . .	02 15 00	⎬ 040 19 04
Gilt spurres ane pair	08 00 00	⎪
Book	30 00 00	⎭

Proppertie.

Castlemilk and Broomhill . . .	038 00 00
Dunwoodie	040 00 00
Burgh of Dumfries	021 01 00

STEWARTRIE OF ANNANDALE.

Argentes 10$^{d.}$ in scotts mony .	00 10 00	⎫
Gume one pund . .	00 10 00	⎬ 012 10 00
Pepper one pund . .	01 10 00	⎪
Book . . .	10 00 00	⎭

Proppertie.

Allmagill	012 06 08
Newbie	060 00 00
Bodisbeck	022 00 00
Kirk Landes of Ibert	016 06 08
Ibert	001 10 00
Penpount	010 13 04
Gallowbanks	000 10 00
Burgh of Annand	002 00 00
Burgh of Lochmaban	002 00 00
Burgh of Sanchar	005 00 00
Suma of this Shyre & Stewartie extendes to the soume of	285 01 00

ANNANDALE. *Memorandum* that ther are severall few dewties in the
Stewartrie of Annandale, which doe not compt be the rolls,
nor hath ever boin chairged therby which are allocat for keeping of the castell of Lochmaben to the Earle of Annandale,
which shall be more fully & particularlie sett doune amongst
the improvements so that ther being no castell now upholden
the rent which will be about 400lb. which with 32 mairts att
10lb. the peice will extend to 720lb.

LANRICK.   LANRICK SHYRE.

Payed be the Shirriff for book blench & Castellwairdes viz.:

Money	01 13 04	
Argentes 19d. in scottes money .	00 19 00	
off wax halfe ane stane . .	08 00 00	
Gilt spurres 2 pair . . .	16 00 00	
more of blench ferme . . .	02 00 00	076 12 04
one Harie noble . . .	08 00 00	
Castellwairdes . . .	20 00 00	
Book	20 00 00	

Proppertie.

Lesmahago by Duke of Hamiltoun of few .	154 00 00	
And of blench dewtie . . .	050 00 00	
Viccars Landes by Lindsay . .	001 06 08	
Hamiltoune & Kirkleyring viz.: 40lb. for Hamiltoune		
& 6d. for ilk aiker of 140 aikers of Kirklering		
3lb.	043 10 00	
Hospitall of Glasgow	033 06 08	
Barronie of Glasgow	333 06 08	
Bot now as being a part of the Bishoprick of		
Glasgow the samyne is not paid but deduced . .		333 06 08
Monkland of blench dewtie . . .	100 00 00	
Thankertoune by Ja. Hamiltoun . .	010 00 00	

Proven of monoy 95^{lb.} 7s. & for 32 bolls corn win att   LANRICK.

5s. the boll	103 07 00		
Lead minerall	333 06 08		
bot now it is not payed for the cause mentioned in the following observationes & so ought to be deduced			333 06 08
Burgh of Rutherglen	013 00 00		
wherof ther is deduced which is payed to the Colledge of Glasgow . . .			011 00 00
Burgh of Glasgow	013 06 08		
Burgh of Lanrick	040 00 00		
The Medrops	014 06 08		
Glentores of money . . .	04 00 00		
It. 2 bolls oats att 4^{lb.} 3s. 4^{d.} . .	08 06 08		012 06 08

Suma of the Charge of this Shyre extends to   .   .   1331 16 00

Suma of the deductions extend to   .   .   677 13 04

So ther rests of free money the soume of .   654 02 08

Observationes.

Lesmahago is a part of the Abbacy of Kellso, and the reddendo insert in the Marquis of Hamiltones new chartor, extending to 200^{lb.} consists of the old few dewties contained in the Marquis Chartor of his oun proppertie. And the particular few dewties contained in the remanent Vassalls of the saids landes ther old infeftments are ordained by ane decreet of the Lordes of Session, in anno 1636, to be payed in to the said Marquis for his relieff of the forsaid few dewties, with 4^{lb.} 10s. in augmentatione of the same, which maks in all 154^{lb.} And 50^{lb.} for the teyndes great & small of the saids landes, which is the just blench dewtie contained in the chartor, of new erectione, granted to the Marquis of Hamiltoune. So it would appear that ther hes bein no particular blench dewtie paid

H

LANRICK. for that erectione, nether for a proportionall relieff of Kellso
—wherof it wes a pairt. And in anno 1614 it compts with
Kellso for the soume of 266^{lb.} 13s. 4^{d.}

The blench dewtie of Monkland wes never compted for in
the rolls, these landes being ane 100^{lb.} land, and a pairt of the
Lordschip of Newbottle, who by his chartor is oblidged to free
the Lord Lothian as a pairt of blench dewtie of Newbottle,
and for which the said Lord Lothian in anno 1625 had a
deduction. This blench dewtie wes allocat to Doctor Baillie,
Keeper of the Liberarie of Hollyrood - house, bot since is
compted for & paid in.

Hospitall of Glasgow did compt in anno 1658 & ought yet
continually to compt tho it hes not compted since the Kings
restauratione.

The Lead Mineralls are not now compted, tho above in the
Charge, because the Lord Hoptoune pretends ane ryght to
the same upon ane grant from the King for building of ane
Kirk in that place. The originall few is a proportionall pairt
of the Lead or gold myne that should be win, bot of late
his Majestie hes granted this few to the Laird of Hattoun &
so ought to be deduced in manner forsaid.

Proven, uther wayes called the prebendarie of Ballamarkie,
did formerly belong to Mr Wm. Baillie president of the Colledge of Justice, as prebendar therof, who for the bettering &
augmentatione of the rentall, and in speciall for the soume
of 1000^{lb.} paid to him did dispone the samyne landes & haill
few dewties therof to Tho. Baillie for yeirly payment of 95^{lb.}
7s., & 32 bolls of horse corne or 5s. for ilk boll; 8 duzone
poulltrie or 12^{d.} for the peice. The chartor is dated the 10th
Aprill 1562, and it is provyded that no reductione or nullitie

of the infeftment shall be persewed except for the payment of the few dewties, & also shall not uther wayes intend any reductione on the same untill such tyme as the forsaid soume of 1000^lb be first repayed.

This few dewtie of Proven falling in to the King be Act of Annexatione of Kirklandes the King dispones the few dewties to Sir John Prestoun of Pennicook, president of the Session, & to his sone efter his decease, who is dead within thir 5 or 6 yeirs, & therfor these few dewties ought to be compted for, and paid in according as is above said.

The Medropes & Glentores are a pairt of the barronie of Monkland, bot it is conceaved not to be included in the blench dewtie, bot rather to be of the old few, & so ought to compt for the same now, by & attour the forsaid blench dewtie. They have never as yet compted, bot of late since his Majestis restauratione. There are severall uther fewers of the Monkland that tho they be not oblidged to pay a proportionall pairt of the blench dewty forsaid, yet they are lyable for payment of the severall few dewties contained in thair chartors, as the proportion of the old fewes befor the erectione, which shall be more enlarged in the improvements.

KIRKCUD-
BRYGHT.

KIRKCUDBRYGHT STEWARTRIE.

Payed for book and blenches yeirly viz. :

Money	. . . .	00 13 04	
Argentes	. . . .	01 06 06	
Gloves one pair	. . .	03 00 00	
Whytt spurres one pair	. .	01 00 00	
Broad arrowes 7	. . .	03 10 00	39 09 10
2 bolls oatts .	. . .	[blank]	
one spar haulk	. . .	[blank]	
Book .	. . . .	30 00 00	

Proppertie.

St Marie Ile, of few .	. .	121 00 00
Burgh of Stronraver .	. .	004 00 00
Burgh of Kirkcudbryght	. .	009 13 04

Suma of this Stewartrie is   .   .   .   174 02 10

Which is free money ther being no deductiones.

WIGTOUN.

WIGTOUN SHYRE.

Payed yeirly for book and blenches viz. :

Money	. . . .	00 00 02	
Argentes	. . . .	00 04 00	030 04 02
Book .	. . . .	30 00 00	

Proppertie.

Duncow	. . . . .	082 13 04
Burgh of Wigtoun	. . . .	020 00 00
Burgh of Newgalloway	. . .	006 13 04

Challmerlane of Galloway conforme to the particular
    rentall following :

Suma of this particle is   139 10 10

LORDSCHIP OF GALLOWAY.

The Landes and barronie of Buthill . .	245 06 08
Thrave Grainge & Kelltoune Grainge . .	103 06 08
Airdes-Over, Midle & Nether . . .	024 03 02
Halfe of Nether Sanik . . .	008 03 04
Uther halfe of Nether Sanik . . .	009 06 08
Halfe of Whytpark	007 16 08
The uther halfe therof . . .	008 03 04
Grainge of Sanik	004 13 04
Dunrod Sanik	028 13 04
Meillfeild	004 17 00
Largevey	004 13 04
Craginvey	051 13 04
Cressok	002 00 00
Barskey	001 06 08
Logane	016 00 00
Augmentatione therof . . .	002 04 04
Meikle & Litle Clothege . . .	008 00 00
Cloyark	001 14 08
Corsock	006 06 08
Largemoir, Knockskenny, Barskeoch, midle & nether	
Stranglaskein with the fishing . .	025 00 00
Augmentatione therof . . .	002 13 04
Over Barskeoch	006 08 08
Drumbey	006 00 00
Augmentatione therof . . .	001 15 08
Barnetaggart	007 04 00
Garvarie	008 00 00
Stewindew	008 06 08
Ardinlosk	004 16 00
Cubboyes & Dalcarnethame . . .	007 04 00
new augmentatione of Ardinlosk, Cubboyes &	
Dalcarnethame . . .	001 13 00
Culcraiges	009 12 00
Corscraig, Cassinvey, Cauldale & Barley .	036 00 00
Augmentatione of the saids landes .	004 08 00
Cullven	005 06 08
Pollinzask	000 18 00
Chappelltoun	008 00 00
Barskeant	015 11 08
Craigtoune	006 13 04
Glenrie	002 08 00

WIGTOUN. Logane	006	08	00
— Barscracth	006	08	00
Tostrie	009	12	00
Drumstinchell	004	16	00
Reidbank	004	16	00
Oversanik	024	00	00
Milne of Sanik	009	12	00
Almernes	030	06	08
Craigmoir	009	12	00
Augmentatione therof	000	06	08
Corkanders	021	00	00
Auchinskeant .	004	10	00
Auchinvey	003	00	00
Auchinloss	001	06	08
Glentoskin	002	04	04
Closbyart	002	13	04
augmentatione Auchinskeant & the last 4	001	09	00
Southwoek	006	00	00
Broadland	004	06	08
Barclay	006	00	00
Eist Medic	003	08	04
Tullindach	007	10	00
Park & Largevey	008	02	00
Moit & Dallry	000	06	08
Pluntoun	000	13	04
Gaittwell & Knockinvayne	002	00	00
Pockincrew	002	13	04
Forrest of Buchine & libertie of fishing	023	13	04
Grainge of Spottes	035	10	00
Castellmaynes of Kirkcudbryght	003	00	00
Logane	004	00	00
Milne of Culvene	005	06	08
Knockeane	008	00	00
Killdarach	004	06	08
Kervattock	005	00	00
Lesnocks, Lochtappine, Carmultburgh, & Tanny Laddott	048	00	00
Augmentatione therof	001	04	00
Kereghirne	009	16	00
Cairnesckeoch	013	15	00
Clontarch	005	12	00
Pollvey & Dirlleskin vocat	007	03	00
The halfe of Cammy Laddot & Clancharrie	006	18	00
Kerrieburne	008	13	04

Lidisdale	024	00	00
Arboig	017	13	04
Fintallot, Beanch, Glenruther, Glenluthdy, and Garbcrow	024	14	08
Killadane	002	16	08
Knockfrick	005	16	08
Newtoune, Gulldirrie & Ardwhat . .	020	06	08
Stelbindonald, Dallmerk, and Dalbauchtein .	025	00	00
Auldtoun	009	06	08
Fultis, Talynes, Largis, Ballgregant & Blairmaking	026	13	04
Grainge of Balldoune	042	00	00
Madincroft	003	10	00
Blaidnot	003	10	00

It. for Knockfin of oatmeill—6 bolls { att 100^{lb.} }
Grainge of Balldoune oatmeill—12 bolls { the chall. } 075 00 00

Landes above Crie, of Mairts—13 { att 10^{lb.} }
Landes under Crie . 21 { the peice } 340 00 00

Suma of the challmerlainrie of Galloway as it is presenttlie compted extends to . .	1687	17	8

Wherof ther is to be deduced as followes :

First of old Challmerlaine fee	120	00	00
And by ane Contract betwixt the Thesaurer and the Challmerlane in anno 1633 ther is allowed him, by and attour the said old fee, for his extraordinary paines . .	100	00	00
Item, for the Landes of Culven	005	06	08
Item, for Southweck	006	00	00
Item, for Borland	004	06	08
Item, for Logane	004	00	00

All which are chairged be the old & presentt rentalls And by ane act of Exchequer upon the production of ane Chartor dated the last day of Aprill 1557, it is found that Ja. Lindsay of Wauchop holds the said landes waird, and so ought to be deduced.

Item, for the landes of Gaitwells & Knockinvaine because the samyne landes ly not in Galloway . . .	002	00	00
Item, for Craiginvey as superfluently chairged conforme to ane Act of Exchequer dated 29th July 1612 yeirs . .	043	05	00

Suma of this Shyre of Wigtoun as it presenttlie compts in the Shirriff burrow & proppertie rolls extends to the soume of . .	1837 08 06		
Suma of the haill deductiones extend to .	284 18 04		
So ther rests of free money the soume of .	1552 10 02		

Observationes & differences
betwixt the forsaid presentt rentall & the old rentalls
in anno 1522, 1601 & uthers.

The Lordschip of Galloway being the Kings proppertie feudi
firma feudifirmarum, and, by Act of Parl. Ja. 6, Par. 11th
Cap. 30; and Ja. 6, Parl. 15th Act 230, all dispositiones
made & granted therof are decleired voyd & null as is more
particularlie inlarged in page 1. The victuall by the abone-
writin rentall being only 18 ·bolls, and that was formerly paid
be the old rentall extending to 30 challders is ether supprest
in this presentt rentall, or utherwayes given away for further
clieiring wherof the particular differences follow :—

Grainge & Spottes be the forsaid presentt rentall payes

only	035 10 00	
Bot be the old rentalls it payes over & above the said money of victuall 5 chall. att 100ᶫᵇ· pʳ chall.	.	500 00 00
Milne of Culven be the presentt rentall payes only	005 06 08	
Bot be the old rentalls it payes also 1 chall. meill		100 00 00
Milne of Kellton compts not be the presentt rentall Bot be the old rentall it payes 8 bolls meill . .		050 00 00
Milne of Sanik be the presentt rentall payes only	009 12 00	
Bot be the old rentall payes also 1 chall. 4 bolls meill		125 00 00
Grainge of Balldoun be the presentt rentall payes of mony . . .	042 00 00	
And of victuall 12 bolls is . .	075 00 00	
Bot be the old rentall it payes of money 42ᶫᵇ· And of meill 19 chall. So the rentalls differ be 18 chall. 4 bolls is in money		1825 00 00
Mylne of Blednocht compts not be the presentt rentall Bot be the old rentalls it payes 1 chall. 6 bolls meill		0137 10 00

Liddisdale be the presentt rentall payes only . 024 00 00
 Bot be the old rentalls it payes 24$^{lb.}$ of money
And of meill 7 chall. is 0700 00 00
  So the differences betwixt the presentt & old rentalls
   extend to the soume of 34 chall. 6 bolls which att
   100$^{lb.}$ per chall. is 3437 10 00

AIR SHYRE.

Payed be the Shirriffe for book & blenches, viz. :
Money	05 17 07	
Argentes . . .	00 12 00	
One pair gilt spurres . .	08 00 00	045 09 07
One pair whyt spurres .	01 00 00	
Book	30 00 00	

BAILLIARIE OF CARRICK.

Argentes 4$^{d.}$ in scotts money .	00 04 00	
1 pair Gilt spurres .	08 00 00	
wheat 8 bolls att 100$^{lb.}$ per chall.	50 00 00	088 04 00
Book	30 00 00	

BAILLIARIE OF KYLSTEWART.

Money	01 07 07	
Argentes 6$^{d.}$ in scotts money . .	00 06 00	
2 pair whyt spurres . .	02 00 00	013 13 07
Book	10 00 00	

BAILLIARIE OF CONNINGHAME.

Money . . .	00 13 04	
Argentes 22$^{d.}$ in scotts money .	01 02 00	
pepper 1$^{lb.}$ 3 quarters . .	02 02 06	034 17 10
One pair whyt spurres .	01 00 00	
Book . . .	30 00 00	

I

Proppertie.

Receaver of Carrick, Leswet & Monybridge .	100 00 00	
Therinzean by the E. of Loudoun . .	020 00 00	
A part of Trabench by the said Earle .	020 06 08	
The uther part of Trabench be the Lord Cochrane	083 06 08	
Kylsmure Lordschip be the Earle of		
Loudon of few · .	200 00 00 ⎫	
of blench dewtie . . .	066 13 04 ⎬ 286 13 04	
of blench dewtie for the teyndes of	⎬	
the haill Landes lying in Barne-	⎬	
muire	020 00 00 ⎭	

Wherof ther is deduced conforme to ane Contract betwixt the King and the said Earle, dated 4th
Septr. 1630, and ratified be Act of Parliament
in anno 1633 .   .   .   .   .   .   200 00 00
And for the blench dewtie of the saids teinds because
it is presumed that they are a pairt of the
blench dewtie of Kyllsmuire Lordschip .   .   020 00 00

Kilwinning Lordschip of blench dewtie .	040 03 04	
Dundonald by the Lord Cochrane . .	032 02 00	
Burgh of Air	020 00 00	
Burgh of Irving	007 06 08	
Suma of this Shyre & bailliaries ex-		
tends to . . .	792 03 01	
Suma of the deductiones extend to . .		220 00 00
So ther rests of free money . . .		572 03 01

Differences betwixt the old and present rentalls.

Leswalt and Monibridge in the rentall
    1603 payed of money .   .   179 06 10
with 18 bolls oat meill att 100 merk
    the boll is   .   .   .   075 00 00
Bot be the presentt rentall it payes only of money 100 00 00
    So the rentalls differ be the soume of   .   .   154 06 10

Alex^r. Stewart of Garley pretends a ryght to the said victuall,
bot it hath never been produced nor instructed, & therfor it
ought to be compted in.

Suma of the differences patet.

Observationes.

Kylsmuir by the rentall 1611 payes only of blench ferme 56^{lb.} 13s. 4^{d.} conforme to ane Chartour granted to the E. of Loudoun, dated the last day of Junij 1608, and in the rentall 1613 it payed 66^{lb.} 13s. 4^{d.} of blench dewtie. The said Lordschip of Kylsmur paid 200^{lb.} of few dewtie, bot be ane contract betwixt the King & the Earle of Loudoune, dated the 4th day of September 1630, the few dewties are dischairged, bot it shall not att this tyme be convenient to sett doune the heids of that Contract, but reserved to be placed amongst the discoveries & improvements of the revenew.

There is also ane uther contract betwixt the King & the Earle of Lowdoune dated the 10th Martch, in anno 1634, in which contract the Earl of Lowdoune resignes his ryght of the Lordschip of Kyllsmure in favoures of his Majeste for payment of 3200 merks, off the which ther is 1400 merks to be payed out of the Exchequer for the Shirriffship of Air. Whilk two contractes, groundes, & causes therof & the maner of the payment of the soumes of money therin contained, shall be enlarged amongst the discoveries & improvements.

This 200^{lb.} of few dewtie of Kyllsmure with the few dewtie payable out of Killwining, gives occasion, from the severall Conceallments therof, to touch in generall the nature of those fewes which ought to be payed notwithstanding of the blench dewties compted for. Be the Act of Parliament 1633 ther is ane particular clause declairing that the Lordes of Erectiones shall bruik these landes which were the proppertie befor the date of the generall surrender, they holding the same of his

AIR. Majeste & paying the few fermes and few dewties contained in
the old infeftments.

Amongst uther abuses of the revenew this was not the
least, that, after the Kings generall decreet & determinatione,
severall lordes of Erectione did purchase & buy in parcells of
landes from thair respective vassalls, who resigning in thair
favoures obtained new infeftments of the same, and so consolidate the ryght of the superioritie in thair persones.

There hes been much debate in the Exchequer about this
busines & uther points of the Lordes of Erectione, which shall
be more propperly spoken to in ane uther place then heir,
bot in respect that it concernes the revenew & few dewties
which should be payed in (tho now altogither supprest) the
Kings care by his Letters & the Exchequers dilligence by thair
acts will (notwithstanding they containe severall uther things)
evidence the preventing of the prejudice & give ane arryse
in the persewance of the same.

Coppie of his Majestis Letter anent Erectiones that no signatur
passe theranent in prejudice of the late Acts of Parliament
in anno 1633, presented the 9th Novr 1633 :—

"C. R.

"Whereas divers good & profitable acts & statutes
were made in our favoures, in our late parliament holden
in Junij last, & speciallie anent the Superiorities of Erectiones,
Regallitie of Erectiones, chainging of holdings from waird to
blench; annulling of infeftments of our annexed proppertie
disponed be any uther holding then in few ferme, Prohibitione
to our Vassalls to dispone waird landes without our consent,

& ane act that all the Church Landes pertaining in proppertie AIR.
to the Lordes of Erectiones should hould of us in few ferme,
for payment of the old few ferme dewties. Therfore it is our
pleasure that no signatur be past in Exchequer, which may
derogate to the saids acts & statutes made in our favoures
except wee be speciallie consulted theranent, and that yee
have our particular warrand for that effect. Whythall the
5th October 1633."

Ane uther of his Majestis Letters.

" C. R.

"Right trustie & well beloved Cousin & Counsellor, Right trustie & well beloved Cousines & Counsellors
wee greitt yow well. Forasmuch, as the superiorities of all
erectiones pertaineth to us by the late Act of Parliament made
in our favoures : reserveand to such titulars of erectiones who
subscribt the generall surrender these few maills till they be
satisfied therfor, conforme to our generall determinatione.
And forasmuch as divers of the Vassalls of Erectiones, as wee
are informed, are willing to advance the money for buying
the few maills to our use, they haveing retentione in thair
handes of thair few maills for such yeirs, efter the advanceing
of the money, as in reason & equitie may compence the money
to be advanced be them. And seeing wee approve this course,
and are willing that those that advance have retention for
ther few maills for such space of yeirs as yow shall think
fitt & reasonable : therefor, it is our speciall pleasure that yow
cause intimatione heirof to be made to all our leidges, who
have interest, be open proclamatione att the mercat cross of
Edinburgh to the effect such of the vassalls as is, or shall be,

AIR. willing may come in befor yow & agree with our Thesaurer or Thesaurer depute for advanceing of such moneyes, & receave warrand & securitie be Act of Exchequer for retentione of the saids few maills & few fermes for the space to be agreed upon. And because ther hath bein heirtofore some scruple made what shall be compted superioritie, whereanent wee shewed our royall pleasure be 2 severall Lettres registrat in our books of Comission : therfore, wee have thought good to acquaint yow therwith, & with the equitie of our proceedings therin, which is that in justice all is to be compted superioritie to which the Titulars of Erectiones had not lawfull ryght of propperty befor thair erectione, or whereof they had not acquired ryghts of proppertie, & be vertue of these ryghts had bein in possession befor the generall surrender. And wee will yow to proceed according to these generall rewells, and in the meane tyme it is our speciall pleasour that yee passe no signatur of any Kirklandes, pertaining to erectiones, in favoures of the saids Lordes of Erectiones, or in favoures of any uther on thair resignatione, bot of that which wes thair proppertie in maner forsaid to be holden alwayes of us in few ferme, according to the late Act of Parliament made theranent. And because wee are informed that some Titulars of Erectiones intend to ingrosse againe to them thair superiorities, in haill or in part, be prosecuting resignationes from thair Vassalls wherupon they intend to passe new infeftments & then to give subaltern ryghts & fewes to those who have resigned : it is our will & pleasour that no such signatur be exped of the said superiorities in our prejudice, which recommending to your caire wee bid yow fairwell. From our court at Whythall 8th October 1633."

The Lordes of Exchequer ordained the same to be registrat AIR.
in thair bookes, & also ordained Letters of publicatione att
the mercat croce of Edinburgh to be direct therupon, except
that part of the Letter anent what shall be compted superioritie. The Lordes referred the samyne to ane further consideratione & were desired to think on ane answere therto.
There wes also ane Act of Exchequer made in December following wherof the tenor followes :—

Act anent Superiorities of Erectiones. What is to be compted
superioritie? The Lordes ordaines all to be compted superioritie
to which the Titulars of Erectiones had not lawfull ryght of
proppertie before ther Erectiones, or wherof they had not acquired ryghts of proppertie & be vertew of these ryghts had
bein in possession therof befor the generall surrender, and
Letters to be directed heiron if neid be. There is no report
of this made to the King till August 1634 att which tyme
the King gave a particular Comissione to the then Lord Chancellor & uthers to consider the abuses of the revenew & Exchequer. In returne wherof, & for preventing of the same
they amongst uthers gave returne to this article which shall
be more fully enlarged in the discoveries & improvements of
the revenue as well toward the redeeming the few dewties of
Erectiones as to the severall particulars aforsaid.

Killwining of old ane Monastrie Ordinis Tironensis founded
be Hugo Morvell Constabularius Scotiæ, one of the four slayers
of Thomas Bacquet, Archiepis. Cantuariensis. Off late Killwining payed nothing bot 40 : 03 : 04 of blench dewtie, bot it
ought to compt for $12^{lb.}$ 12s.; 3 hens; 13 capones; 2 cariages
as in the rentall 1642 of few, which ought to be added to the
forsaid charge & differeth therfor in . . 17 02 00

DUMBARTOUNE SHYRE.

Payed be the Shirriff for book & blenches viz.:

Money	00 00 01		
Argentes 3^{d.} in scotts money . .	00 03 00		
One pair gilt spurres . . .	08 00 00	031 03 01	
One pair gloves . . .	03 00 00		
Book	20 00 00		

Proppertie.

Assyse aill of the west sea 2 bolls malt .	012 00 00		
Cardross & Comrie 10 mairts att 10^{lb.} the peice	100 00 00		
Which mairtes are allowed to the Keeper of Dumbartoun castell and so ought to be deduced . .		100 00 00	
Burgh of Dumbartoune . . .	007 10 04		

Suma of this Shyre extendes to	150 13 05	
Suma of the deductiones . . .		100 00 00
So there restes of free money . .		50 13 05

Observationes.

The *Assyse Aill* of the west sea is ane old dewtie payed to his Majeste, for the aill that is drunken & spent att the fishing of the west sea, and hes been sett ordinarlie for 2 bolls of malt yeirly.   In anno 1509 & 1519 & of late the same wes sett to Arnecaple for yeirly payment of the saides 2 bolls malt.   This dewtie ought to be sett, bot ther is hardly anything payed since anno 1646.

The *mairts of Cardross & Comrie*, with the fermes of dewties therof, are assigned to the Castell of Dumbartoun be act of parliament K. Ja. 6, par. 9, Act 8th.

BUTE SHYRE.

Payed yeirly bo tho Shirriff for book & blenches viz. :

Argentes in scottes monoy 3ᵈ . .	00 03 00 ⎫	
2 pair whyt spurres . . .	02 00 00 ⎬ 012 03 00	
Book	10 00 00 ⎭	

Proppertic.

Burgh of Rothsoy		006 00 00	
Buto Lordschip, of money . .	162 15 04 ⎫		
11 chall. 15 bolls beir att 100 merks	795 10 00 ⎪		
10 chall. oats pryco forsaid . .	666 13 04 ⎪		
Milno of Rothsyo { of meill 1 ch. 8 bolls	100 00 00 ⎬ 2134 18 08		
{ of mairts 41 att 10ˡᵇ·			
{ tho peice .	410 00 00 ⎭		

All which monoy victuall money and mairtes of tho
said Lo. of Bute is assigned for keeping of
tho Castell of Dumbartouno be Act of Parlᵗ·
Ja. 6. pa. 9 Act 8th And therforo ought to
be deduced 2134 18 08

Suma of tho haill money victuall
money & uthers arrysing from
the Shirriff burrow & proppertic
rolls for this Shyro extendes to 2153 01 08

Suma of the deductiones . . . 2134 18 08

So ther rests of free money yeirly payed . 18 03 00

ARGYLL SHYRE.

Payed be tho Shirriff for blenches yeirly :

Money	00 00 11 ⎫	
ono pʳ· gloves out of Killmouns .	00 06 00 ⎬ 000 09 11	
Ono chalomond Reid out of Lorne	⎪	
Argentes 3ᵈ· in scotts monoy . ·	00 03 00 ⎭	

K

Proppertie.

Coull & Rosnceth payes as followes :

Dummuino within the Lo. of Cowell	018 00 00 ⎫	
Glenderowallie . . .	013 06 08 ⎬	
Barronie of Rosnocth . .	041 00 00 ⎬ 512 06 08	
2 pᵗ of Glenderowallie of mairts 44 att 10ᵗʰ· the peice . .	440 00 00 ⎭	
Inneramblo & Ballinab . .		062 02 11
Colonsey Ardnamurchan & Swynart .		457 14 01
Oronsay		005 01 08
Arrosse in Mull . . .		130 00 00
Kintyre & Jura . . .		2400 00 00
Terrie		1666 13 04
Ila		6000 00 00
Wherof deduce for the cause mentioned in the following observationes . . .		. . 5500 00 00
Largie . . .		0200 00 00
Assyse herring of the west seas . .		1000 00 00
Burgh of Inverayray . . .		0006 00 00
Suma of this Shyre as it comptes in the Shirriff burrow & Proppertie rolls extendes to . .	12,440 08 07	
Suma of the deductiones extend to .	. . 5500 00 00	
So ther restes of free money . .	. 6940 08 07	

Observationes & differences
betwixt the old & presentt rentalls of this Shyre.

Colonsey Ardnamurchan & Swynart be the presentt
rentall . . . 0457 14 01

Be the old rentalls they payed as followes, viz. :

1287 stone meill being 143 bolls att 48s. the boll is . .	0343 04 00	
1287 stone cheise att 26s. 8ᵈ· is .	2049 06 08	
81 bolls 2 f. 1 p. ½ ⅓ malt att 6ᵗʰ· the boll . . .	0489 11 03	
60 mairtes att 10ᵗʰ· the peice .	0600 00 00	
34 wedders att 40s. the peice is .	0068 00 00	
All which extendes to .	3550 01 11	
So the rentalls differ be the soume of . .		3092 07 10

Inveramble & Ballinab be the presentt rentall payes   0062 02 11
Be the old rentalls they payed as followes, viz. :

Mairtes 7 & $\frac{111}{8820}$ p^t mairt att 10$^{lb.}$ the peice . .	75 01 08	
Weders 7 & $\frac{111}{8820}$ p^t att 40s. the peice	14 00 04	
55 stone cheise att 26s. 8$^{d.}$ the stone	73 06 08	
55 stone meill being 6 bolls at 48s. the boll . . .	14 08 00	
Geise 7 & $\frac{111}{8820}$ p^t att 6s. the peice	02 09 04	
Foulls 7 & $\frac{111}{8820}$ p^t att 3s. the peice	01 03 04	
All which extendes to the soume of . .	180 09 04	

So the rentalls differ be the soume of   . . . 0118 06 08

Kintyre & Jura be the presentt rentall   .   2400 00 00
Be the old rentall North Kintyre payed, viz. :

4 chall. 13 bolls malt att 6$^{lb.}$ the boll is . .	462 00 00
311 & $\frac{1}{4}$ stones meill being 34 bolls & $\frac{1}{2}$ att 48s. the boll .	082 16 00
605 & $\frac{3}{4}$ stones cheise att 26s. 8$^{d.}$ the stone . . .	807 13 04
one kow pryce therof . .	010 00 00
6 mairtes att 10$^{lb.}$ the peice .	060 00 00
41 & $\frac{1}{4}$ wedders att 40s. the peice	083 00 00

South Kintyre payes 25 chall. 9 bolls

2 f. malt att 6$^{lb.}$ the boll is .	2454 00 00
868 & $\frac{1}{4}$ stones meill being 96$\frac{1}{2}$ bolls pryce . .	231 12 00
326 & $\frac{3}{4}$ stones cheise pryce forsaid	435 13 04
57 & $\frac{3}{4}$ mairtes pryce forsaid .	577 10 00
47 & $\frac{3}{4}$ weders att 40s. the peice .	094 10 00

Jura payes 20 mairtes pryce forsaid .   200 00 00

180 stone of meill being 20 bolls pryce forsaid . . .	048 00 00
80 stone cheise pryce forsaid .	106 13 04
All which extendes to the soume of . .	5656 08 00

So the rentalls differ be the soume of   .   .   3256 08 00

ARGYLL. *Arross* in Mule be the presentt rentall payes . 130 00 00
——   Bot be the rentall in anno 1649 it
            payed . . . 230 00 00
            So the rentalls differ be the soume of . . 0100 00 00
            Suma of the haill differences betwixt the old and
            presentt rentalls, as is particularlie above
            sett doune, extendes to . . . 6567 02 03

Assyse of herring of the west seas being a dewtie which is a pairt of his Majesties proppertie, and wes annexed to the Croun in anno 1593 be Act of Parl. Ja. 6, par. 13 Act 176. And in anno 1632, 33, 34, 35, 36, & 1634 [*sic*] it payed of tack dewtie 44 last of herring. And in anno 1620 the samyne paid yeirly 1000$^{lb.}$ of tacke dewtie be Mr Jo^n Archbald.

This assyse of herring being a dewtie which is payed both in this Shyre & in the Shyre of Haddingtoun & in uther places wher ther is any fishing of herring, it is thought necesar to cleir the nature of it, & what uther dewties are payed for the fishing. And first the Excyse of every boat that slayes herring upon the west coast payes 5$^{lb.}$, and on the eist coast every boat payes 6$^{lb.}$ as they are distinguished be the distance of place & difference of tyme.

Secondly, the ground leive payes 36s. upon every last.

Thirdly, the teithes of the herring for the Ile fishing 40s. And at Dumbar the teith herring is taken up *ipsa corpora*.

Fourthly; the gadge is 4s. each last.

Fifthly, the Admiralls dewtie is 20s. on each boat.

Sixthly, the customes of herring transported is 24s. for ilk last.

1. As to the first, ther is but one excyse payed for Dumbar & the Heiks, because it is bot one fishing of the very same scoolls of herring, a litle differing both in tyme & place, bot

if these boats happen that same yeir to goe to the Iles they ARGYLL.
pay a new excyse because it is a severall & distinct fishing.

2. The ground Leive, is for a piece of ground designed
be the Landlord to the merchant upon agreement to make
herring on thair ground for *devottes* & sea wair to cover the
heides of thair barrells while the grein herring setle & be sufficiently pyned for packing & barrelling.

3. The teithes, befor the proces att the instance of the
Laird of Craigie, ther wes never any teind dewtie craved in
the Iles from the slayers of the herring ther; bot in Clyd
ther is some Churchmen & uthers haveing ryght from them,
who hes some small dewtie of every boatt according to the
bignes & quantitie of the boatt & success of the fishing. In
Dumbar the teindes of the herring is payed to 2 severall
persones viz: the one halfe therof of late wes payed to the
Laird of Aitkine as haveing ryght therto be the minister as
parson of Dumbar; the uther halfe payed to the parson of
the parish from whence the fish boatt comes.

4. The gadge belonging to the toune of Edinburgh & thair
deputes who receaves 4s. for ilk last, and 13s. 4ᵈ· for the act of
cautione bearing that the 3ᵈ pairt of the herring to be salted
shall be sold within this Kingdome conforme to the Act of
Parliament.

5. The Admiralls dew, of old called Verum, which is 10s.
for the coble, bot now in Dumbarr they take 20 or 40s.
And it seimes agreeable to reason that all boatts, birleinges
and busches, pay not alyke, bot that they pay according to
ther burding & be the last. Off old ther wes litle or no
respect had to the Admirall in Ile fishing, because the merchants choyced ane Admirall amongst themselves who uplifted
all these fynes dew to the Admirall; bot the Tacksmen of the

ARGYLL. excyse doe oftymes behave themselves as Admirall, & uplifts the dewties therof.

This small custome of 24s. on the last is never altered, nor highted that the merchants may be encouraged to venture on such a hazardous & uncertaine a commoditie both for tyme, which falls out sometyme late, sometyme aire, & for place sometyme heir somtyme ther. And this is taken up rather for acknowledgement then custome; as ane ship pound of wax inward & 16s. outward for drawing in comerce & money be tradeing with a forraigne & not native commoditie.

Ila: the few dewtie therof is set in tack to the Duke of Lennox for yeirly payment of the soume of 500^lb. bott the propper few dewtie of the same is 6000^lb. befor chairged so ther is deduced 5500^lb. And the said soume of 500^lb. payed in yeirly.

RENFREW.

RENFREW SHYRE.

Payed yeirly be the Shirriffe for book & blenches viz.:

Money	10 15 00	
Argentes 24^d. in scottes money . .	01 04 00	
Gloves one pair taxed 4^d. . .	00 00 04	
One pair whyt spures	01 00 00	048 02 08
one pund pepper	01 10 00	
one pund cumin seed	00 13 04	
Broad arrowes 6 pair	03 00 00	
Book	30 00 00	

Proppertie.

Craig of Blantyre	002 00 00
Lordschip of Paislie of blench dewtie . . .	133 06 08
Burgh of Renfrew	005 06 08
Suma of this Shyre extendes to . .	0188 16 00

Which is all free money ther being no deductiones.

STIRLING SHYRE.

Payed yeirly be the Shirriff for book & blenches viz.:

Money	. . . .	19 11 02	
Argentes 11ᵈ in scotts money .	.	00 11 00	
Gilt spures 3 pair	. .	24 00 00	
Gloves one pair	. . .	00 03 00	050 15 02
pepper one pund & 7 pairts of a pund .	02 00 00	
Whyt spures one pair .	. .	01 00 00	
one Cairt full of hay .	. .	01 10 00	
Book .	. . . .	02 00 00	

wherof the haill blenches is to be deduced as allocat to the E. of Marr in maner eftermentionat .   048 15 02

Proppertie.

Burgh of Stirling	. . .	006 13 04	
Barronie of Fallkirk .	. .	010 00 00	
Hayning	. . .	94 15 04	106 08 08
Duniepeace .	. . .	11 03 04	

wherof deduce as payed to the minister of Morvingsyde as a pairt of his stipend .   .   .   042 12 10

Winsheillhauch	. . .	006 13 04	
Kirk Landes of Bothkenner .	. .	004 04 00	
Polmond	. . .	030 00 00	
Torwood or Torwoodheid	. .	[blank]	
Kirk Landes of Tillicultrie	. .	002 00 00	
Dennie	. . . .	010 00 00	
Challmerlanrie of Stirling of money	.	442 14 07	
8 chall. 4 bolls wheat att 100ˡᵇ· the chall.	. .	825 00 00	
31 chall. 5 bolls 1 f. 2 p. beir & malt pryce forsaid .	.	3133 11 10	4759 10 05
4 chall. oats att 100 merk the chall.	0266 13 04	
188 Capones att 6s. 8ᵈ the peice	0069 06 08	
36 poultrie att 4s. the peice	0007 04 00	
30 salmond att 10s.	.	0015 00 00	

wherof deduce of Challmerlane fee   .   .   .   010 00 00

Item, to the Serjeand 002 00 00

Item, for Craigingorth as belonging to the Lord Elphingstoune   .   .   .   013 06 08

STIRLING. Item, for the halfe of the landes of Inverallone belong-

ing to the Laird of Keir in money . .	007	10	00
Wheatt one chall.	100	00	00
Beir One Chall.	100	00	00
Oatts one chall.	066	13	04
Item, to the watchmen of the castell of Stirling .	172	00	00
Item, of beir & malt to the Serjeand 1 chall. 4 bolls .	125	00	00

Item, of beir & malt allowed to the Lord Carden

1 chall. is	100	00	00

Item, of Capones 15 evicted be the E. of Airth be

decreet dated the last of febrij 1611 . .	005	00	00

Item, the haill remanent dewties of the said Lordschip
of Stirling extending to 4058$^{lb.}$ 00$^{s.}$ 05$^{d.}$ is
payed in to the E. of Marr & therfor ought

to be deduced	4058	00	05

So the said Lordship payes only 10 merks of yeirly
tack dewtie in maner mentioned in the follow-

ing observationes . . .	0006 13 04		

Suma of the presentt rentall extendes

to . . .	4992 18 03

Suma of the deductiones is . . .   4850 19 05

So ther restes of free money .   141 19 10

Observationes.

The blench dewties of this Shyre extending to 48$^{lb.}$ 15s.
2$^{d.}$ is allocat as pairt of the Lordschip of Stirling to the E.
of Marr & so ought to be deduced.

Falkirk payes the forsaid soume of 10$^{lb.}$ as a pairt of the
Lordschip of Hallyroodhouse, and barronie of Brughtoune, conforme to ane Chartour dated 13 Dec$^{r.}$ 1607 which shall be
further enlarged in Edinburgh Shyre wher Hallyroodhouse
Lordschip is compted for.

Torwood, or *Torwoodheid*, payed be the old rentalls 3$^{lb.}$
6s. 8$^{d.}$ with 20 cariages of beiff, and ther wes allocat to the
Keeper of Torwood ane Chalder victuall, bot be ane contract

betwixt the King & the Lord Forster, dated the 4th Novr. 1636, the King did sett to him the Torwood and Torwoodheid in few, for payment of the soume of 333^{lb.} 6s. 8^{d.} which is now assigned and payed to the E. of Marr as Keeper of the castell of Stirling. It ought not to be allowed bot yeirly compted for in the proppertie roll, because it wes the Kinges propper wood, for which he gave to the Keeper therof out of the Lordschip of Stirling one chalder of victuall, which victuall the said E. of Marr hes now. And the King haveing sett out this Torwoodheid in few for yeirly payment of the said few dewtie 333^{lb.} 6s. 8^{d.} which ought not to be allowed to the said E., bot compted for & payed in, in respect that he hes both the said chalder victuall formerly allowed to the Keeper & also the said few dewtie of 500 merk.

Chalmerlane of Stirling; As to the serjeands fee both money & victuall, ther should no such thing be allowed, because ther is no such office now in use. And wher the office ceases the benefite should cease. 2do. All heretable offices are discharged be Act of parliament, and be the Kinges Revocatione particularlie revocked. And by severall instructiones from his Majeste and Actes of Exchequer dischairged to be allowed in any comptes.

Craigingorth: ther is allowed for thir landes 13^{lb.} 6s. 8^{d.}, bot ther is no reasone nor ground for allowing the same; it being in all preceeding Rentalls charged & compted.

Halfe Landes of Inverallon: both victuall and money of thir landes is evicted be ane decreet of the Lordes of the Session alleadgeing that the same holdes blench; bot be the contair in the rentalls in anno 1502, 1503, 1600, 1612 the haill landes of Inverallon payes 10^{lb.} of money 2 chalder wheat

L

STIRLING. 2 chalder beir, 2 chalder oats.   The one halfe of the landes of Inverallon constantly payes & comptes & how the uthir halfe can be discharged it is thought hard.   Bot in respect it is alleagit to be founded on ane decreet of the Lordes of the Session it may att presentt be past, and shall be more exprest in the improvements.

For the allowance given to the watchmen of the castell of Stirling, it is found be the Comisioners appointed for considering of the burdings & unnecesar chairges of the revenew, 7th May 1634, that the Captaines & Keepers of the Castells haveing great fees & allowances for keeping of the same ought to have no allowance for the watchmen & souldiers except it appear uther wayes be thair infeftments.

The Lordschip of Stirling rentes are divyded in money & victuall.   The money rent is assigned for keeping the Castell of Stirling be Act of Parl. K. Ja. 6 par. 9th, Act 8th, and by ane Contract betwixt the King & the E. of Marr in anno 1641, by which Contract the said Earle oblidges himselfe to resigne the heretabill offices of Shirriff and Baillie of Stirling for which the King wes to pay him the soume of 5000$^{lb.}$ sterling; and 3000$^{lb.}$ sterling restand to him as the arreiars of his pensione of 300$^{lb.}$ sterling yeirly, makeing in all the soume of 8000$^{lb.}$ sterling.   By the forsaid contract the King did sett to the said E. of Marr the haill victuall fermes of the said Lordschip of Stirling for the space of 25 yeirs for yeirly payment of 10 merks.   And by ane new signatur, under his Majestis hand in anno 1660, His Majeste in consideratione that the rents of said Lordschip were uplifted be the Englishes the tyme of the usurpatione did adde ten yeirs to the said tack.   And so the haill rentes of the said Lordschip of Stirling

ought to be deduced, except the soume of 10 merks of tack STIRLING.
dewty which is payed yeirly be the E. of Marr.

And because the said E. of Marr his ryght to the said
Lordschip was not thought legall, bot may be recalled and
reduced be his Majeste, att leist being but ane tacke for ane
certaine & determinate tyme the same will fall in againe to the
Exchequer. It is therfor thought fitt to observe the differences
betwixt the rentalls of the said Lordschip of Stirling, as it
payed and compted, befor the allocatione therof in maner forsaid. And as it payed be the rentall 1612 & 1603 viz.:

By the said old rentall it payed of beir 35 chall. 4 bolls; bot be
the presentt rentall it payes 31 chall. 5 bolls 1 f. 2 p.
So the rentalls differ be 3 chall. 14 bolls 2 f. 2 p. att
100^{lb.} per chall. is 391 08 00
By the old rentalls of wheatt 9 chall.; bot be the presentt rentall
8 chall. 4 bolls. So the rentalls differ be 12 bolls wheat
pryce forsaid 075 00 00
By the old rentall 4 chall. oates which agrees with the presentt
rentall. By the old rentall 10 chall. meill & 12 bolls;
bot be the presentt rentall ther is no meill payed. So
the rentalls differ be the haill meill which at 100 merks
per chall. extendes to the soume of . . .   714 13 04

Suma of the differences of this Shyre is . <u>1181 01 04</u>

CLACKMANAN SHYRE. CLACK-
MANAN.

Payed be the Shirriff for book & blenches yeirly viz.:

For the Landes of Hiltone & Bread croft .	00 03 00	⎫
For Alloway one pair Gilt spurres .	08 00 00	⎪
For the Landes of Chamburry 1^{d.} monetæ .	00 00 01	⎬ 18 04 02
For Broomhills & Rosholme 1^{d.} monetæ .	00 00 01	⎪
For the blenches of Iavestoune 1^{d.} argentis .	00 01 00	⎪
Book	10 00 00	⎭

Proppertie.

Armblo landes of Clackmanan	004 03 04
Eister Kenneth	002 00 00
Stewart Bank	000 06 08
Suma of this Shyre extendes to . .	024 14 02

Which is all free money ther being no deductiones.

LINLITHGOW SHYRE.

Payed yeirly be the Shirriff for Blenches book and Castellwairdes as followes :

Money	00 03 04
Argentes 12^d in scottes money	00 12 00
Whyt spurres one pair .	01 00 00
Castellwairdes . .	06 17 08
Book	20 00 00

28 13 04

Proppertie.

Bining Lordschip of blench 1 pair gloves	03 00 00
Teynds of Priest feild . .	01 00 00
Kirk Landes of Bining .	02 13 04
Knock & midle quarter .	03 12 00

0010 05 04

Coalls of Meidhope by Sr Rob. Drummond .	0000 13 04
Torphichen of yeirly few . .	0066 13 04
Nether Newlistoune . . .	0027 03 05
Carlowrie be Samuel Drummond . .	0000 13 04
Over Newlistoune	0009 00 00
Briestmylne	0003 00 00
Craigtoune	0000 10 00
Panstead alias Salin . . .	0004 00 00
Viccars landes of Lennie . .	0007 13 04

Lordschip of Linlithgow of money .	218 13 04
Wheat 6 chall. 5 bolls 2 f. 2 p. att 100^{lb} . .	635 03 00
Beir, malt, & meill 8 chall. 9 bolls is .	857 16 03
Oats, 6 chall. 14 bolls 1 fir. att 100 merks . .	459 07 06
Poultrie 42 att 4s. the peice .	008 08 00

2179 08 01

All which ought to be deduced as being allocat
and assigned for keeping the palace of Linlithgow in maner specifit in the following
observationes 2179 08 01
Burgh of Queensferry 0003 00 00
Burgh of Linlithgow 0052 10 00

Suma of the presentt rent of this
Shyre . . . 2393 03 02

Suma of the deductiones extend to . . 2179 08 01

So ther remaines of free money yeirly payed in . 213 15 01

Observationes.

Torphichen Lordschip is thought to be non of the Lordes
of Erectiones, bot only for the Landes called St Johne Landes,
which landes were mortified and founded of old for the mentainance of the Knights of the Hospitall of Jerusalem, whose
chairge wes to defend and conduct such devote Christians
who were in use to take pilgrimage, from all places of the
Christian world, to visite the grave & sepulchere of our Saviour
Jesus Christ in Jerusalem from incursions & roberies of the
Hagarines & uther Brigaines & guarding also the pilgrimes
within the Hospitall then builded in Jerusalem for receaveing
of them, which Hospitall was dedicat to St John & which
Knights were no wayes Ecclesiasticall persones, but one
Christian fraternitie of Noblemen & Gentlemen professing
armes. Wherupon the Lord Torphichen did supplicat the
parliament, in anno 1633, desireing that the Lordschip of
Torphichen nether as to the superioritie, nor proppertie,
should be included in the Generall act of his Majestis determinatione anent the Lordes of Erectiones, which Petition
the Parliament did remitt to the Secreet Counsell to try and

consider the same, but not to determine therin till his Majeste should be further acquainted therwith.

In anno 1635 the Lord Torphichen compts for the blench dewtie of the said Lordschip att 333 : 06 : 08. Bot he haveing represented to the Exchequer that ther was severall persones who ought to relieve him of a pairt of the said blench dewtie. And therfor desired that they might be chairged for the same yeirly; and to that effect gave up a list of severall persones heritors of the landes following viz. :

Hallyairdes	.	.	.	.	66 13 04	
Arnestoune	.	.	.	.	40 00 00	
Maines of Marie Culter		.	.	.	08 10 00	
Kincousie	.	.	.	.	01 06 08	
Tilburies	.	.	.	.	01 06 08	
Auchinlowines	.	.	.	.	01 06 08	209 03 08
Thankertoune		.	.	.	10 00 00	
Temple	.	.	.	.	49 00 00	
Temple hall	.	.	.	.	17 13 08	
Inglistoune	.	.	.	.	10 06 08	
Briestmylne	.	.	.	.	03 00 00	

Which reliefe of 209 : 03 : 08, with the soume of 120$^{lb.}$ 04s. 06$^{d.}$ then payed in be the said Lord Torphichen, will not make up the totall of the said blench dewtie be 4$^{lb.}$ 6s. 8$^{d.}$

In anno 1642 & 1647 and since, the said Lord Torphichen only compts for 66$^{lb.}$ 13s. 4$^{d.}$ and that conforme to ane Act of Parliament in anno 1633. In which case the forsaid blench dewty of 500 merks will not be made up be the soume of 57$^{lb.}$ 9s. 8$^{d.}$ for which he is to compt—57 : 09 : 08. For it seemes strainge that any pretence of ane Act of Parliament in anno 1633 can be allowed in anno 1645. Wheras it was requisit in anno 1635 & he necessitat to compt for the haill.

Linlithgow Lordschip, and severall fewars therof, hes not

compted in Exchequer thir many yeirs; it being allocat and
assigned for keeping the Palace of Linlithgow, and so ought
to be deduced, which shall be more fully & particularlie spoken
to amongst the improvements.

Suma of the differences patet.

BATHGATE SHYRE.   BATHGATE.

Lochtwill 1ᵈ· monetæ .	00 00 01	} 0010 00 01
Book . . .	10 00 00	

EDINBURH SHYRE.   EDINBURH.

Payed yeirly for blenches book & Castellwairdes viz. :

Money . . .	. 00 06 08	
Argentes 3ˢ· 4ᵈ· in scottes money	. 02 00 00	
Pepper one pund . .	. 01 00 00	
Gume one pund . .	. 00 10 00	
Libri Thuris . . .	. 03 06 08	63 10 00
Gloves 3 pair . .	. 09 00 00	
One haulkheid (sic) . .	. 00 13 04	
Gilt spures one pair . .	. 08 00 00	
Castell wairdes . .	. 18 14 00	
Book . . .	. 20 00 00	

REGALITIE OF MUSSILBURGH.

Book .	. 02 00 00	0002 00 00

Proppertie.

Arnestoune .	.	040 00 00
Howburne .	.	002 00 00
Kinges stables	.	004 08 08
Kinges meadow	.	014 06 08

EDINBURGH. Cannogate & Leith be the provost & baillies of
    Edinburgh 020 00 00
Kings work in Leith 005 16 00
Heriotes Hospitall 033 06 08
The peice ground neir Hallyrood-house . 000 06 08
Newbottle Lordschip 283 00 00
Inglestoune & Briestmylne . . . 013 06 08
Hallyairdes . . . . 66 13 04 ⎫
New augmentatione . . . 00 03 04 ⎬ 066 19 08
Auld Listoun for the rigges . . 00 03 00 ⎭
    Wherof ther is only 100 merk to be allowed
        for relieff of the Lordschip of Torphichen
        the augmentatione being lately added
Tocksheid holl 009 08 08
Temple 049 00 00
Eister Temple for one pair gilt spures . 08 00 00 ⎫
And of few dewtie . . . 08 19 00 ⎬ 0016 19 00
Todishauch 0001 04 00
Teyndes of the Deane . . . 0002 00 00
Kirknewtoune 0010 15 04
Cramound mure 0002 00 00
Hallyrood-house Lordschip of blench dewtie . 0200 00 00
    Wherof ther is deduced for the causes
      mentioned in the following observationes .   100 00 00
Park of Hallyrood-house 200 bulks of
    mutton att 40s. the peice is . 400 00 00 ⎫
Hay 6000 stone att 2s. the stone . 600 00 00 ⎬ 1000 00 00
    Which ought to be deduced as being disponed to Sr·
    Ja. Hamiltoun in manner mentioned in the
    following observationes . . .   1000 00 00
Burgh of Edinburgh payes sterlingorum monetæ
    34lb· 13/4d· extending in scottes money to . 0346 13 04
Wherof ther ought to be deduced as payed to the poor
    of Corstorphin 20lb· ster. extending in scottes
    money 0200 00 00
Item, to the Abbot & Convent of Dumfermling . . 0050 00 00
Item, to the Trinitie Hospitall of Edinburgh . . 0061 13 04

    Suma of the Shyres of Bathgate & Edinburgh
      and Regallitie of Mussillburgh extendes
      to 2197 02 01

    Suma of the deductiones extend to . . . 1411 13 04

    So ther remaines of free money . . 785 08 09

The Barronie of Brughtoune, being comprehended within the Lordschip of Hallyrood-house did pay 60[lb.] as ane proportionall pairt of the blench dewtie of the said Lordschip. And now the toune of Edinburgh possesseth and enjoyes the haill barronie of Brughtoune, and comptes & payes yeirly therfor under the designatione of Cannogate & Leith 20[lb.], so that the old & presentt rentalls differ be the soume of . 040 00 00

Newbottle Lordschip, of old ane Monastrie Ordinis Cistertiensis founded be David I. King of Scotland in anno 1140, and erected in ane Lordschip to the E. of Lowthian be chartour, dated 15th October 1591, for payment of the blench dewtie of 400[lb.] Bot by ane chartour granted to Robert E. of Lowthian, dated 3d Febrij 1620, the said blench dewtie is reduced to 283[lb.] befor chairged which shall be more fully enlarged amongst the improvements. So that the old & presentt rentalls differ be . . . 117 00 00

Halyroodhous, of old ane Monastrie called S. Crucis Hallyruidhouse of the order of St Augustine founded by Da. I. King of Scotland in anno 1144. And erected in ane Lordschip to John Lord Hallyroodhouse, be Chartour dated att Whytthall the 10th Dec[r.] 1607, for payment of the soume of 200[lb.] of blench dewtie ; of the which soume the landes of Auldhammer called Whitkirk payes 100[lb.]; the landes of Polmond belonging to Duke Hamiltoune payes 30[lb.]; Falkirk payes 10[lb.] & Brughtoune payed 60[lb.] which makes up the haill 200[lb.] All which is particularlie sett doune in the rentall 1618, bot ther is nothing now compted for the same; except Falkirk for 10[lb.], Polmond 30[lb.], and Brughtoune under the name of Cannogate & Leith 20[lb.]

Park of Hallyroodhouse payed of old 600 mutton bulks which wes plenished and reserved for keeping of his Majestis

M

EDINBURH. house, with 6000 stone of hay which is compted for in anno
1633 att 40s. for ilk mutton bulk, and 2s. for ilk stone of
hay. Extending in all to 1000$^{lb.}$ befor chairged, bot the same
being now disponed to Sir James Hamiltoune as Keeper therof,
who payes nothing for the samyne tho the former Keepers
payed as said is. And to be deduced, bot it is strange that
the Keeper shall pretend such a ryght therto, as if it were his
proppertie, & not to make the samyne furthcoming to his
Majeste ether by paying what formerly it paid or give his
Majeste the use of the same. So by this the Keeper of any of
his Majestis house may extrude him fra the possession of the
same.

Suma of the differences betwixt the old & presentt
rentalls as is befor sett doune extendes to   157 00 00

HADDING-
TOUNE.

HADDINGTOUNE SHYRE.

Payed be the Shirriff for book blenches & Castellwairdes viz.:

Argentes 3s. 1$^{d.}$ in scottes money	. 01 17 00	
One broad arrow . .	. 00 10 00	
Gilt spures 3 pair . .	. 24 00 00	075 07 00
Castellwairdes . .	. 29 00 00	
Book	. 20 00 00	

Proppertie.

Chalmerlaine of Dumbar of money .	134 11 08	
390 pair Cunings att 13s. 4$^{d.}$ the pair . . .	260 00 00	
30 chall. wheat small mett att 100$^{lb.}$ the chall. .	3000 00 00	6554 17 11
30 chall. beir att 100$^{lb.}$.	3000 00 00	
2 chall. 1 p. oats att 80$^{lb.}$ per chall .	0160 06 03	

Wherof deduce for a pairt of the Links that is
    overblowen—

Conings 153 pair att 13s. 4ᵈ· the pair 102 00 00		
Item to the chalmer. of fee of wheat 1 chall. 4 bolls . . 125 00 00		
Item to him of beir 1 chall. 4 bolls . 125 00 00		
To the Serjeand of wheat 2 bolls . 012 10 00	2983 05 00	
of beir . . . 2 bolls . . 012 10 00		
To the aires of Mᵗ Wᵐ· Kellie 13 chall. 2 f. wheat . 1303 02 06		
Item of beir to him—13 chall. 2 f. 1303 02 06		

The assyse of the herrring of the east sea   .   1200· 00 00

    Which ought to be deduced for the causes con-
    tained in the following observationes . . 1200 00 00

Ballincrieffe of money . 40 10 00		
3 chall. 12 bolls beir att 100ˡᵇ· . 375 00 00		
49 Capons att 6s. 8ᵈ· the peice . 016 06 08	0484 14 00	
251 poultrie ½ at 4s. the peice . 050 06 00		
300 pair doves sold heretabillie for 4 merk . . 002 13 04		

1000 cherryes payes nothing.

Loch-hill of few & augmentatione . . 0013 10 00

Prora & Fenton of blench dewtie as a pairt of the
    Lordschip of Newbotle . . 0017 00 00

Prestoune Grainge of few . . . 0044 00 00
And of blench dewtie . . . 0060 00 00

Beill { of money . . . 44 04 06		
8ᵈ· argentes in scotts money . 00 08 00	0068 12 06	
3 pair Gilt spures . 24 00 00		

Sᵗ· Germaines be the Earle of Wintoune . 0009 13 04

Gosfuird { of few . . 16 00 00		
24 Capones att 6s. 8ᵈ· . 08 00 00	0033 12 00	
48 poultrie att 4s. . . 09 12 00		

Friers landes of Lufnes . . . 0014 00 00
Ruch-law of yeirly few . . . 0026 13 04
Wester Gamellsheills of few . . . 0013 06 08
Staniepeth & Hartrumwood . . . 0026 13 04
Templehall and Paistoune payed be the Laird of
    Arnestoune John Pringle & Robert Hepburne 0018 15 08
Parisflatt & Viccarsfauld . . . 0002 16 08
Friers Landes of Dumbar . . . 0020 00 00
Priorie of Northberwick of blench ferme . 0154 10 00

HADDING- TOUNE.	Kingstoune as a part of the Lordschip			
	of Cardros of blench dewtie .	26 08 00	} 0047 01 04	
	Friors Landes of Dirletoune of few .	20 13 04		
	Kirk Landes of Lauder and teynds therof .		0001 00 00	
	Kirk Landes of Cavers . . .		0003 00 00	
	Lordschip of Haddingtoune of blench dewtie .		0026 13 04	
	Tuninghame Lordschip of money .	115 09 05	} 0915 19 05	
	of wheat 5 chall. att 100lb. .	500 00 00		
	of meill 3 chall. att 100lb. .	300 00 00		
	one pund wax . . .	000 10 00		
	which ought now to be deduced for the causes specifit in the following observationes .		. .	0915 19 05
	Burgh of Dumbar		0004 00 00	
	Milnes of Dumbar		0013 06 08	
	Cockenie burgh { of burrow maill .	06 13 04	} 0008 06 08	
	{ for one gold penny .	01 13 04		
	Burgh of Northberwick . . .		0001 00 00	
	Burgh of Haddingtoune . . .		0130 00 00	
	Suma of the presentt rent of this Shyre is . . .		9988 09 10	
	Suma of the deductiones extend to .		5099 04 05	
	So ther restes of free money		4889 05 05	

Observationes.

First, as to the blenches, ther is only compted of late be the Shirriff for the blenches the soume of 18lb. ; for Castellwairdes 29lb. ; for book 20lb. ; which in the haill extendes only to the soume of 67lb. 7s. So ther is a differ of 8lb. which is for a pair of gilt spurres that is payed out of the Landes of Byres, and which wes remitted to the Lord Binning the Secretarie in the compts in anno 1615. And in that same compt ther is remitted to Ormistoune, then Justice Clerk, ane uther pair gilt spures, but therefter the one pair is compted for and the uther ought to be lookt efter.

Castell wairdes be the presentt rentall payes 29lb. as is

befor chairged, bot be the rentalls in anno 1450, and uthers,
they are compted for att 51$^{lb.}$ 19s. so the rent. differ be —
22 : 19 : 00.

Challmerlanrie of Dumbar: ther is allowed & allocat to
the aires of Mr W$^{m.}$ Kellie the number of 26 chall. 1 boll
wheat & beir.   This victuall being few ferme, as a part of
the Lordschip of Dumbar, wes given to the Lord Holdernes
be King James 6, for his good service, in saveing his Majeste
from Gowries Conspiracy.   King Charles of blessed memorie
wes most desirous to have these few fermes in againe, and
by his severall letters directed to his Thesaurers, which may
be sein, he desired them to transact for the saides few fermes
or utherwayes to reduce them legallie.   Att last by ane letter
from his Majeste, dated 10th Novr 1634, ther wes ane transaction that they should sell the few fermes att 2000 merks per
challder.   Conforme therunto Mr Cornelius Ingles for himselfe,
and as haveing warrand from the rest of the aires portioners
of the said Mr Wm Kellie gave in the rentall which extends
only to 22 chall. 12 bolls 2 pecks victuall as the rentall yet
extant bears.   Bot how ther is now 26 chall. one boll wheat
& beir allowed to them is uncertaine; wherfor it would be
inquired for.

There is also 2 bolls wheat and 2 bolls beir allowed to the
serjeand of Dumbar, but ther is no such office att presentt and
with the demission of the officer benefits cease.

The Assyse Herring of the east seas thir 3 or 4 yeirs
hes payed nothing, the samyne wes sett to Sir Adam Blair
and Sir John Strachen, bot they justly had deduction of thair
tacke dewtie & this yeir it wes in Collectorie, and nothing
gotten for the same.   In anno 1656, 57, 58, and 1659 it

payed 130[lb.] ster.; and in anno '1598 it payed 1120 dry killing, and in anno 1614 it payed 2000[lb.] scotts and 1300[lb.] of Grassume.

Ballincrieffe bo the presentt rentall payes only .		40 10 00
Bot be the old reutall it payed . 47 08 08		
So the rentalls differ be . . .		006 16 08
Be the presentt rentalls of beir 3 chall. 12 bolls is	375 00 00	
Be the old rent. 7 chall. 12 bolls 2 f. is . . . 778 02 06		
So the rentalls differ bo 4 chall. 2 f. is		403 02 06
Be the presentt rent. no wheat payed, bot be the old rent. it payes 13 cha. 1 boll 1 f. 3 p. is		1308 11 10
Be the presentt rentall 49 Capons is . .	16 06 08	
Be the old rent. 55 capons is . 18 16 08		
So the rentalls differ be 6 capons is . .		002 10 00

Loch-hill is a pairt of the Lordschip of Ballincrieffe and is sett in few to Mr David Borthwick for payment of 13[lb.] 6s. 8[d.] as is befor chairged.

Prestoun Grainge be the presentt rentall payes of blench dewtie 60[lb.] and 44[lb.] of few dewtie. Bot it has not compted for the few dewtie these many yeirs; yet it ought to compt for the same as a part of the old few before the erection.

Northberwick of old ane Cloister Ordinis Cistertiensis founded be Duncane Earle of Fyfe, and wes erected in ane priorie to S[r.] John Home conforme to his chartour, dated the 7th July 1609, for payment of 154[lb.] of blench dewtie, which blench dewtie wes assigned to Sir John Prestoun of Pennicook and his sone, dureing thair lyfetymes who are both lately dead; and so the same ought to be compted for, and payed in. There is also compted for in anno 1623, 26, and 1630, over and above the forsaid blench dewtie, the soume of 23[lb.] 16s. 8[d.],

which seemes to be for few dewtie, in respect that ther are
severall fewars lyable in payment of thair particular fewes :
as Etherine Craig of Ballgoun & uthers; for in the rentall
1515 this 154$^{lb.}$ is compted in the Shirriffe Roll as the blench
dewtie of the maines of Northberwick.

Tuninghame Lordschip did compt for, in anno 1603, the
particulars contained in the chairge, bot now it ought to be
deduced as being allocat to the Archbishop of St Andrewes
& to the Lordschip of Mellrose as is more particularlie sett
doune in the rentall 1611.

Burgh of Dumbar payes 4$^{lb.}$, & for the mylnes therof 17$^{lb.}$
6s. 8$^{d.}$ And that conforme to ane Act of Exchequer wherof the
tenor followes :—

Apud Striveleing the 20 July Anno mdcxxviii per Cancel-
larium &c. Item, it is divysed & ordained that forsameikle
as the toune of Dumbar were summonded be our So: Lords
precept to compeir & make compt reckoning & payment of
thair burrow maills, mylne & uthers thair intromissione, the
baillies of that burgh being personallie presentt alleadged
that they were never in use, since the forfaulter of the Earle
of March to make compt of the premiss. And therfor the
Lordes Auditores of Exchequer made the rolls to be sought,
in the which it was found, in ane compt made be umquhile Hew
Spencer, Stewart of Merch, holden att Edinburgh the first day
of September the year of God [illegible—? 1536] & xxxvi. wher
the said Stewart was chairged in his comptes of 4$^{lb.}$ of burrow
maill of the said burght, and of 15$^{lb.}$ 6s. 8$^{d.}$ for the mailles
of the mylnes of Dumbar. And therfor ordained the Ballies,
Councill, & Comunitie of the said burgh of Dumbar to compeir
yeirly to make compt reckoning & payment of thair burrow

HADDING-
TOUNE.
—

mailles, mylne mailles, & uthers thair intromissione ilk yeir in tyme comeing, sicklyke as uther burrowes of this realme doe, & that under the paine of the unlaw of the Exchequer & tinsaill of thair freedome.

Suma of the differences betwixt the old & presentt rentalls extend to.   .   .   1743 10 00

PEARTH.

PEARTH SHYRE.

Payed be the Shirriff for book & blenches viz:

Money . .	. 17 13 04	
Argentes 2s. 8ᵈ in scottes money	. 01 12 00	
One Leopard or Gray hound .	. 05 06 08	064 00 00
One pair gilt spures . .	. 08 00 00	
One pund pepper . .	. 01 10 00	
Book	. 30 00 00	

STRATHERNE STEUARTRIE.

Payed yeirly to the Shirriff for book & blenches viz:

Money . . .	. 00 00 07	
Argentes 13ᵈ in scottes money	. 00 13 00	030 19 07
Broad Arrow heids . .	. 00 04 00	
Book	. 30 00 00	

Proppertie.

Stratherne Challmerlanrie of money	. 910 05 09	
Mairtes 44 & ½ mart att 10ˡᵇ. the peice . .	. 445 00 00	1355 05 09
Wherof deduce of Challmerlane fee	. 180 00 00	
Landes of Tillibanchorie .	. 004 00 00	. 0194 00 00
Landes of Auchtertyre .	. 010 00 00	
Discheor & Toyeor of money .	. 170 00 00	
Item, 2 mairtes . .	. 020 00 00	0190 00 00

Scoone & Elcho Lordschip   .   .   .   1000 00 00

Archalony 0048 00 00

Culross Lordschip   .   .   .   0066 13 04

Collheughs of Culross .   .   .   0002 05 00

Huntingtour of money   .   0192 10 00

    Wheat 14 bolls att 6$^{lb.}$ 5s. the boll 0087 10 00

    Bear 32 chall. 1 boll 1 f. 1 p.

      att 100 merks the ch. . 2138 16 00

    Meil 71 chall. 9 bolls 3 p. att

      100 merk the cha. . 4771 12 02   7374 06 10

    Capones 154 att 6s. 8$^{d.}$ the peice 0051 06 08

    Poultrie 568 att 4s. . 0113 12 00

    Geese 30 att 10s. . 0015 00 00

    One boar . . 0004 00 00

    All which is deduced as is specifit in the

      following Observationes .   .   . 7374 06 10

The peice ground within the sea mark att Walli-

    feild 0001 00 00

Muiredge fewar   .   .   .   0010 00 00

Strathbrane of money .   .   . 176 19 04

    Stirks 21 att 3$^{lb.}$ the peice . 063 00 00

    Kiddes 52 att 10s. the peice . 026 00 00

    Butter 29 stone & ½ att 40s. the

      stone . . . 059 00 00   0340 06 08

    Capons 24 att 5s. . 006 00 00

    Swyne 2 att 4$^{lb.}$ . . 008 00 00

Item, of old and new augmentatione . 001 06 08

    All which is deduced for the reasones men-

      tioned in the following observationes .   . 0340 06 08

Kinclevin Lordschip .   .   .   0484 00 00

    which is deduced as in the following observa-

      tiones is contained 0484 00 00

Eglismagrigill   .   .   .   [blank]

Culmalundies   .   .   .   0000 07 08

Couper Lordschip { of few . . 04 03 08 } 0208 03 08
                { of blench dewtie . 204 00 00 }

Monteith Chalmerlanrie of money . 526 13 04

    oat meill & beir 10 chall. 9 bolls

      at 3s. 4$^{d.}$ per boll . 28 03 04

    oates 5 chall. at 3s. 4$^{d.}$ the boll . 013 06 00 0810 08 04

    Mairtes 24 att 10$^{lb.}$ the peice . 240 00 00

    muttones 15 att 3s. the peice . 002 05 00

PEARTH. Wherof ther is deduced of chalmerlane fie 100 00 00 ⎫
—   Item to him as more fee .   . 014 00 00 ⎪
       Item for the mentainance of Stir-   ⎪
           ling castle   .   .   . 478 11 01   ⎪
       Item, for the landes of Letter belonging   ⎪
           to the Laird of Kipponrose because   ⎬   0603 07 09
           they hold waird .   .   . 000 16 08 ⎧ ·
       Item, to the Keeper of the castell of   ⎪
           Douno out of the fermes of the   ⎪
           mylne & mylne Landes of Canmes   ⎪
           & uther landes 3 chall. 12 bolls   ⎪
           oatmeill pryce forsaid   .   . 010 00 00 ⎭
       Burgh of Culross   .   .   .   .   0010 00 00   ·
       Burgh of Pearth 0240 00 00
           Which is deduced as is mentioned in
           the following observationes .   .   .   0240 00 00

              Suma of the presentt rent of this Shyre
                  extends to   .   .   12,235 16 02

              Suma of the deductiones extend to   .   .   9236 00 07

              So ther restes of free money   .   2999 15 07

Observationes.

Stratherne Challmerlanrie : There is deduced to the Challmerlane for the landes of Auchtertyre 10$^{lh.}$, which ought not
to be deduced in respect these landes are chairged in the
rentall only for 20$^{lb.}$ in anno 1612, the haill Challmerlanrie
being in the rentall 910$^{lh.}$ of money. And so ther being no
more chairged ther ought no more to be deduced, for the
reason which is given for deduction therof (is as being over-
chairged with 30$^{lh.}$) is not to be respected because ther is no
more chairged nor compted for but 20$^{lh.}$

Item, there is allocat to the Challmerlane. of fee 180$^{lb.}$
which exceedes the old fee ther being, be all former accompts,

only allowed to him 100^{lb.}, bot this addition is for his extraordinary paines.

Scoone Lordschip of old ane Monastrie of the order of S^{t.}
Augustine founded be K. Alex^{r.} I. Cognomen fers, Rex Scotiæ,
and erected in ane Lordschip to Sr. David Murray now Lord
Scoone be Chartour, dated the 18th August 1608, for payment
of the forsaid blench dewtie of 1000^{lb.}

Culross Lordschip of old ane Monastrie Ordinis Cistertiensis
founded be William M^cduff Earle of Fyfe, and erected in ane
Lordship to John Lord Colvell be chartor, dated att Roystoune
the 20th January 1609, for yeirly payment of 100 merks, bot
he hes not compted thir many yeirs alleadgeing that he ought
not to compt therfor, bot that the severall & particular fewars
should compt for the same which is ane mistake for he as Lord
of the Erection ought to compt therfor.

Huntingtour falling in to his Majeste be the forfaulter of
the Earle of Gowrie wes annexed to the Croun in anno 1600
Ja. 6, Par. 16, Act 2^{d.} & did yeirly compt as is befor chairged,
& wes disponed to William Murray one of his Majestis bed
chamber, who disponed the samyne to the Earle of Tillibardine,
who sinsyne, by his Majestis favour, hes gotten the whole lands
holden blench of his Majeste.

Strathbrane, being a pairt of the Earle of Gowries landes
wes disponed be his Majeste to S^{r.} Wm. Stewart for his good
service done to his Majeste the tyme of Gowryes Conspiracy,
for payment yeirly of the few dewties befor chairged, & wes
allowed as being allocat to him in all former compts till anno
1634. Att which tyme ther wes ane actione intented of reduction & improbatione of his ryght, who therupon did take ane
new Chartor from his Majeste containing ane reddendo of the

PEARTH. few dewties befor charged, & accordingly did compt for the same then, but never since, & therfor they ought to be called for, notwithstanding that he pretendes that pairt of the saids few dewties are now allocat & assigned to the singers of the Chappell Royall, & the pryces of the casualities converted to small soumes, which shall be more fully enlarged in the Improvements.

Kinclevine Lordschip is a pairt of his Majestis proppertie disponed be his Majeste to the late Lord Kinclevin as keeper of the castell therof, & therefter disponed be the King to Robert Leslie as Captaine & Keeper of the said castell for the space of two 19 yeirs. Therefter the said Robert Leslie assignes his ryght & tacke, which is dated 4th Novr. 1646, to S^r. W^m. Stewart under this provisione & declaratione, that, if the same should be quarrelled, the said Robert Leslie oblidged him to refound the soume receaved from the said S^r. W^m. for the same. The few dewties therof did alwayes compt, as is befor chairged, & ought yet to compt & not to be deduced as shall be more fully inlarged amongst the improvements.

Eglismagrigill is yeirly called in the Exchequer table, but it never compts because the same is included in the Lordschip of Lyndors & so ought not to compt per se.

Burgh of Pearth payes 24^lb. st., but the same is allowed to the Hospitall, and for upholding the Land staills of the bridge. And now they have no Hospitall nor bridge to be upholden & therfor it ought to be called for, which is in scotts money 240^lb.

Coupar Lordschip of old ane Monastrie Ordinis Cistertiensis founded be Malcolme, Cognomine Virgo, King of Scotland & erected in ane Lordschip to Ja. Lord Coupar be ane Chartor, dated the 20 December 1607, for payment of the blench dewtie PEARTH. of 200^{lb.}

Monteith Lordschip be the presentt rentall payes of
 money . . . 526 13 04
 Be the rentall 1502 it payes of
 money . . . 707 00 00
  So the rentalls differ be . . . 180 06 08
Be the presentt rentall of beir & oatmeill 10 chall. 9 bolls.
Be the old rentall 20 chall. 7 bolls
 beir & meill . . . 1362 10 00
  So the rentalls differ be 9 chall. 14 bolls pryce forsaid 658 06 08
Be the presentt rentall of oats 5 chall. pryce forsaid.
Be the old rentall 19 chall. oats is 1900 merks.
  So the rentalls differ be 14 chall. is . . . 933 06 08
Be the presentt rentall 24 mairts att 10^{lb.} the
 peice is . . . 240 00 00
Be the old rentall 68 mairts att 10^{lb.} is 680^{lb.}
  So the rentalls differ be 44 mairts is . . . 440 00 00
Be the presentt rentall 15 muttones att 26s. 8^{d.} the peice.
Be the old rentall 43 muttones is . 37 06 08
  So the rentalls differ be 28 muttones is . 037 06 08
Be the presentt rentall ther is no calves payed.
Bot be the old rentall 9 calves att 2^{lb.} . 018 00 00
Be the presentt rentall no wedders payed.
Bot be the old rentall 20 wedders att 26s. 8^{d.} the peice is . 026 13 04
Be the presentt rentall no salmond payed.
Be the old rentall 260 salmond att 10s. the peice . 130 00 00
Be the presentt rentall no swyne payed.
Bot be the old rentall one swyne att 4^{lb.} . . 004 00 00
Be the presentt rentall the Chalmerlaine hes of
 fee . . . 100 00 00
More to him of fee . . . 014 00 00
Be the old rentall ther is only allowed of fee 100^{lb.} so
 ther is 14^{lb.} which ought not to be allowed to him seeing
 no Challmerlaine had the said office had more fee . 014 00 00

  Suma of the difference betwixt the presentt rent.
  and the rentall in anno 1502 extendes to . 2442 00 00

FYFFE SHYRE.

Payed be the Shirriff for Book & blenches viz. :

Money	.	.	10 00 03
Argentes 7s. in scottes money	.	.	04 04 00
One pund wax	.	.	00 10 00
Gloves 2 pair	.	.	06 00 00
Pepper 2 pund	.	.	03 00 00
Cucumer seed 1 pund	.	.	00 13 04
2 hens	.	.	00 12 00
Book	.	.	30 00 00

} 054 19 07

REGALITIE OF DUMFERMLING.

Book .   .   .   004 00 00

REGALITIE OF PITTINWEYME.

Book .   .   .   002 00 00

Proppertie.

Graingo Muir fewer .	.	019 10 03
Fewar of the Kirk Landes of Dairsie .	.	003 06 08
Fewar of the Kirk Landes of Kinghorne eister		024 00 00
Ballmerinoch Lordschip of few .	20 06 08	
Item, 26 poultrie att 4s. the peice	05 04 00	} 126 10 08
Item of blench dewtie .	. 101 00 00	
Cumerlands . . .	.	000 13 04
St Colme Lordschip . .	.	066 13 04
Birkinsyde, besyde Faulkland, called Ladyes chappell		002 01 00
Kinghorne Barronie 3lb. 15s. ster. in scotts	.	045 00 00
Tenement & Hospitall in Inverkeithing	.	004 06 08
Friers Landes in Inverkeithing	.	000 13 04

Fyffe Chalmerlanrie of money .   1100 00 00 ⎫
    wheat 32 chall. 9 bolls 3 f. att
      100$^{lb.}$ p$^{r.}$ chall.   .   3257 08 05 ⎪
    of beir & meill 64 chall. 9 bolls
      2 f. 3 p. 2 Lep. att 80$^{lb.}$ p$^{r.}$
      chall. .   .   .   5167 11 10 ⎪
    oats 5 chall. 5 bolls 1 f. 3 p. att   ⎬ 13469 17 04
      100$^{lb.}$ p$^{r.}$ chall.   .   3489 06 05 ⎪
    Capons 643 att. 6s. 8$^{d.}$ the peice
      compting 5 score to the 100   0214 06 08 ⎪
    Poultrie 946 att 4s. the peice is 0189 04 00 ⎪
    of Geese 96 att 10s. the peice is 0048 00 00 ⎪
    one Boar pryce therof   .   0004 00 00 ⎭

Deductions out of the Challmerlainrie of Fyffe—

For the Chalmerlaines fee of money	0200 00 00
To the Challmerlaine of wheat 2 chall. . . .	0200 00 00
To him of beir & meill 2 chall. is . . .	0160 00 00
Item, for reparatione of the Pallace of Faulkland of money .	0032 00 00
of beir & meill 6 chall. pryce forsaid . .	0480 00 00
of oats 9 chall. pryce forsaid . . .	0600 00 00
Poulltrie 96 att 4s. the peice . . .	0019 04 00
Geese 16 att 10s.	0008 00 00
Item, for Landes impeallit to the park of Faulkland of money .	0029 09 00
of beir & meill 2 chall. 8 bolls . . .	0200 00 00
of oates 11 chall. is . . .	0733 06 08
Capones 16 is	0005 06 08
Poulltrie 72	0014 08 00
Geese 12	0006 00 00
Item, to the minister of Faulkland of money . . .	0005 00 00
One boll wheat	0006 05 00
of beir & meill one boll	0005 00 00
Item, disponed be infeftment to the Laird of Creich in money .	0006 00 00
of beir & meill 1 chall. 4 bolls . . .	0100 00 00
of oates 2 chall. is . . .	0133 06 08
Capons 12	0004 00 00
Item, disponed be infeftment to the Lord Bawaird of money .	0005 00 00
of oates 2 chall. 8 bolls 2 p. is . . .	0167 03 09
Poultrie 18 pryce forsaid . . .	0003 12 00
Item, disponed to the E. of Kellie, of money . . .	0048 00 00
of wheat 9 chall. 900$^{lb.}$ . . .	0900 00 00
beir & meill 11 chall. is	0880 00 00
Capones 120 pryce forsaid . . .	0040 00 00

FYFFE. Item, to the castell of Edinburgh of wheat 14 chall. 5 bolls 1 fir.   1432 16 03
        beir & meill 17 chall. 12 bolls   .   .   .   1420 00 00
      Lyndors Challmerlainrie of money   173 18 04 ⎫
            of beir 14 bolls 2 f. 8 p. att 6^{lb.}   ⎬ 0265 05 10
            5s. the boll is .   .   091 07 06 ⎭
        wherof deduce of Challmerlaine fee   .   .   0066 13 04
      Dumfermling Lordschip sett to the E. of Dumferm-
            ling for yeerly payment of 100 merks of
            tack dewtie 0066 13 04
      Burgh of Dumfermling   .   .   .   0000 06 00
      Burgh of Inverkeithing   .   .   .   0006 00 00
      Burgh of Earles Ferrie   .   .   .   0001 00 00
      Burgh of Bruntisland 0001 13 04
      Burgh of Kinghorne 0002 10 00
      Burgh of Kirkcaldie 0001 14 00
      Burgh of Dysart 0002 10 00
      Burgh of Pittenweymo   .   .   .   0002 00 00
      Burgh of Craill 0011 00 00
      Burgh of Anstruther ester   .   .   0001 00 00
      Burgh of Anstruther wester   .   .   0000 06 08
      Burgh of St Andrewes¹   .   .   .   0006 13 04
      Burgh of Coupar 0017 06 08
            Suma of the present rent of this
                shyre of Fyffe & Regallities of
                Dumfermling & Pittenweymo
                extend to   .   .   14209 11 04

            Suma of the deductiones   .   .   .   7908 11 04

            So ther restes of free money yeirly paid in   .   6301 00 00

Observationes & differences betwixt the old & present Rentalls.

Grainge Muir by the presentt rentall payes 19^{lb.} 10s. 03^{d.}
as is befor chairged as the pryce of 4 bolls 3 pecks wheat;
1 chall. 8 bolls 1 fir. beir; one chall. 8 bolls 1 fir. oates; 12
geese, 8 capones, 12 poulltrie, 12 dukes, all which victuall &
graine is liquidat to 6s. 8^{d.} the boll, the geese 12^{d.} the peice,
capons & poulltrie to 8^{d.} the peice & the dukes to 6^{d.} the peice,
makeing in the haill the said soume which makes ane dim-

inutione of the old rentall, bot if they were estimat att the FYFFE.
ordinar rates the same would extend to the soume of 263^{lb.} 2s. 9^{d.}
so the rentalls differ be the soume of .   .   243 12 06

Balmerinoch Lordschip, of old ane Monastrie Ordinis Cistertiensis founded be Emergarda Queen to William King of Scotland, erected in ane Lordschip to James Lord Balmerinoch be
Chartour, dated att Whithall the 10th day December 1607, for
payment of the forsaid blench dewtie of 101^{lb.}

St Colme, called the Ile or Monastrie of St Colme Ordinis Cistertiensis founded be Murdoch E. of Fyffe & erected
in ane Lordschip to Henry Stewart be Chartor, dated the 7th
Martch 1604, for payment of the blench dewtie of 100 merks,
which blench dewtie hes not been compted nor payed thir
many yeirs. Bot of late the Countes of Murray as lyfe-rentrix
hes compted for the same for some few yeers. And for the
preceeding yeirs, yet resting, the E. of Murray is to be called.

Chalmerlane of Fyffe comptes be the presentt rentall in
money victuall & uthers as is befor chairged for 13,469^{lb.} 17s. 4^{d.}
which differs from the old rentalls in anno 1512, 1526, 1600 &
1612 in maner particularlie following viz. :

Be the presentt rentall in that quarter
    of Lindors the Landes called
        Old Lindores payes of money .   40 00 00 }
Item 64 poulltrie is .   .   06 08 00 } 0046 08 00
Be the said old rentalls it payed of money 50 00 00
    off poulltrie 100 .   .   . 12 16 00
        So the rentalls differ be .   .   .   0017 04 00
Be the presentt rentall in that quarter of Edin the
    landes of Ardct payes . . .   0027 06 08
Be the said old rentalls it payed . 29 06 08
        So the rentalls differ bo .   .   .   0002 00 00
And by ane Act, dated the 2d January 1616, the Commissioners
    deduces them 5^{lb.} 6s. 8^{d.}

O

FYFFE. And in anno 1612 it payed in augmentatione of the
—   rentall of that pairt of the landes of Ardett
belonging to Mr Wm Murray, which is not
chairged in the said rentall one quarter peck
wheat and als much beir.   Be the presentt
rentall in that quarter of Edou the landes
called Luthrie payes .   .   .   0074 06 08
Be the said old rentall it payed   . 80 06 08
So the rentalls differ be 0006 00 00
Which 6$^{lb.}$ was deduced be the saids Lord Commissioners in
anno 1516 for the sterilitie of the ground.
Be the presentt rentall in that quarter of Largo the
landes called Kings barnes payes   .   0040 00 00
Be the said old rentalls it payed   . 66 13 04
So the rentalls differ be 0026 13 04
Off the which 40 merks ther wes 20 merks given doune and
deduced for the sterilitie of the ground.
Be the presentt rentall ther is deduced as payed to
the Minister 1 boll wheat & 1 boll beir; and
to the Chalmerlane 2 chall. wheat & 2 chall.
beir.
Be the rentall 1635 ther is nothing deduced as paid
to them.
So the rentalls differ be 4 chall. 2 bolls victuall   . 0412 10 00
Be the presentt rentall ther is no oynions payed.
Bot be the old rentalls ther is 4 barrells onions payed
att 10s. per barrell.
So the rentalls differ be the said oniones   0002 00 00

There are severall uther particulars which might be observed
in this rentall which shall be enlarged amongst the Improvements.

Lyndores Lordschip of old ane Monastrie Ordinis Cistertiensis founded be David Earle of Huntingdun, brother to
William King of Scotland, & erected in ane Lordschip to Patrick Lord Lyndors be Chartour, dated att Pearth the last day
of Merch 1600.   It is divyded to witt: One pairt therof lying
att Lyndores & the uther pairt therof lying beyond the Cairnie-
month, which is called Logie Fintray, and Compts in Aberdein
shyre.   There might be very much debate of this in behalfe

of his Majeste and his interest, which in its propper place
shall be enlarged.

Dumfermling Lordschip of old ane Monastrie St Benedicti
Monachi Nigri found[ed] be David I. King of Scotland and
Margret his Queen. It is now sett in tacke to the Earle
of Dumfermling for payment of the yeirly Tacke dewtie of
66^{lb.} 13s. 4^{d.} befor chairged. Bot in respect the said Tacke
will expyre, & the same may fall in againe it is thought neces-
sar to sett doune the particular rentall therof as is compted
and payed befor the said Tack viz. :

First of money	4731	04 08
of wheat 15 chall. 15 bolls 5 p. att 100^{lb.}	1583	04 00
of beir 57 chall. 9 bolls att 80^{lb.} the ch. .	4605	00 00
whyt oatts 65 chall. 5 bolls 9 p. att 100^{lb.}	4356	10 02
black oatts 39 chall. 1 boll 10 p. att 40^{lb.}	1564	00 00
oatmeill 9 chall. 4 bolls 2 f. 2 l. att 100^{lb.}	0618	17 06
Pepper 3 pund att 30s. the pund . .	0004	10 00
Cheise 30 stone att 40s. the stone . .	0060	00 00
Butter 7 stone att 3^{lb.} the stone . .	0021	00 00
Coalls 22 Loades att 3s. the Load . .	0003	06 00
Lyme 20 chall. att 48s. the chall. . .	0048	00 00
Capons 298 att 6s. 8^{d.} the peice . .	0099	06 08
Poulltrie 918 att 4s. the peice . . .	0183	12 00
Extending to the soume of .	17,878	11 00

So the presentt rentall differs from the forsaid old rentall
in the soume of 17,811 17 08

There wes severall deductiones & allocationes out of this
old rentall, which would have exhausted a great part therof,
which (in respect the same is now sett in tacke) shall not
be necesar to mentione bot shall be more fully enlarged
amongst the Improvements of the Revenew.

Suma of the differences betwixt the old & presentt
rentalls of this Shyre extendes to . 18,521 17 06

FORFAR.

FORFAR SHYRE.

Payed be the Shirriff yeirly for book & blenches viz.:

Money	01 17 01	
Argentes 18ᵈ in scottes money .	00 18 00	
One pair whyt spurres .	01 00 00	
One pair gilt spurres . .	08 00 00	
One pair gloves . .	03 00 00	
One pund ginger . .	01 10 00	0047 08 05
One broad Arrow . .	00 10 00	
Pcits 3 Cairtfull . .	[blank]	
One Duke [duck] . .	00 13 04	
Book	30 00 00	

Proppertie.

Abirbrothok Lordschip of blench ferme .	0500 00 00	
Bot now it is allocat & so ought to be deduced as is contained in the following observationes . . .		0500 00 00
Brechin & Navarr	0333 06 08	
Bot now it ought to be deduced for the cause mentioned in the following observationes		0333 06 08
Restennet	0020 00 00	
Fettercairnie Challmerlanrie of money . 57 06 04	0059 11 04	
Item, 3 mairts att 15s. the peice . 02 05 00		
wherof deduce for the causes specifit in the following observationes		0003 06 08
Teilling and Pollgavie of money . 66 13 04		
Of oats 2 chall. att 100 merks par chall. 133 06 08	0232 00 00	
of Capons 96 att 6s. 8ᵈ the peice 032 00 00		
Burgh of Forfar	0008 13 04	
wherof ther is deduced as payed to the Chapline of Finevine .		0006 13 04
Burgh of Abirbrothok . . .	0002 00 00	
Burgh of Dundee	0130 00 00	

Suma of the presentt rent of this Shyre is . . .	1332 19 09
Suma of the deductiones extendes to . .	0843 06 08
So ther rests of free money yeirly payed in the soume of	489 13 01

Observationes.

Aberbrothok Lordschip of old ane Monastrie Ordinis Tironensis founded be William King of Scotland, and erected in ane Lordschip to the Marquis of Hamiltone conforme to his Chartor, dated the 8th Febry. 1608, for the yeirly payment of 500[lb.] of blench dewtie befor chairged, which hes not bein payed now thir 40 yeirs. Bot since that tyme the King was pleased to buy in these landes, and gave & disponed the same to the Earle of Panmuir.

Breichen & Navarr in anno 1600 compted for 288 : 17 : 04, and in Augmentation therof 34[lb.] 10s. 4[d.] which extendes in all to the soume of 323 : 7s. 8[d.]; and in the rentall 1614 it payes the soume of 333[lb.] 6s. 8[d.] befor chairged, which few dewtie is be Act of Parliament King Ja. 6 Par. 9 Act the 8th assigned & allocat to the Captaine and Keeper of the Castell of Stirling & therfor ought to be deduced.

Restennet of old ane cell of the Monastrie of Jedburgh founded be K. Alex[r.] I. Cognomen fers, and erected to the Earle of Dirltoune, 10th Merch 1615, for payment of the blench soume of 20[lb.] befor chairged, which wes assigned to severall persones & last to William Law who is dead.

Fettercarne of old called the Thanage of Fittercarne did compt in the rentall 1520, 1534, & 1600 for 77[lb.] with 3 mairts att 15s. the peice : is in all 79[lb.] 5s., wherof ther is deduced 20[lb.] for the landes of Durney or Killmakewin, and 3[lb.] 6s. 8[d.] to the Chapline of the Cathedrall Kirk of Breichen for praying for the soull of Robert Erskine. And in that rentall the compter wes ordained to instruct the warrandes for the saids deductiones att the next compt.

KINCAIRDINE SHYRE.

Payed to the Shirriff for book & blenches viz.:

Money	02 11 09	
Argentes 9ᵈ in scottes money . .	00 09 00	
1 pʳ gloves	00 03 00	089 17 01
1 chall. oatmeill	66 13 04	
Book	20 00 00	

Proppertie.

Altrie Lordschip	140 00 00
Craigmylo	041 07 06
Burgh of Montrose	037 06 08

Suma of the presentt rent of this Shyre extendes
to 308 11 03

Which is all free money.

In the blenches of this Shyre ther is one chall. meill att 100 merks which hes not bein compted for, nor payed, thir many yeirs bygone, because the same is alleadged to be dew to the Earle of Marschall, bot ther wes ane band granted be Robert Keith, Shirriff depute of Kincairdine, of the date the 2d August 1636, wherby he bindes & oblidges him in name of the said Earle Marschall, Shirriff principall of Kincairdine, that he shall ethere make compt & payment to the Exchequer of the said chall. meill wherwith the said Shirriff wes yeirly chairged in his comptes, for the yeirs resting then last by past, betwixt the date of the said band & the 14th day of Novʳ then nixt 1636, or els should instruct that the said Shirriff wes not lyable in payment therof; he getting Letters of relieff for chairging the partis lyable to refound the same as the said band yet extant. It seemes this particular hes never bein cleired, both in respect of the said band yet extant, & that ther is no act found wherin the same is determined.

Altrie by chartor, dated 29 September 1592, granted to the Lord Keith payes of blench dewtie 140$^{lb.}$ befor chairged, which hes not bein payed thir 20 or 30 yeirs, bot ought to be compted for & payed be the E. of Marischal.

Craigmyle payes 41$^{lb.}$ 7s. six$^{d.}$ which hes not beein compted, nor payed in Exchequer since the yeir 1633, because the samyne wes allocat to Mr Henry Cheap, Advocat who is dead 14 yeirs or therby, so that now the fewar therof ought to be chairged for the same.

ABERDEIN SHYRE.

Payed be the Shirriff for Book & blenches yeirly viz. :

Money	05 10 00	
Argentes 2s. 9$^{d.}$ in scottes money .	01 13 00	
Gilt spurres 2 p$^{r.}$ . .	16 00 00	054 13 00
Ginger ane pund . .	01 10 00	
Book	30 00 00	

Proppertie.

Kinnimuck		021 09 02
Ruthveins & Over & Nether Ballnatrad .		002 00 00
2 pairt of Cowell . . .	06 13 04	
with 2 pairt of a mairt sold by in-feftment for . . .	00 10 00	007 03 04
Pettmedden by the Baillies of Aberdeen .		006 00 00
Pittendreich		009 06 08
Deir Lordschip		005 11 00
Greincoattes & Tullilair . . .		0003 11 08

ABERDEIN.	Marie Culter			0008 00 00
—	Tilliburies			0001 06 08
	Nather Dyce			0008 00 00
	Ballbythan as a pairt of the Challmerlanie of Logie			
	Fintray . . .			0022 16 08
	Kincowsie			0001 06 08
	Auchlownies			0001 06 08
	Eister & Nather Disblair . . .			0045 00 00
	Wester Disblair . . .			0018 18 04

Mylne of Fintray of money .   07 05 08
    Capones 6 att 6s. 8ᵈ· the peice   01 16 00
    Poulltrie 6 att 3s.   00 18 00 } 0014 01 08
    1 wedder att 40s.   02 00 00
    One boll oats . .   02 02 00

Kintoire Garvioch of money .   213 10 00
    of mairts 11 att 8ˡᵇ· the peice   088 00 00
    6 duzon Capons att 6s. the peice   021 12 00
    1 chall. 2 bolls beir att 100 the } 0423 18 00
     chall . . .   072 00 00
    6 duzon poulltrie att 3s. the
     peice .   .   028 16 00

All which is deduced for the causes mentioned
   in the following observationes .   .   .   0423 18 00

Logie Fintray payes 563ˡᵇ· 7s. 2ᵈ· with one boll
   meill att 48s. wherof 21ˡᵇ· 9s. 2ᵈ· befor
   chairged be the fewar Kinnimuiks & 22ˡᵇ·
   16s. 8ᵈ· be the fewar of Ballythan is a
   pairt. So ther is payed be the Challmer-
   laine yeirly 0519 01 04
with one boll meill att 48s.   .   .   0002 08 00
wherof deduce of Challmerlaine
   fee of money .   .   63 00 00 } 0065 08 00   0065 08 00
   And the said boll meill .   00 08 00

Oneill Croce of money .   19 03 04 } 0020 13 04
   mairts 2 liquidat to 15s. the peice   01 10 00
wherof deduce as paid to the Bishop of Aber-
   dein & uthers haveing ryght 0001 06 08

Kinnadies 0008 00 00
   Bot it is allocat to the Earle of Marr as a pairt
   of the Thanage of Kintoir and so ought to
   be deduced 0008 00 00
Kirtoune of Bourtrie 0011 17 00
Taveltie 0006 13 04

Burgh of Aberdein	0214 06 08	
wherof deduce as paid to the poor of the Hospitall of S⁺ Mayor . . .	. .	0100 00 00
Burgh of Kintoir	0006 00 00	
Burgh of Inverurie	0004 13 04	
Suma of the presentt rent of this Shyre is . . .	1448 02 08	
Suma of the deductiones . .	.	0598 12 08
So ther rests of free money the soume of		849 19 10

Observationes & differences betwixt the old & presentt rentalls.

Ruthvens, Ballnatrad & 2 part of Cowell payes be the presentt rentall as is befor chairged 9ᵇ. 3s. 4ᵈ, with the 2 part of ane mairt sold be infeftment for 10s. And in the rentall 1635, 38, 42, 45, and 1647 Ruthveines and 2 part of Cowell payes 9ᵇ. 3s. 4ᵈ with 2 part mairt. Bot in the rentall 1606 Cowell compts be itselfe att 10ᵇ. & one mairt; and in the rentall 1588 & 1614 Ruthveines comptes be itselfe att 2ᵇ. conforme to ane Chartour granted to Robert Dugood of Auchinhove.

Deir Lordschip of old ane Monastrie Ordinis Cistertiensis founded be William Cumin Earle of Buchane in anno 1218.

Kintoir and Garioch payes yeirly as is befor chairged, wherof ther is allocat to the Bishop of Aberdein 4ᵇ. 4s. and to Alexʳ. Ogilvie of Auchterhous 3ᵇ., & the rest therof to the Earle of Marr, and so the samyne ought to be deduced in maner forsaid.

Logie Fintray is that part of the Lordship of Lyndors lyand beyond the Mounth, and be the presentt rentall as is befor chairged, payes 563ᵇ. 7s. 2ᵈ, bot be the rentall

P

ABERDEIN. 1649 it payes 573$^{lb.}$ 7s. 2^d So the rentalls differ be
10$^{lb.}$ 10 00 00

    There is deduced 63$^{lb.}$ with one boll meill of Challmerlaine
fee off the presentt rentall, and the few dewtie of Kiminmucks
extending to 21$^{lb.}$ 9s. 2^d, and 22$^{lb.}$ 16s. 8^d for the few dewtie
of Ballbythane as is befor chairged is a part of the dewty of
Logie Fintray.

    Suma of the differences patet.

BAMFF SHYRE.

BAMFF.

Payed be the Shirriff for book & blenches as followes :

Money	00 06 09 ⎫	
Argentes 7^d in scotts money . .	00 07 00 ⎬ 10 13 09	
Book	10 00 00 ⎭	

Proppertie.

Pittendreith be the Lord Oliphant . .	00 03 04	
Burgh of Bamff payes yeirly . .	33 06 08	
wherof ther is deduced as payed to the Kings Colledge of Aberdein . . .		12 13 04
Burgh of Cullen payes yeirly . . .	21 12 00	
Suma of the presentt rent of this Shyre is . . .	65 15 09	
Suma of the deductiones is . .		12 13 04
So ther rests of free money . . .		53 02 05

ELGIN & FORRES SHYRES.

Payed yeirly be the Shirriff for book and blenches viz.:

Money	05 00 04		
Argentes 10ᵈ· in scotts money .	00 10 00		
Broad Arrowes 7 . .	03 10 00	} 0039 02 02	
Pepper 1 unce . .	00 01 10		
Book	30 00 00		

Proppertie.

Unthank		0002 00 00
3 bolls 2 f. beir att 4ˡᵇ· 3s. 4ᵈ· the boll .		0014 11 08
Kinloss Lordship { of few yeirly .	14 15 00 }	0214 15 00
{ of blench yeirly .	200 00 00 }	
Saltcoats		0010 00 00
2 part Duffes & 3ᵈ· part of Saltcoats .	26 00 00 }	
One chall. beir & 12 bolls 2 f. att 100	}	0144 15 00
merk per chall. . .	118 15 00 }	
3 parts of Duffes 4 chall. 9 bolls beir is .		0304 03 04
Pluscardin { of few dewtie . .	100 00 00 }	0120 00 00
{ of blench dewtie .	020 00 00 }	
Levinshauch fewar . . .		0002 00 00
Beafort & Beulie . . .		0013 06 08
Vrquhart Lordschip be the Earle of		
Dumfermling of blench dewtie .	366 13 04	
Item, for the fishing of Spey . .	004 00 00	
Item, for the few dewtie of the mans		
dowcoatt and yairdes in Elgine	002 00 00	
Item, for the few dewtie of the presentors		
house ther . . .	002 13 04	
Item, for ane house in Inverkeithing .	004 06 08	
Item, for the Kirktoune of Fyvie &		
prior mylne . . .	085 00 00	} 0464 17 04
Item, for the Mairs landes of Pittencrieff		
1ᵈ· argent. . .	000 01 00	
Item, for the blench dewtie of the Lord-		
schip of Fyvie 1ᵈ· argentis .	000 01 00	
Item, for the landes of Moynes 1ᵈ·		
argent. . .	000 01 00	
Item, for the Patronage of the Kirk of		
Fyvie 1ᵈ· Argent. . .	000 01 00	

ELGIN & Burgh of Elgin 0013 06 08
FORRES. Burgh of Forres 0002 16 00

Suma of the presentt rent of this
Shyre . . . 1345 13 10

Which is all free ther being no deductiones.

Observationes.

Kinloss of old wes a part of the Thanage of Kintoir erected in ane Monastrie by David I. King of Scotland of the order of St Augustine in anno 1136; and erected in ane Lordschip to the Lord Bruce of Kinloss be Chartor, dated 3d May 1608, for payment of the blench dewtie befor chairged. These landes are wodsett be Thomas Earle of Elgin to Brodie of Lethane who hes ryght to the few dewties of the samyne be vertew of the said wodsett ryght, ay and while the landes be redeemed be payment of the soume for which they are wodsett. Bot the said Earl of Elgin and Brodie of Lethane thair ryghts therto shall be more fully enlarged & cleired in the rentall of the Kirk Landes.

Pluscarden of old ane Priorie Ordinis Valliscaulium and therefter Ordinis Nigri Monachi founded be Alex[r.] 2d King of Scotland & John Bisset, & payes the blench dewtie befor chairged conforme to ane Chartor dated 25th July 1636.

Beaufort & Beulie of old ane Priorie Ordinis Valliscaulium founded be the said King Alex[r.], & payes the blench dewtie befor chairged conforme to ane Chartor in anno 1581.

NAIRNE SHYRE.

Payed be the Shirriff yeirly for the book   010 00 00

Proppertie.

Pittendreich be [blank] Douglass	.	.	004 00 00
Vrquhart & Glenchairne	.	.	144 13 04
Burgh of Nairne	.	.	004 00 00

Suma of the presentt rent of this
Shyre extendes to   .   162 13 04

Which is all free money.

ROSS & INVERNES SHYRES.

Payed yeirly be the Shirriff for Ross Shyre:
One pair gloves   .   .   03 00 00 }
1 pund pepper   .   .   01 10 00 }   0004 10 00

Payed yeirly be the Shirriff for book & blenches out of Invernes as
followes:

Money	.	.	00 01 04
Argentes 15ᵈ in scotts money	.		00 15 00
Cævum called greese one pund	.		00 10 00
Pepper 2 pund	.	.	03 00 00
Gloves 2 pair	.	.	06 00 00
Book	.	.	30 00 00

0040 06 04

Proppertie.

Glenmoristoun	.	.	0027 06 08
Trouternes of few	.	.	0266 13 04
Fewar of Northuist & Slait	.		0257 06 08
Fewar of the Lewes	.	.	2000 00 00
Chalmerlane of Ross & Ardmanoch			
of money	.	.	877 6 0

ROSS &
INVERNES.
—

Beir & meill 43 chall. 14 bolls 1 f. 1 p. att 100 merk the chall, is . . .	2926 06 07	
Oats 6 chall. 6 bolls att 50 merk the chall. .	0212 10 0	
Mairts 42 att 10ᵗᵇ the peice	0420 00 0	
muttones 47 & ¼ pᵗ att 20s. the peice . .	0047 05 0	
Capons 5 score & 2 att 3s. 4ᵈ	0017 00 0	
Hens 74 score att 1s. 8ᵈ the peice . .	0123 06 08	

4623 14 04

wherof deduce to the Challmerlaine of fee . 0963 06 08

Delnie, of money . .	0098 19 00
beir & meill 53 chall. 7 bolls 3 f. 3 p. att the forsaid pryce	3566 08 02
Oats 5 chall. 4 bolls pryce for- said . . .	0150 00 00
Mairts 25 pryce forsaid .	0250 00 00
Muttones 22 pryce forsaid	0022 00 00
Capones 48 pryce forsaid .	0008 00 00
Hens 86 pryce forsaid .	0007 03 04

4102 10 06

Miltoun of Meddat 6 chall. 3 bolls beir att 100 merk 0412 10 00

Burgh of Invernes of money & 1 pund pepper att 30s. 0058 16 08

wherof deduce as paid to the poor of the said toune . 0010 00 00

And formerly paid to the Chaplaine of Murray & now to the said poor 0000 08 08

Suma of the presentt rent of this Shyre is . . . 11793 14 06

Suma of the deductiones is . . . 0973 15 04

So ther restes of free money . . 10819 19 02

Observationes.

Northuist & Slait pays of few dewtie be the presentt rentall the soume of 257ᵗᵇ 06 : 08, and be the rentall 1647 & 1655 it payes 259 : 06 : 08; so the rentall differs be 40s.

Lewes by ane chartor, dated the 11th July 1610, wes holden taxit waird for payment of 180 merks of taxt dewtie dureing the tyme of the waird, & 900 merks for the mariage with 80 merks for the relieffe. In anno 1633 the King haveing intended action of Reduction & Improbatione against the Earle of Seaforth for reduceing of thir landes to the Croun which wes accurately dispute. And the Earle of Seaforth not willing to contend with his Majeste, or fearing his oun ryght, did petition the King for a ratificatione of the same, which his Majeste refuseing he did againe petition his Majeste to take his condition & ryght to his Majestis consideratione. In August 1635 the King, by his reference & letter, did referr the tryall of that busines to a select number of the Lords of Counsell, togither with some of the Lords of Session for takeing tryall of his said ryght and to make report to him. Which Lords haveing both heard the Kings Advocat and the said E. att large they returned a report to his Majeste on the 20th January 1636. Wherupon the said Earle of Seaforth by his humble supplicatione and submissione, submitted his ryght to his Majestis oun determinatione. Wherupon his Majeste wes pleased to enter in ane contract, with the said Earle, in the which contract the said Earle tackes & accepts these landes holden few of his Majeste for yeirly payment of the said few dewtie of 2000$^{lb.}$ And resignes the toune, Castell and Port of Stronua [Stornoway] in favoures of the King ad perpetuam remanentiam. Which contract was registrat the 13th March 1637, and ane Chartor past therupon of the same date. The Kings Majeste wes att that tyme exceedingly earnest for the recovering of that castell, burgh and port of Stronnua intending to make the same very advantagious to his Majestis Kingdomes, and to stop the fishing of uthers in these seas. Yet, notwithstanding that his Majeste now hes undoubted ryght to the same, throw the distractiones of the tymes his Majestis ryght has not been looked efter.

Ross & Ardmanoch is a part of his Majestis proppertie, and is annexed to the Croun be Act of Parl. K. Ja. 3d Par. 8 Act 71. And the haill lands of the said Lordschip of Ross and Ardmanoch (except some few) are in non entrie thir 60 yeirs. In the rentall 1503 Ross compts be itselfe & payes of victuall 105 chall. 8 bolls. And in the rentall 1507 Ardmanoch compts be itselfe att 25 chall. 10 bolls makeing in the haill 131 chall. 2 bolls victuall; bot be the presentt rentall they compt only as is befor chairged 115 chall. 3 bolls 1 fir.

So the Rentalls differ be 15 chall. 14 bolls 3 f. att 50$^{lb.}$ per chall. is 795 14 06

Be the said old rentalls Ross & Ardmanoch payed of mairts 69. Bot be the presentt rentall they pay only 67 mairts. So the rentalls differ be 2 mairts att 10$^{lb.}$ the peis is . . 020 00 00

Suma of the differences of the old & presentt rentalls of Rosse and Ardmanoch extendes to . . . 815 14 06

There is also deduced out of the Challmerlainrie of Ross & Ardmanoch which wes assigned in Pension to the Earle of Desmond of money   381 00 00
Item, of beir malt & oatmeill 9 chall. 8 bolls is   633 06 08
oats 1 chall. 8 bolls att 50 merks per chall.   050 00 00
mairts 8 att 10$^{lb.}$ the peice . .   080 00 00
muttones 12 att 20s. the peice .   012 00 00
Poulltrie 23 att 20$^{d.}$ the peice . .   001 18 04

Extending in all to the soume of .   1158 05 00

Bot now the said Earle is dead severall yeirs since & therefore the Challmerlaine ought to compt for the same.

CROMARTIE SHYRE.

Payed yeirly be the Shirriff for the book .					006 00 00

Burrow & Proppertie Maills.

Burgh of Cromartie .	.	.	.	013 06 08
Burgh of Rosemarke .	.	.	.	003 00 00
Burgh of Dingwall .	.	.	.	005 00 00
Suma of the Rent of this Shyre extendes to .	.	.		027 06 08

Which is all free money.

SUTHERLAND SHYRE.

One pair gilt spurres .		08 00 00	
Money .	.	00 00 02	18 00 02
Book .	.	10 00 00	

Proppertie.

Mullochie Fewar [sic] .	.	.	04 00 00
Burgh of Dornoch .	.	.	02 00 00
Suma of this Shyre is .			24 00 02

Which is all free money.

CAITHNES SHYRE.

Two pair doves	.	.	00 10 00	10 10 00
Book .	.	.	10 00 00	

Suma of this Shyre patet.

Q

ORKNEY & ZETLAND.

In anno 1606 the Lordschip of Orkney wes sett out in few to Patrik Earle of Orkney for the few dewtie of 2073$^{lh.}$ 6s. 8$^{d.}$ yeirly.

The Earle of Orkney haveing efter this contracted severall debts, and becomeing insolvend for the payment of which debts ther were severall executiones of law against him ; and particularlie att the instance of S$^{r.}$ John Arnot, Thesaurer Depute, who not only did compryse the Lordschip of Orkney from him, bot also obtained the gift of his escheate and lyferent, and declarators therupon Anno 1611. And the said comprysing wes expyred for the soume of 300,000$^{lb.}$ scotts. The Earle of Orkney then reteiring for obviating the payment of that and uther debts S$^{r.}$ John Arnot addresses to the King and Counsell, and uses all kynd of legall dilligence, and att last obtained Letters of Treasone, fyre, and sword. And therupon sends ane Herauld with displayed coatt & trumpet chairgeing him to rander his persone & house, which also he opposed with force & disdaine. Wherupon the King and Counsell sent forces and took both him & his sone, and for this and uther gros acts of treasone and oppression they were forfaulted.

In anno 1610 there is Commissione given to the Bishop of Orkney (being on the place) to take up the rent of the said Earldome of Orkney besyde what was payed to himselfe, and to be comptable. The King haveing resolved to make purchase of this Earldome, and to cleir the ryghts and wryttes,

His Majestie by adyce of his Counsell and Advocat for the
tyme did transact with Sr. John Arnot. And therupon wrytes
to Sr. Gideon Baillie, the Thesaurer Depute, to agree with S^{r.}
John Arnot, who accordinly did compt and reckon with him;
and therefter payed and gave him securitie for what wes
resting. And Sr. Gideon took assignatione from Sr. John
to his Majeste ad remanentiam as the contract superscryved
be his Majeste att Thebolls in England and Edinburgh, the
21 September & 29th October 1612 bears: ratifyed in Parliament the 3d October 1612.

The ryght of the landes being now consolidat in the Kings
persone, the first of Aprill 1622 there was a tack granted
to Sr. John Buchanan for 45,000 merks, and the Customes att
1600 merks.

In anno 1623 the Lordschip of Orkney wes sett to William
Dick for the lyke soume of 45,000 merks & Customes 1600
merks, which tacke wes assigned to John Stewart of Coldinghame who transferred that ryght to Sr. Robert Douglass of
Blackerstoune & uthers.

The 13th January 1632 there is ane pensione of 50,000^{lb.}
granted to the Earle of Mortoune ad vitam, in recompence of
10,000^{lb.} sterling dew by precept to the said Earle, for payment wherof his Majeste assignes the said Earle to this Tack
dewty of Orkney.

On the 23d December 1636 Orkney wes sett to Sr. William
Dick for 35,733^{lb.}; to which Tack the Earl of Mortoune also
getts ryght.

Att Oxford, 22d Aprill 1643, by ane contract his Majeste
wodsetts and dispones to the Earle of Mortoune the said
Lordschip of Orkney & Zetland redeemable for 30,000^{lb.} ster.

ORKNEY &
ZETLAND.
—

viz. 10,000$^{lb.}$ ster. as the redemptione of Zetland & 20,000$^{lb.}$ ster. as the redemptione of Orkney. This contract containes severall uther clauses.

The 23d Aprill 1662, ane signature of new is granted to the Viscount of Grandishome upon the conditiones aforesaid, and ane Band given be him declaring the same to be for the use of the Earle of Mortoune & Lady Grisell Middletoune & thair children.

His Majeste haveing taken the Condition of his revenew to consideratione ordaines the Commissioners of the Thesaurie to doe all legall dilligence for reduceing the forsaid ryght, as appears by the Kings letter dated the 29th September 1668 yeirs; which accordingly wes done, and the said ryght reduced, and in the parliament therefter 1669 annexed to the Croun. And ever since Orkney & Zetland were rouped, and sett in Tack as ane part of his Majestis Proppertie.

Haveing spoken so farr of the first branch what is to be agitate in Exchequer, which is his Majestis proppertie, with a distinctione what it wes befor King James went into England; and what the presentt Conditione of it is, I shall only sett doune for the further cleiring a particular List of what of his Majestis proppertie is disponed of late, leaving the particulars of the same with the severall conversiones & uther allocationes to be sett doune in the article of the decay of the revenew viz. :—

Out of	Air Shyre	3,000	Out of	Pearth Shyre		14,991
"	Galloway	0,600	"	Fyffe Shyre		32,468
"	Dumbartone	1,200	"	Forfar Shyre		00,114
"	Argyll	8,000	"	Nidisdale		00,400
"	Stirling	[blank]	"	Annandaile		00,500
"	Linlithgow	1,300				———
"	Edinburgh Shyre	1,860				67,766
"	Haddingtoune Shyre	3,333				

This is by & attour of converting the rentes from ordinarie pryces to small, and inconsiderable; and of many great & considerable conceallments to which both shall be spoke in thair propper place; and so haveing closed this of the proppertie wee shall hasten to speake of the uther particulars, and conclude this with,

GOD BLISS HIS SACRED MAJESTIE.

APPENDICES

APPENDICE

I.

THE RETOURED DEWTIES OF THE HAILL SHYRES FOLLOWS

INVERNESS AND ROSS.

	Lib.	*s.*	*d.*
Imprimis, The Earldome of Ross and Lordship of Ardmanoch in the queens hands worth yearly in time of peace	313	08	00
The Lordship of the Isles	112	00	00
The lands of Petty, Breachly and Strathnern in the queen's hands by reason of feu	012	10	00
The lands of Urquhart and Glenmoriston in the queen's hands	046	00	00
The lands of Cullard be west of Inverness in the queens hands be reason of feu	016	13	04
The lands of Leffaris in the Queens hands	016	13	04
The Earldom of Caithness with tennents & tennandries	200	00	00
The lands of Olryk and Greenland	029	06	08
The lands of Strathullie pertaining to Earldome of Caithness lying within Earldome of Sutherland	036	00	00
Lands of Akergill pertaining to Earl Marischal	030	00	00
Lands of Balnagown with tenents & tennendries	200	00	00
The Earledome of Sutherland with tenents and tenendries	200	00	00
The lands of Lewes, Assint, Coygyet & Waternes	069	06	08
The lands of Dunveggan and Glenelgie Ward	036	05	00
The lands pertaining to Donald M'Kay of Far	013	04	00
The lands of Ardurynes pertaining to said Donald holden of the Cathedral Kirk of Caithness	016	13	04
The lands pertaining to said Donald holden of the Cathedral Kirk of Murray	002	10	00
The lands of Strathourdill	013	06	08
The lands of Ardnamurchis	020	00	00
The lands of Moydert	020	00	00
The lands of Knoydert	020	00	00
The lands of Ardgour	008	00	00
The lands of Locheil	010	00	00
The lands of Lochquhaber pertaining to Earl of Huntly	020	00	00
The lands of Lochquhaber pertaining to Alister M'Cane M'Allister	005	00	00
The lands in Lochquhaber pertaining to Maclean	026	13	04

		Lib.	s.	d.
INVERNESS AND ROSS.	The lands pertaining there to William Mackintosh	053	06	08
	The lands of Achdrome pertaining to John Mackenzie	002	03	04
	The lands of Berridaill	030	00	00
	The lands of Dunbeucht [Dunbeath]	010	00	00
	The lands of Freswick	010	00	00
	The lands of Drumry portaining to the Bishop of Orkney	009	10	00
	The lands of Garloch holden ward	008	00	00
	The lands of Freuchie	024	00	00
	The lands of Inverallan holden ward	004	00	00
	The lands pertaining to the Baron of Cromdal	006	00	00
	The lands of Kingcairne	006	00	00
	The lands of Spanziedow [Spanziedale]	006	00	00
	Lordship of Badzenoch with tenents and tenendries	100	00	00
	The lands of Strathnairn with tenents and tenendries	040	00	00
	The lands of Coulmony	004	00	00
	The lands of Largs	003	00	00
	The lands of Culloden	004	00	00
	The lands of Culcabock	003	00	00
	The lands of Killene	006	00	00
	The lands of Durris	005	00	00
	The lands of Moneak, Cubreact and Obrick	004	00	00
	The lands of Drumcharding	007	00	00
	Lordship of Lovat with tenents and tenendries	254	06	08
	The lands of Cumer and Strathglas	006	00	00
	The lands of Kyntaill, Strathconane, Strathcarron, Kindlochewe, Ferret, the half Drym, halfe Cultelerye pertaining to Mackenzie	032	00	00
	Lands of Incherorey and Dallachnettey	004	00	00
	The lands of Foulis	032	00	00
	The lands of Meikle Tarrell	002	06	08
	The lands of Innerbreakie	002	06	04
	The lands of Kasteard [sic]	003	06	08
	Lands of Lochslyne	001	10	00
	Lands of Artboll pertaining to James Dunbar	001	08	08
	Lands of Artboll pertaining to John Denoon	001	08	08
	Lands of Ussoy [Strathpeffer]	000	03	06
	The lands of Braychar pertaining to the Laird of Kildun	002	10	00
	The lands of Kildun pertaining to the Kirk of Dunfermline	004	00	00
	The lands of Pladdis	007	00	00
	Lands of Bochloche, Lochcarron, Kisseran, & Loch cayne	022	00	00
	The lands of Artboll pertaining to James Corbet	001	08	08
	The lands pertaining to the Prior of Bewling [Beauly]	009	15	06

	Lib.	s.	d.	
The lands of Bewfort pertaining to my lord Lovat . .	002	10	00	INVERNESS
The lands pertaining to the Abbacy of Fearn . . .	100	00	00	AND ROSS.
The lands pertaining to the Bishop of Ross . . .	110	07	00	
The lands of Skibo pertaining to Bishop of Caithness within the Earldom of Sutherland	020	03	04	
The lands within the bounds of Caithness . . .	220	00	00	
The lands of Nuemore holding of the chaplain of the Kirk of Tayne in feu pertaining to George Munro . .	007	10	00	
The lands of Kilmorak held of B. of Ross . .	003	06	08	
The lands of the Kirk holden feu	010	00	00	
The Kirklands pertaining to the Bishop of Moray except the lands of Laggan, Ballyeinespick [Balnespick] in Badzenoch	038	00	00	
The Kirklands of Kilmorack holden of the Bishop of Ross .	003	06	08	
The lands of Logan [Laggan] and Ballyeinespick [Balnespick] .	002	06	08	
	2743	12	00	

TAXT ROLL OF THE SHIRE OF NAIRNE.

NAIRNE.

The Thayndom of Calder . . .	040	00	00
The lands of Geddes and half Rait . .	008	00	00
The baron of Kilraivoks lands . .	016	00	00
The lands of Bryghtmony & Kinstere . .	016	00	00
The lands of Moynes & Golford . .	010	00	00
The barony of Lethen . . .	010	00	00
The barony of Lochloy . . .	010	00	00
The lands of Kynneud . . .	002	00	00
The Bellands and Bellems lands . .	001	06	08
The lands of Pitquhey . . .	001	00	00
The lands of Little Urchney . . .	002	00	00
The Lands of Clavage pertaining to Lord Athol	005	00	00
	121	06	08

THE TAXT ROLL OF THE SHERIFEDOM OF ELGIN AND FORRES.

	Lib.	s.	d.
The lands of Rothes	014	00	00
The lands of Inneis	013	00	00
The lands of Mulben, Balnabrayht, and Aulchaish . .	010	00	00
The lands of Balmukatie	014	00	00
The lands of Ernsyd	002	00	00
The Lairds third of part Duffus . . .	013	06	06
Third Part of Duffus belong to Earle Marischal .	013	06	08
Lands of Correlwood, Greishop, Brytmore and Kinstary .	013	06	08
The lands of Kilmalenok	010	00	00
Pittendreich, Easter Sheriftoun, Levinhauch, Darclene, and Cauldcotts	004	00	00
The lands of Ogstoun & Plewlands	006	00	00
The lands of Westfield	008	00	00
The lands of the half of Pediesfield . . .	[Blank]		
The Muir of Forrest of Longmure	[Blank]		
The lands of Fochabers	004	00	00
The Mure of the boat of Spey	001	00	00
The lands of Innerallan & Glenbeg	006	00	00
The lands of Alter and Dollas	014	00	00
The lands of Tullieglennis	002	00	00
The lands of Sanquhar	010	00	00
The Laird of Burdsyards	001	00	00
The lands of Fleuris	000	06	08
Lands of Grieshop and Brumyshope . . .	004	00	00
The lands of Brodie	010	00	00
The lands of Cowbin	008	00	00
The lands of Drumreach	002	00	00
The Sea croft of Kyntessok	000	06	08
—————— of Dernway	000	06	08
The Laird of Calder for Moyland . . .	002	00	00
The lands of Hills & Haynings . . .	000	06	08
	186	06	06

TAXT ROLL OF THE SHERRIFDOME OF BAMFE. BAMFE.

	Lib.	s.	d.
The lands of the Forest of Enzie propertie and tenendrie .	100	00	00
Lands of the Forest of Boyne propertie and tenendrie .	060	00	00
Lands of Strathoun propertie and tenendrie . . .	040	00	00
Grandonachtie [Glendowachie] propertie and tenendrie . .	020	00	00
Rothiemay and Corakenow [?]	030	00	00
The lands of Troup propertie and tenendrie . . .	020	00	00
The lands of Inverugie propertie and tenendrie . .	040	00	00
Lands of Deskfuird propertie and tenendrie . . .	020	00	00
Lands of Thaynedom of Boyne	046	13	04
The lands of Kilburne	003	00	00
The lands of Tulliecallon	003	00	00
The lands of Inverbroche [sic]	004	00	00
The lands of Lesmurdie	003	00	00
The lands of Keithmuire propertie and tenendrie . .	010	00	00
The lands of Corromes propertie and tenendrie . .	006	00	00
The lands of Abericher [Abirchirder] propertie and tenendrie .	030	00	00
The lands of Drumnakeith propertie and tenendrie . .	003	00	00
The lands of Ratty	016	13	04
Inde to the Kirk xiijs 1111d.			
The lands of Netherdale . . .	008	00	00
Inde to the kirke . . .	003	06	08
Lands of Druirbright and Glenbeg . .	005	00	00
The lands of Carnousies . . .	010	00	00
To the Kirk . . .	001	06	08
The lands of Conway . . .	010	00	00
Lands of Inchervin and Cuvirme [Kilburne] .	005	00	00
To the Kirk . . .	001	08	04
The lands of Gartule	012	00	00
Lands of Balvenie propertie and tenendrie .	040	00	00
The lands of Sandlant . . .	002	00	00
The lands of Durno . . .	010	00	00
To the Kirk . . .	001	00	00
The lands of Baldavie . . .	004	00	00
To the Kirk . . .	002	00	00
The lands of Achanasse . . .	002	00	00
The lands of Ardmallie and Culsarly . .	005	00	00
The lands of Bunchlaw [Bremlaw] . .	001	00	00
The lands of Outlaw and Tibert . .	005	00	00

		Lib.	s.	d.

	Lib.	s.	d.
The lands of Muldavit	001	00	00
The lands of Auchinhamperis . . .	003	00	00
The lands of Strathalvet propertie and tenendrie .	010	00	00
To the Kirk	006	13	04
The lands of Findlater	005	00	00
To the Kirk	003	00	00
The fourt part and eighteen part of Castle field .	000	06	08

The queen's lands that pays yearly to the Exchequer :—

		Lib.	s.	d.
The lands of Pittendrech		008	00	00
The lands of Ordie		004	00	00
to the Kirk . .	001 06 00			
The lands of Blairshinnoch . . .		005	00	00
.to the Kirk . . .	007 00 00			

THE SPIRITUALL LANDS OF THE SHIRE OF BAMFF.

	Lib.	s.	d.
The Kirklands of Rothven	010	00	00
The Bishop of Aberdeen's lands	015	00	00
The lands of Strathieley pertaining to Abbot of Kinloss .	040	00	00
The lands of Strathieley pertaining to Bishop of Moray .	020	00	00
The lands of Galbots pertaining to my Lord Aberdeen . .	006	00	00
The lands of Dunlugus and Muirden	005	00	00
Kirktoun of Strathalvet and Innerichen . . .	004	00	00
The lands of Cuterick [sic, Auchorsk] . . .	001	06	08
The lands of Lychinok [Lithnet]	001	06	08
The lands of Forgline	005	00	00
	737	01	08

TAXT ROLL OF THE SHIREFEDOM OF ABERDEIN.

	Lib.	s.	d.
The barony of Huntly or Strathbogie . .	200	00	00
The barony of Slains the Earle of Erroll's .	100	00	00
The Lord Elphinston's lands of Kildrumy .	060	00	00
The Lord Erskine's lands of Kelly and Balhagardy	040	00	00
The Earle Marshall for Aden . . .	043	00	00
Item, for Kyntore and Skeyne . .	021	10	00
The lord Sinclair for the lands of Newburgh .	021	00	00

	Lib.	*s.*	*d.*
The Lord Forbes propertie and tenandrie . . .	040	00	00
The Lord Borthwick for Aberdoure	030	00	00
James Gordon of Methlick for the same . . .	008	00	00
The Laird of Tulliegowny	002	00	00
The Laird of Johnisleys for the same	002	00	00
The laird of Pitsligo	040	00	00
The Laird of Tulquhon for the same . . .	020	00	00
The Laird of Tollies forbes	012	00	00
The Laird of Brux for the barony thereof . .	018	00	00
The Laird of Asloun for Synnaboth . . .	002	00	00
John Forbes of Bairness	009	00	00
The Laird of Skene	010	00	00
The Laird of Madler for the same and Foulshunter .	009	00	00
The Laird of Thanestoun and Kinnellar . .	003	00	00
The Laird of Clocaroquteyes Forbes . . .	001	00	00
The Laird of Johnstoun propertie and tenendrie .	020	00	00
Laird of Geicht for barony of Sheves . . .	012	00	00
The Laird of Pitodrie for Carvechin and Gilcumstoun .	010	00	00
James Gordon for the lands held of the Queen .	008	00	00
The Laird of Littlefoley	002	00	00
The Laird of Aberzeldie	006	00	00
The Laird of Dalgetty	020	00	00
The Laird of Muiresk for part of Auchterless . .	010	00	00
The Laird of Esselmonth	010	00	00
The Laird of Bokgollie [*sic*, Bucholy] . . .	008	00	00
The Laird of Dunbreck	003	00	00
The Laird of Achmaly [? Achmacoy] . . .	003	00	00
The Laird of Craigiefintry	003	00	00
The Laird of Pitmedden Abercrombie . . .	006	00	00
The Laird of Geight for Fetterletter . . .	001	00	00
The Laird of Balnacraig	003	00	00
William Blakhall for Barraucht and Finersie . .	003	00	00
The Laird of Frendraucht	050	00	00
The Laird of Philorth	020	00	00
The Laird of Fedderat	020	00	00
The Laird of Fyvie for the barony thereof . .	040	00	00
The Laird of Invermarkie for Ardgraine . .	003	00	00
The Laird of Schechin for Balgouny and Fingask .	020	00	00
The Laird of Auchinhuiff	009	00	00
The Laird of Foveran	020	00	00
The Laird of Meldrum	010	00	00
The Laird of Udny and Auchlevin . . .	010	00	00

ABERDEIN.

S

	Lib.	s.	d.
William King for Barraucht and Bourtie	003	00	00
The Laird of Drum	030	00	00
The Laird of Creichie	006	00	00
The Laird of Balquhen	010	00	00
The Laird of Pitcapill	005	00	00
The Laird of Garntullie for Slee, Muncuffer, and Fortrie	009	00	00
Thomas Tulloch for part of Muncuffer	006	00	00
The Laird of Glenbervie for Kemnay	005	00	00
The Laird of Inneraloquhy	003	00	00
Andro Chamber of Stroquhen	003	00	00
The Laird of Halzaird	003	00	00
The Laird of Innermarkie for part of Creithie	001	00	00
The Laird of Dalgarnofintrie	003	00	00
The Laird of Bodom	002	00	00
The Laird of Straloche for part of Creithie	002	00	00
The Laird of Fyvie for part of Auchterless	020	00	00
The Laird of Mayne	006	00	00
Thomas Menzies of Pitfoddels	004	00	00
Jon Grant of Baldallaucht for Inveravan	004	00	00
William Strauchan of Glenkindie for the same	006	00	00
John Leith portioner of Barns for his part	003	00	00
The Laird of Locht for his part of Kyndrocht	000	10	00
John Panton of Pitmedden for his lands of Allachin	006	00	00
Ochterellon	004	00	00
Towie Barclay	020	00	00
Ochtertoun and Logyruif [Logie Ruthven]	003	00	00
Rainstoun and Mosstoun	003	00	00
The Laird of Stanewood for the same & Muchells	020	00	00
The Laird of Ouchterculle	006	00	00
The Laird of Craigor [? Craigievar] for the same	009	00	00
Patrick Leith for his lands of Harthill	005	00	00
Jonnet Leith for Aberzeldie and her part of Barnes	006	00	00
William Blackhall of that Ilk	002	00	00
Thomas Crawfuird [sic, ? Copland] for the lands of Udauch	006	00	00
Thomas Urrquhart for the lands of Fisherie	009	00	00
Thomas Chalmer for Lands of Cults and Methlik [?]	003	00	00
Portioner of Lautheris [Laithers] for the same	006	00	00
James Innes for the lands of Touchs and Pitfour	003	00	00
Gilbert Innes and Alexander Irvine for Rothiebrisbane	001	00	00
Alexander Fraser of Durrous for Beltie	003	00	00
John Strauchan of Lenturk for the same	003	00	00
Andro Wood for his part of Fynersie	001	00	00

	Lib.	s.	d.
The Laird of Mayne for his lands of Rothven .	006	00	00
The Laird of Pitcurre for Drumblait .	009	00	00
Alexander Dunbar for Peltfomerie [*sic*, Pitfindrie]	001	10	00
George Creichton for Conzie .	001	10	00
Laird of Rattie for lands of Ardeone and Buchanstoun .	003	00	00
The Laird of Porterstoun for the same .	003	00	00
James Wood for his lands of Wauss and Birness	006	00	00
William Burnett for Gask	002	00	00
The Laird of Colleroroquhie, Lesley	001	10	00
Lord Glamis for his lands of Buthilrie, Courtistoun, and Drumgowan	020	00	00
The Laird of Kinfaunes for his lands of Lumphanan .	010	00	00
The Laird of Innermarkie for Monycabell [Monycabok]	003	00	00
The Laird of Crabstoun .	002	00	00
William Hay of Urie for Cromongorth	010	00	00
Geo. Gordon for his lands of Durlatheris	010	00	00
The Lord Innermeith for his lands of Durlatheris	020	00	00
Ros of Auchlossin, for Auchlossin	003	00	00
Alexander Gordon for Brakely and Midletoun of Knokmelows .	002	00	00
Alexander Cuming of Culter for his lands of Culter Cuming .	015	00	00
The lands of Drumers pertaining to Wm. Gordon	002	00	00

ABERDEIN.

THE KINGS LANDS WITHIN THE SHIRE OF ABERDEEN.

	Lib.	s.	d.
The lands of Stradie [Strathdee] Cromarr and Braemarr gives yearly to the Exchequer .	600	00	00
Alexander Leslie of Wardess gives yearly by Exchequer .	220	00	00
Item, His Graces lands in Cowll holden feu in Laird of Drums hands .	009	00	00
Item, His Grace's fewlands of O'neill, Kincraigie Muirtoun .	014	16	00

Whereof lib. 13, 10s. to the King and lib. 1, 6s. to the Bishop of Aberdeen which lands are in the hands of Patrick Forbes.

Item, The barons of Inqueist forsaid kenns not perfytlie the Queen's Grace's lands forsaid of old extent, but referrs the same to the Rolls of Exchequr.

THE SPIRITUALL MEN'S LANDS WITHIN SAID SHIRE.

	Lib.	s.	d.
The Archbishop of St Andrews his lands and baronies of Moniemusk .	040	00	00
The bishop of Aberdeens lands of Birse, Tullinessel, Rayne, Davioch .	080	00	00

		Lib.	s.	d.
ABERDEIN.	The Abbot of Abberbrothick lands of Tarves and Fyvie	020	00	00
—	The Abbot of Lyndores lands of Fintry and Coolsamoney	100	00	00
	The Abbot of Deirs lands	020	00	00
	The Abbot of Cowpars lands	004	00	00
	The Abbot of Kinloss lands	000	13	04
	The Pryor of Moniemusk lands and Mayns thereof	005	00	00
	The Parson of Kingcardins lands and barony of O'neill	013	06	08
	The Parson of Turiffs lands of Kirktoun of Turiffe	005	00	00
	The Prior of St Andrew's lands of Kirktoun of Bortie	001	00	00
	The Dean of Aberdeen's lands of Deantown and Dilspro	002	00	00
	The Parson of Balhelvies lands of Blairtoun	001	00	00
	The Principall of the College of Aberdeen's lands of Colyne Badnakeddle Ardrail and Kirktoun of Slains	005	00	00
	The lands of Westshall	006	13	04
	The Parson of Oyne's lands of Kirktown of Oyne	002	00	00
	Mr Arthur Telfer's lands of Kirktoun of Obyne	000	10	00
	The Viccar of Forogis [Forgue] lands of the Kirktoun thereof	001	00	00
	The Theasaurer of Aberdeens lands of Kirktoun of Daviot & Mounie	003	06	08
	The Archdean of Aberdeon's lands of the Kirktown of Rayne	003	06	08
	The lands of Spittell of the Sub-chantorie	002	00	00
	The Parson of Innernochty lands of Kilbothick	002	00	00
	The Chantor of Aberdeens lands of the Kirktown of Auchterles	001	00	00
	The Kirktoun of Kikrymorie [sic, Kildrummie]	000	10	00
	Pittentorg pertaining to the parson of Cuishny	000	10	00
	The Kirktoun of Glenbucket	000	10	00
	The Parson of Cletts lands, ane plough of Christs Kirk	000	10	00
	The Parson of Moniemusks lands of Bavak	001	00	00
		2571	02	08

KINCARDIN.

RETOUR OF THE LANDS IN THE SHERIFFDOM OF KINCARDIN.

	Lib.	s.	d.
The Barrony of Tullieboy	003	00	00
Park of Drum and Badarow	002	00	00
Straichan and Culperso	020	00	00
Leyes	010	00	00
Durris	010	00	00
Crechnitillie Regis	002	00	00
Fineone [also Findone]	008	00	00

	Lib.	s.	d.
The Baronie of Cowie viz. Elsich, Muchalls and Urie . .	020	00	00 KINCARDIN.
Fettereso	020	00	00 —
Uras	010	00	00
Dunottar	005	00	00
Hiltoun and Linniger	005	00	00
Barony of Glenbervy and Barres, Auchkedie and Inchmarlo pertaining to the Laird of Glenbervy in all retoured to .	027	00	00
Thanestoun	002	00	00
Easter Kynneff, Buitift and Largisland with the pendicles .	006	00	00
Pitcarvy	005	00	00
Allerdes	010	00	00
The barony of Arbuthnot	020	00	00
The other nine parts of Innerbervy pertaining to Earl Marischall, the laird of Arbuthnot, Halgreen & Mr David Lindsay .	003	00	00
Benholme	010	00	00
Slains and Fawside	001	00	00
The lands of Arbirnie	001	00	00
Balhauder [Balhandro]	005	00	00
Laurantoun	010	00	00
Jaickistoun Skidrickmur	002	00	00
Craigie	006	00	00
Bardrepertoun [Wardropertoun]	004	00	00
Canterland & Cuningstoun	005	00	00
Morphie Meikle	010	00	00
Morphie Fraser	010	00	00
Haltoun and Balmalidie	005	00	00
Englishmadie	003	00	00
The Baronie of Barnis	015	00	00
Dulledies	004	00	00
Dissoloun [Discloune]	003	00	00
Woidcomes [Woodtone]	002	00	00
Newdesk	002	00	00
Balfour	001	00	00
Balmayre	010	00	00
Craignestoun & Drumellie	002	00	00
Glenshauch	002	00	00
Drumtochtie	001	00	00
The Barony of Monydnis	010	00	00
Cairntoun	005	00	00
Coulie	003	00	00
Portertoun	001	00	00
Whiterigs and Redmyre	002	00	00

		Lib.	s.	d.
KINCARDIN.	Middleton	006	00	00
—	Halkertoun	006	00	00
	Thornetoun	005	00	00
	Easter Strache	002	00	00
	Pittarow	003	00	00
	Drumnager	002	00	00
	Garvock	020	00	00
	Nether Craigneston	002	00	00
	Wester Kyneff	003	00	00
	The thanedom of Fettercairn, Aberlethnot pertaining to John Wood, John Strachan, and to the Laird of Brodland in the haill	006	00	00
		378	00	00

THE TAXT ROLL OF ANGUS.

QUARTER OF DUNDIE.

	Lib.	s.	d.
Imprimis, The barony of Keithymore pertaining to the Earl of Buchan his pairt thereof	005	00	00
The barony of Newtyre and Ochtertyre in the hands of my Lord Oliphant and Pitcur	020	00	00
Tullibodies part of Keithymore	010	00	00
The barony of Nevay	005	00	00
The barony of Esse	010	00	00
The Haltoun of do.	002	00	00
The barony of Glamis	025	00	00
The lands of Powrie-Ogilvie with Wester Powrie	018	00	00
The lands of Thornetoun	004	00	00
The lands of Wester Drumnone	002	10	00
The lands of Easter Drumnone	002	10	00
The lands of Haystoun & Scrogiefield	004	00	00
The lands of Brigtoun Straichane	006	00	00
The lands of Innerichtie	004	00	00
lands of Kincaldrum with tenents and tenendries	013	06	08
The barony of Innerarity	020	00	00
The lands of Meikleour	004	00	00
The lands of Kirkbuddo	003	00	00

	Lib.	s.	d.
The barony of Duny .	050	00	00	ANGUS.
The lands of Achinleck	004	00	00
The lands of Easter Brightie .	003	00	00
The lands of Ardowrie	003	00	00
The lands of Lawis and Baldowy	003	00	00
The Kirktoun of Monyfuith .	003	00	00
The Grange of Monyfuith	006	00	00
The lands of Athebetoun [? Auchedin] .	005	00	00
The lands of Balmossy and Eglismuth .	006	00	00
The lands of Balgillo Gray	003	00	00
The lands of Lumlathin	005	00	00
The lands of Kingany with Legisland .	003	00	00
The lands of Unoquhy	003	00	00
The lands of Finlarge .	002	00	00
The lands of Wester Brichtie .	008	00	00
The lands of Garryes .	003	00	00
The lands of Maynes of Balumbie	003	00	00
The Westfield of Dundie	001	00	00
The barony of Dudhope with tenents and tenendries .	015	00	00
The lands of Drumgeith	001	00	00
The lands of Pitcarro .	002	00	00
The lands of Gotherestoun	000	13	04
The Maynes of Strathduchtie [sic]	002	00	00
The lands of Whytefield	002	00	00
The lands of Balmurie	003	00	00
The halfe lands of Tiling, Campbell	010	00	00
The other half therof, Maxwell	010	00	00
The lands of Balkello	000	10	00
The lands of Baltherome [sic] .	002	00	00
The barony of Auchterhous	013	06	08
The lands of Scottistoun	003	00	00
The lands of Hedderlaw alias Henrystoun	005	00	00
The lands of Adamestoun	002	00	00
The barony of Lundie	012	00	00
The lands of Ardblair and Baldowrie .	006	00	00
The lands of Erlistradichtie Maynis	002	00	00
The lands of Petty	005	00	00
The lands of Pitcur, Gask, and Balgovie	005	00	00
The lands of Balewry [sic]	005	00	00
The lands of Wester Kelor	005	00	00
The lands of Balgillowy, Blair	005	00	00
The lands of Ledcrieff 3 lib. .	001	00	00

		Lib.	s.	d.
ANGUS. The lands of Baldovan	.	001	00	00
— The third part lands of Miltoun Craig	.	003	00	00
The lands of Claverhouse	.	002	00	00

QUARTER OF KYREMURE.

	Lib.	s.	d.
The lands of Panlathie and third part of Pitcomry	003	00	00
The two part lands of Pitcomry	001	00	00
The lands of Pitmowis	002	00	00
The barony of Craigs, Glenegley Wester Dary, Easter Craigs and Overcraigs 20 lib.	010	00	00
The lands of Wester Craigs	002	00	00
The lands of Drumsloquyes	003	00	00
The lands of Auchrany beside Airlie	002	00	00
The lands of Baithlowmanes	002	00	00
The lands of Formnal and Fornathie	005	00	00
The barony of Linthrathin	020	00	00
The lands of Glenquharitie	001	00	00
The lands of Easter Campsie and Balnavele	005	00	00
The lands of Wester Campsie	005	00	00
The lands of Cruden Barclay	005	00	00
The Maynes of Airlie	005	00	00
The land of Redy & Kynaltie	005	00	00
The lands of Baikie, propertie and tenendrie	020	00	00
Longlands quarter of Brydestoun	001	00	00
The lands of Cuikston and halfe of Blacktoun	003	00	00
The lands of Ruthven Davie	005	00	00
Brigtoun of Ruthven with the Mill	002	00	00
The barony of Clova	010	00	00
Lands of Cortaquhey propertie and tenendrie	010	00	00
The lands of Glenprossen	004	00	00
The Kirktown of Keyremuir with the Mill	004	00	00
The Laird of Logies part of Kirktoun	000	05	00
The barony of Innerquharitie	010	00	00
The lands of Cramonthynche [sic]	002	00	00
The lands of Kintyre	002	00	00
The lands of Balnagarno	002	00	00
The lands of Kineroquhies Easter and Wester	003	00	00
The lands of Auchluhie	002	00	00
The lands of Glaswell and Carnbirnis [? Tulbirnis]	004	00	00
The lands of Balmukaties	006	00	00

	Lib.	*s.*	*d.*
The barony of Logie Wischart	010	00	00 ANGUS.
The barony of Finaven and Forest of Platane with tenendries .	040	00	00
The halfe lands of Balingstor leyes	002	00	00

QUARTER OF ABERBROTHOK.

The lands of Rossie of that Ilk	008	00	00
The lands of Ullishawin	003	00	00
The lands of Baldovie, Melville . . .	002	00	00
The lands of Dysert	003	00	00
Lands of Anainie	001	00	00
The lands of Fullertoun	002	00	00
The lands of Bonytoun	003	00	00
The landes of Baynemoyes [also Balnamounis]. . .	002	00	00
The lands of Little Carcary	002	00	00
The lands of Fetheys	007	00	00
The lands of Kynnell, propertie and tenendrie . .	020	00	00
The lands of Kynblathmont	010	00	00
The barony of Innerkelor	020	00	00
The lands of Kinnaird Carnegy	002	00	00
The lands of Connansyth	006	00	00
The barony of Guthry	010	00	00
The lands of Gardin with Prescock and Leock . .	007	00	00
The lands of Lunan, Ruthven and Drumkilbo each of them £5	015	00	00
The lands of Balmashanar	004	00	00
The lands of Flymingtoun	003	00	00
The lands of Modway [Woodway] and Pochgarroch [Polgaroch]	008	00	00
The lands of Incheoch, Annastoun Bowlane . . .	003	00	00
The lands of Achterforfar	002	00	00
The lands of Balglassy	006	00	00
The lands of Melgund Cramond	006	00	00
Lands of Melgund, Beaton	006	00	00
Innerpefferis and Haltoun	004	00	00
Barony of Kellie	020	00	00
Barony of Panmure with tenendries, etc. . . .	040	00	00
The lands of Panbryd	005	00	00
The lands of Curings, Tirungis	006	00	00
The lands of Balgyes, M'Gill	004	00	00
The lands of Old Montrose	013	06	08
The lands of Muir Mylnis	001	00	00
Lands of Meikle Carcanry	004	00	00
Lands of Muir Leddriwood	004	00	00

T

QUARTER OF BRECHIN.

	Lib.	s.	d.
The lands of Newbigging, Chambers	001	10	00
The halfe lands of Arrot of that Ilk	005	00	00
The lands of Luchland	005	00	00
The lands of Cuikston beside Brechine . . .	001	00	00
The lands of Carreldston	010	00	00
The lands of Balnabreich	003	00	00
The lands of Watterston	006	00	00
The lands of Kynaber	005	00	00
Lands of Burnfield	005	00	00
The barony of Tanadaes	020	00	00
The lands of Memas	004	00	00
The lands of Wester Ogil	005	00	00
Kinzaltie propertie and tenendrie pertaining to the Earle of Buchan	014	00	00
The barony of Ferney	020	00	00
Barony of Menmuir propertie and tenendrie . .	020	00	00
Lands of Boigtoun and Balhavie	005	00	00
Lands of Glenesk	050	00	00
Lands of Dunloppie	013	00	00
Lands of Pearth and Balloquhy	010	00	00
Lands of Gallauray, Oliphant	006	00	00
Lands of Craigois	003	00	00
Barony of Dune	020	00	00
Lands of Pitforkie	002	00	00
Feu lands of temporality of Brechin . . .	020	00	00
	1129	18	04

THE TAXT ROLL OF THE SCHIREFDOM OF PEARTH.

Foulis in the hands of Gray	020	00	00
Kingudie in hands of Scrymgeor . . .	020	00	00
Longforgan in hands of Lords Gray and Glamis . .	020	00	00
Inchistures Lord Glamis & Kinnaird . . .	015	00	00
Polgavie in hands of Hay of Yester and Maxwell .	006	00	00
Barony of Balegirno, Lord Crichton & Dirleton .	015	00	00
Foss in hands of Earl of Athol . . .	005	00	00
Kinnaird in hands of Lord Kinnaird . . .	014	00	00

	Lib.	s.	d.
Rait in the hands of Bruce	014	00	00
Cardney held by the Earle of Rothes	010	00	00
Buttergask, Colace, Kinossie Langlands	015	00	00
Buttergask in hands of Lord Gray	005	00	00
Barony of Aberdalgie, Gask and Dupplin held by Lord Oliphant	032	00	00
Barony of Ruthven & pertinents	030	00	00
Barony of Craigie in hands of Ross	020	00	00
Barony of Kinfauns in hands of Charteris, Chambers and Ross	015	00	00
Gairntullie in the hands of Stewart	010	00	00
Monyvaird in hands of Toshach	010	00	00
Glastoun in the hands of Herring	015	00	00
Callie in the hands of Butler	002	00	00
Muirtoun of Ardblair in hands of Blair	004	00	00
Barony of Rattray in the hands of Atholl	016	00	00
Tullibarnie with the pertinents in the hands of Murray	030	00	00
Kincairn in hands of Lord Graham	020	00	00
Strowan in the hands of Athol, Robertsons of Faskally and Strowan	020	00	00
Lude in the hands of Inchmartin	005	00	00
Earledom of Atholl	050	00	00
Lochwood and Forest of Cluney	010	00	00
Barony of Weyme held by Menzies	020	00	00
Moncriefe	015	00	00
Quarterum Oliphant of Pitcathlie	001	00	00
Barony of Ogilvie in hands of Murray	020	00	00
Barony of Alyth in hands of Earl of Crawford	030	00	00
Barony of Baltrodie in hands of Crawford	016	00	00
Ardormey in Scryngeors hands	004	00	00
Inchmartin in the hands of Ogilvy	010	00	00
Abernethy (exceptis terris admiralitatus)	050	00	00
Logieamond held by Hay	020	00	00
Hiltoun and Kirktoun Maillars	010	00	00
Aberuthven in Lord Grahams hands	010	00	00
Kelty in the hands of Bonar	005	00	00
Blair-strowie in hands of Barclay	005	00	00
Kippenross in hands of Kinross	010	00	00
Ardargie in hands of Oliphant	...		
Polmais, Cunningham Murray	005	00	00
Rodger fieldie held by Livingston	005	00	00
Ochtermuchany in hands of Cunningham	020	00	00
Fingask in hands of Dundas	005	00	00
Keir in the hands of Stirling	025	00	00

PEARTH.

		Lib.	s.	d.
PEARTH.	Glenegles in hands of Haldane	020	00	00
—	Fordell in hands of Scrymgeor	010	00	00
	Bandoch in Earl of Crawfords hands	006	00	00
	Pitfour in hands of Cochrane	004	00	00
	Abernytie in hands of Crichton	010	00	00
	Meigle in Earl of Crawford's hands	020	00	00
	Monorgan, do.	006	00	00
	Kneeland in hands of Earl Marischal	001	00	00
	Wester Eslundie [Esindy] in hands of Blair	002	00	00
	Forleyis held by Laird of Moncur	002	00	00
	Easter Eslundie held by Dowhill	004	00	00
	Unthank in hands of Moncur	002	00	00
	Kinloch in hands of Lindsay & Scrymgeor	010	00	00
	Kinmonth in hands of Tullie and Ramsay	005	00	00
	Archalzae in hands of Oliphant	002	00	00
	Drumlochie in hands of Chamber	004	00	00
	North & West Ballo held by Scrymgeor	001	10	00
	Duncrub in the hands of Rollok	005	00	00
	Three quarter of Monzie (Scotts)	012	00	00
	Thanesland of Dynning in hands of Rollock	003	00	00
	Kippens held by Haldan	005	00	00
	Murthlie held by Abercromby	010	00	00
	Muling held by Ferguson	002	00	00
	Forgendenie held by Crichton and Halliburton	020	00	00
	The Lordship of Methven	030	00	00
	The Lordship of Monteith	100	00	00
	The barony of Errol	100	00	00
	Lands of Kinnoull	020	00	00
	Barony of Innermeith	020	00	00
	Lands of Balhousie	005	00	00
	Cartock held by Barclay of Towie	010	00	00
	Luncartie held by Pitscottie	005	00	00
	Bamffe held by Ramsay	015	00	00
	Pitwhannartie held by Keir	004	00	00
	Barony of Drummond, Cargill and Kingcardin held by Lord Drummond	100	00	00
	Gormock held by Butter	005	00	00
	Finlarit held by Campbell	030	00	00
	Auchmayat held by James Campbell	002	00	00
	Glensheoch, Glendorch in hands of Arthur Campbell	006	00	00
	Bovane, Craigor, Easter Arquhalzie in hands of Macnab	003	00	00
	Lands of Ardchastle and Defaunes, held by Inverpeffrey	004	00	00

	Lib.	s.	d.	
Tulliechetill in hands of Riddoch	010	00	00	PEARTH.
Barony of Strathyre held by Buchanan . . .	010	00	00	
Ardowan held by Haldan & Napier	020	00	00	
Ragortoun held by Crichton and Ruthven . . .	020	00	00	
The Ladie Banden 3rd part therof	002	00	00	
Cortley held by Methven	020	00	00	
Barony of Moncur	030	00	00	
Easter Elcho, Balchabrane and Craigtown Weymiss . .	004	00	00	
The temple lands of Muthill	020	00	00	
Moness held by Fleming	002	00	00	
Drumsewan	002	00	00	
Fandowie	002	00	00	
Glendovack held by Balwearie	010	00	00	
Strathardle in hands of Maxwell Weymes & Scott . .	030	00	00	
Lukie, Strowie held by Bishop of Dunblane . . .	005	00	00	
Cultmalindie held by Bruce	010	00	00	
Carnbaldie in hands of Bonar	005	00	00	
Barony of Ochtergavin (Ross)	002	00	00	
Cuthilgourdie held by Douglas of Pitcairn . . .	015	00	00	
Ratovin (?) held by Rattray	000	10	00	
Barony of Kelor held by Lochleven	010	00	00	
Easter Moncreiffe	002	00	00	
Wester do.	002	00	00	
Tibbermalloch	002	00	00	
Dalpatrick 3 parts	003	15	00	
	1598	15	00	

RETOUR OF FREEHOLDERS OF STRATHERNE.

	Lib.	s.	d.
Boirland pertaining to Drummond	060	00	00
Wester Cambuschiney pertaining to James Chisholm of Cromlix and Malcolm Kinross of Kippenrate equallie . .	003	06	08
Pitzellony pertaining to John Drummond . . .	003	00	00
Coudoun pertaining to John Murray of Aberuchill . .	002	00	00
Comry	005	00	00
Duchlag in hands of Alex. Drummond of Megor . .	002	00	00
Orchill pertaining to Mungo Graham	004	00	00
Cowgask pertaining to my Lord Gowrie . . .	005	00	00
Cultiequhey	005	00	00
Half of Ardoch pertaining to Cultiequhey . . .	000	13	04
Dundovan Lindsay pertaining to Lord Lindsay . .	005	00	00
Quarter of Monzie pertaining to Andro Toscheoch . .	004	00	00

		Lib.	s.	d.
PEARTH.	Fossoquhey	015	00	00
—	Auchlinistyes pertaining to Lord Marr . .	005	00	00
	Strathie-chamber pertaining to Bothayock younger . .	005	00	00
	Strathie-boyes	002	00	00
	Pitmadie pertaining to Walter Tullock . . .	003	06	08
	Rossie Elphinstoun . . . . . : .	005	00	00
	Colquhylie pertaining to John Drummond and James Chisholm of Cromlin	005	00	00
	Megors pertaining to Alexander Drummond . .	005	00	00
	Clauchadroinn pertaining to Patrick Cairney . .	002	00	00
	Panholls pertaining to William Graham . .	008	00	00
	Tullieallan	020	00	00
	Carnbo Stewart pertaining to Garntullie . .	001	00	00
	Arnebeg pertaining to the Laird of Glenurchie . . .	005	06	08
	Darro pertaining to him	002	13	04
	Edinkip „ „	005	00	00
	Kingartmor „ „	005	00	00
	Eisthill with the hill pertaining to James Chisholm . .	002	13	04
	Dauchlewny pertaining to Henry Stirling of Ardoch .	003	00	00
	Balhaldie pertaining to the Laird of Drumquhasill .	008	00	00
	Drumess [Drumness] pertaining to the Laird of Keir .	002	00	00
	Kippenrate	003	06	08
	Culyngs Drummond pertaining to Alex. Drummond of Megors	003	06	08
	Kilbryd pertaining to my Lord Grahame . .	020	00	00
	Dullaries pertaining to Patrick Murray of Ochtertyre .	004	00	00
	Ouchinpheloch pertaining to John Murray of Strowan and Alexander Drumond of Megors . . .	002	00	00
	Straid pertaining to Strowan	005	00	00
	Finglen pertaining to him and William Reddoch .	005	00	00
	Auchinboyes and Ballinlews pertaining to the Laird of Durie .	006	00	00
	Freuch [or Fornoth] pertaining to James Chisholm .	005	00	00
	Drumshork pertaining to Alexander Drummond of Megor .	000	13	04
	Garvoch held by Graham	005	00	00
	Summa . .	268	06	09

RETOUR OF THE FREEHOLDERS IN MONTEITH.

	Lib.	s.	d.
Burnbank, Boirfield, Culziechat, and Easter Arnat pertaining to Laird Muschet	005	00	00
Arnegivoun, Forrester and Campbell . . .	005	00	00
Gartmoir pertaining to Elizabeth Erskine . . .	005	00	00

	Lib.	s.	d.	
Gartavertoun pertaining to Andro Macfarlane . . .	002	00	00	PEARTH.
do. „ to William Graham . . .	001	00	00	
Achyle pertaining to James Stirling	001	00	00	
Brochoill pertaining to Baron Leitch	000	06	08	
Boquhoples pertaining to Laird Norie	008	00	00	
Drumgzie pertaining to John Drummond . . .	003	00	00	
Drumgzie pertaining to Patrick Graham . . .	000	06	00	
The lands pertaining to George Graham of Boquhople . .	005	00	00	
Torrie Wester pertaining to Walter Graham . . .	001	00	00	
Dullator pertaining to my Lord Argyll . . .	002	00	00	
Callintowie [sic] and Cambuswallace pertaining to Duntreath .	006	00	00	
Boquhople and Brockland Wester pertaining to Keir . .	003	06	08	
Leny pertaining to the Laird of Leney . . .	008	00	00	
Drumgzie pertaining to Donald Campbell *alias* Robertson .	003	00	00	
Balemart pertaining to Walter Buchanan . . .	001	05	00	
	060	04	04	

TAXT ROLL OF THE SHERIFDOME OF FFYFE.   FFYFE.

QUARTER OF EDYN.

	Lib.	s.	d.
The barony of Arngosk with Kippo	016	00	00
Cathokill	001	00	00
Bacanquell [Balcanquill]	003	00	00
Pitincartie and Lady Urquhart	002	00	00
The Easter part of Strathmeglo	003	00	00
Easter Pitlour	003	00	00
Wester Pitlour	003	00	00
Demperstoun with Lagytslands	003	00	00
Westerdron	004	00	00
Redie	001	00	00
Hildron	001	00	00
The barony of Balnabreich	015	00	00
Dunbug	008	00	00
Cullerney	005	00	00
Balmediesyde	004	00	00
Pitanchope	003	00	00
Easter Lumbany	003	00	00
Wester Lumbany	003	00	00

		Lib.	s.	d.
FFYFE.	Pitcairley [Pittarlie]	004	00	00
—	Mugdrum	001	00	00
	Parbroth, Ladisfrone, Seatoun . . .	008	00	00
	Ladisfrone Barclay	001	00	00
	Lochmalenny	002	00	00
	Creich	002	00	00
	The barony of Monquhany with the annuell of Ferney	010	00	00
	The two Kynsleiff	004	00	00
	Myrecarny	004	00	00
	Pitblade	004	00	00
	Hilcarny	004	00	00
	Kilmarone	005	00	00
	Tor	001	00	00
	Killock [also Lilock]	001	00	00
	The Month	004	00	00
	Cringask [Kingask]	001	00	00
	Pittincreiff	003	00	00
	Foxtoun	002	00	00
	Wester Ferney	010	00	00
	Drumclothop	001	00	00
	Wester Rankellor	002	00	00
	Kilquhiss	001	00	00
	Carslogie with Tornakiters . . .	005	00	00
	Easter Forret with the annuell . . .	005	00	00
	Torcaithlock with the annuell . . .	003	00	00
	Kittedie and Craigfarquhar . . .	004	00	00
	Cruvy, Brighouse and Logie . . .	006	00	00
	The barony of Cruvy in propertie . .	024	00	00
	Lucklaw	002	00	00
	Torforret	001	00	00
	Neather Caithlok	003	00	00
	Segy	004	00	00
	Luchers Bruce	005	00	00
	Luchers Forbes with the tenendrie . .	008	00	00
	Luchers Ramsay	005	00	00
	Muncuris lands	010	00	00
	The Rynd	001	00	00
	Thaynslands [vocat Thamslands] . .	002	00	00
	Strauchanrig lands [sic] . . .	000	10	00
	The quarter of Mortoun or Kippeshaid . .	001	00	00
	The barony of Machatoun with tenents and tenendries	008	00	00
	Litle Friertoun [sic]	001	00	00

	Lib.	s.	d.
Floshill	002	00	00 FFYFE.
Innerdavet Lightoun . . .	003	00	00
The Ferrie boat . . .	003	00	00
The Newtoun . . .	002	00	00
Innerdavet Lessells . . .	002	00	00
Laverock law . . .	001	00	00
Sandfurd Nairne and Litle Newton .	002	00	00
Balcomonth	002	00	00
Kinneir	003	00	00
Ballmullo	003	00	00
Pitcullo	003	00	00
The fie lands of Lindores . .	001	00	00
Craiglands of Friertoun . .	010	00	00

THE CONSTABULARIE OF CRAILL.

	Lib.	s.	d.
Bawbett	001	00	00
Kilduncan	001	00	00
Cuikstoun	001	00	00
The barony of Cammo . . .	005	00	00
Newhall and Letham	004	00	00
Balcomy	004	00	00
Randerstoun	003	00	00
Wilmestoun	003	00	00
Pincartoun and Pittcowie . . .	002	00	00
Ardrie	002	00	00
Reidwalls	002	00	00
Barnis	005	00	00
Caplowy [also Caplie] . . .	005	00	00
Anstruther	005	00	00
Balhousie and Gordounshall . . .	005	00	00
Balmonth	003	00	00
Drumravock	001	00	00
The barony of Carnbie . . .	010	00	00
The barony of Kellie . . .	020	00	00
Abercrombie	005	00	00
Balcaskie and Ewingstoun . . .	008	00	00
Ardross	010	00	00
Kilbrathmont	006	00	00
Rerris [Rires]	004	00	00
Sandfuird Duddingstoun . . .	003	00	00
Kingcraig	004	00	00

U

		Lib.	s.	d.
FFYFE. Lathallan	. .	004	00	00
— Banniell	. .	001	00	00
Cassingray	. .	004	00	00
Stratharlie	. .	002	00	00
Pitcruvie	. .	001	00	00
Edindownie	. .	001	10	00
Gibblistoun	. .	003	00	00
Cameron	. .	001	10	00
Balcornie [Balcormo]	.	003	00	00
Langsyd	. .	000	10	00
Keirns	. .	002	00	00

QUARTER OF LEVIN.

	Lib.	s.	d.
The barony of Lundie	020	00	00
The barony of Tassis	006	00	00
The barony of Craighall	012	00	00
The third part of the barony of Craighall	006	00	00
Easter Pitscottie and Duray	004	00	00
Rumgallie	002	00	00
Wester Tarbet and halfe of Balwearie [? Balbirnie]	010	00	00
Sipsies	001	00	00
The two parts of Cassindillie	001	10	00
Carskendow	004	00	00
Skelpie	000	10	00
The barony of Quyhtlie	010	00	00
The barony of Pitlessie	004	00	00
Burnturk	003	00	00
Dabufield [? Downfield]	002	00	00
Cletty	003	00	00
Castlefield of Cowpar	002	00	00
Coleistoun	001	00	00
Dury	006	00	00
Drumare	005	00	00
Kennowie	005	00	00
Donyface	003	00	00
Litle Balcurroquhey [Balcuryquhy]	001	00	00
Meikle Balcurroquhey	005	00	00
Duving	002	00	00
Auchtermorny	004	00	00
Caraldstoun	002	00	00
Pyetstoun	001	00	00

	Lib.	s.	d.
Ramelry	004	00	00
Ballingall	002	00	00
Holkethill	003	00	00
Ramsays Forther	004	00	00
Wester Lathrisk	004	00	00
Orky.	001	00	00
Easter Lathrisk	003	00	00
Fairley's lands	000	10	00
The south syde of Balbirny	002	00	00
Bruntoun and Dalginche	012	00	00
Markinch Easter	005	00	00
Markinch Wester	002	00	00
Tretoun and Newtoun	009	00	00
Schethin	005	00	00
Balgony, Miltoun Hospitall with pertinents	002	00	00
The Maw	003	00	00
Wemyss Easter	010	00	00
Wemyss Wester	014	00	00
Tulliebreck	001	00	00
The East part of Dysert	012	00	00
The West part of Dysert	008	00	00
Ravinscraig, Wilstoun and Carnbarry	002	00	00
Wester Touch	001	10	00
Innerteill	005	00	00
Skeithney	002	00	00
Easter Strathour	002	00	00
Auchinmontie	004	00	00
Kymmonth [Kinninmonth]	002	00	00
Cardownie	003	00	00
The barony of Leslie with Strathanny and Pitcairne	020	00	00
Glasslie	002	00	00
Ballo.	001	00	00
Coneland	005	00	00
Bandone	002	00	00
Coule	001	00	00
Powrane	000	10	00
Kilgour	001	00	00
Cashe	002	00	00
Wester Urquhart and Middle Urquhart	003	00	00
Lippe Urquhart	001	00	00
Corstoun	002	00	00

FFYFE. —

THE QUARTER OF INNERKEITHING.

	Lib.	s.	d.
Balraine	002	00	00
Wester Balelie	001	00	00
The barony of Aberdour—viz., the Maynes, Dauchie, Humbers and two Balbartains	020	00	00
Glasmouth with the pertinents	020	00	00
The Castlerigs of Kinghorne	000	10	00
Easter Pittedie	001	10	00
Wester Pittedie	001	10	00
Tyrie, Sefield, and Grange . . . :	010	00	00
Lord Glamis land in Kinghorne . . .	012	00	00
Dalgathie	005	00	00
Cowcairny	003	00	00
The barony of Fordell	016	00	00
Pittadro	005	00	00·
Balbrogie and Castelland	007	00	00
Deulls (?) and Spenserfield	004	00	00
Hillfield, Brodland, and Mill land . . .	010	00	00
The barony of Rossyth	016	00	00
The Wester part of Lochersrie [Locherschyre] . . .	014	00	00
The Loch heid	001	00	00
Lochgellie	003	00	00
Ludfinnante [or Lumphanan ?] . . .	003	00	00
Pitcarne and Cowquhales	006	00	00
Raith, Glenistoun and Powgull . . .	003	00	00
The Easter part of Lochorshire . . .	004	00	00
The Muirtoun, Strarudie, and Drumdonald . .	002	00	00
The two part of East Newtoun . . .	001	00	00
Balbathie	002	00	00

THE QUARTER OF DUNFERMLING.

	Lib.	s.	d.
Pittencrieffe, Galorig and Clune . . .	004	00	00
Urquhart	005	00	00
The twa part of Pitfirren	001	10	00
Pitconnaquhies	002	00	00
Pitdones	005	00	00
Half Carno (also Garno)	001	10	00
Bredland, Sawline, Sandiedub (?) . . .	002	00	00
Black Saulen	001	00	00
Cleishes	004	00	00

	Lib.	s.	d.	
The lands of Crambeth except Lindsay's part .	004	00	00	FFYFE.
Lindsay's part of Crambeth and Cleish .	005	00	00	—
Touchindad (?) . . .	000	10	00	
Allardyce with annuell of Cranbeth . .	001	00	00	
Cowdrane with the Maw . . .	004	00	00	
Tullieboill	005	00	00	
	950	10	00	

TAXT ROLL OF THE SHERIFDOME OF CLAKMANAN.

CLAK-
MANAN.

The barony of Menstrie . . .	020 00 00
The barony of Tulliebody . . .	020 00 00
The barony of Sauchie . . .	020 00 00
The barony of Alloay and Forrest . .	040 00 00
The barony of Clakmanan . . .	020 00 00
The barony of Shambodie . . .	020 00 00
The barony of Kennet . . .	002 00 00

KIRKLANDS IN THE SHERIFDOME.

The patrimony of Cambuskenneth	026 13 04
Maynes of Doller, Bank, Craighead, and Sheirdale, held of the Abbey of Dunfermline	020 00 00
The lands of Dollerkill, held of the Bishop of Dunkeld .	005 00 00
The barony of Tulliecultrie the King's propertie . .	020 00 00
	213 13 04

TAXT ROLL OF SHERIFFDOM OF STIRLING.

STIRLING.

The barony of Hayning	020 00 00
The barony of Callender	040 00 00
Auchincloich	005 00 00
Cattescleuch	002 00 00
Polknaif Levingston	001 00 00
Ramsay Lands pertaining to Mr Henry Foulis . . .	005 00 00
Daders [sic, Dalderse]	006 13 04

		Lб.	s.	d.
STIRLING.	Skaithmure	002	10	00
—	Castlecary	002	10	00
	The barony of Alveth and Kerse	040	00	00
	The barony of Arthbissat with Sandiland's lands	015	00	00
	The barony of Harbertshyre in propertie and tenendrie	060	16	08
	The Laird of Garden for a piece of land of Torwood and Gunershaw	002	00	00
	The barony of Elphinstoun	026	00	00
	The lands of Quarrell	002	10	00
	The barony of Beam with pertinents	025	00	00
	Polmais Cunningham	005	00	00
	His lands in Slamanan	002	00	00
	His lands in Arthbe, Powfouls, and Powknave	006	00	00
	His lands of Bothaldie	002	00	00
	His lands of Bissetlands beside Stirling: Heddefield, Torbrex, and Levielands	003	00	00
	The barony of Baquhadrock	005	00	00
	The barony of Bannockburn with tenents & tenendries	026	06	08
	Cambusbarron	008	00	00
	Goldenhuif [Cultinhuiff]	010	00	00
	Cangler	012	00	00
	Meikle Sauchie	008	00	00
	Dundaffemur	020	00	00
	Half of Inverallen	001	10	00
	Athray	019	00	00
	Queenshauch	001	00	00
	Morningside	016	00	00
	Whyterig	001	00	00
	The barony of Touchfrazer	020	00	00
	Gargunnoch	020	00	00
	Leckies Easter and Wester	020	00	00
	Culbeg and Culmore	006	13	04
	The barony of Boquhan	020	00	00
	Torrenterran with part of Slamanan	007	00	00
	Carden with the annexis	010	00	00
	The barony of Bochlyvie with the tenendries	030	00	00
	The barony of Fintrie	030	00	00
	The barony of Mugdock with the tenendries	040	00	00
	Kilsyth	016	00	00
	The barony of Auchtermony	016	00	00
	The barony of Buchanan	040	00	00
	My Lord Kilmaures lands with Croyes	013	06	08
	The Laird of Merchistonns lands	040	00	00

	Lib.	s.	d.
The lands of Blairinvaddes	005	00	00 STIRLING.
Drummekill Buchanan	004	00	00
Drumquhassils lands	020	00	00
Glengarnoch lands with Cameron	036	00	00
Duntreith lands	023	06	08
The Letter	005	00	00
Brainshogle	005	00	00
Ballikinraine	005	00	00
Glenegles lands of the barony of Haldau . .	030	00	00
Emboig, Cunningham and Kessane . . .	006	13	04
Houstoun's lands	012	00	00
Auchintroig	005	00	00
Finnick, Cashie, and Gartscairy	013	06	08
Garthnell	003	06	08
Gartquharran, or Gartfarran, Buchanan . .	002	10	00
Bulwhynning, Cameron and Camquhell . .	008	00	00
Culcreigh [? Culcreuch]	010	00	00
Balcorroch	013	00	00
Glorat and Baldrain	011	00	00
Craigbarnet with the tenendries . . .	016	00	00
Bandeith	010	00	00
Ballewne Buchanan	002	10	00
Ballewne Lennox	002	10	00
Bardowrie with the tenendries	030	00	00
Auchinhowie with the tenendries . . .	009	00	00
Colquhouns Glen	009	00	00
Craigroskan	010	00	00
Kilmardenny	005	00	00
Fergustoun	003	06	08
	1046	06	08

RETOUR OF THE SHIRE OF LANERK. LANERK.

NETHER WARD OF CLIDSDALE.

		Lib.	s.	d.
Cambusnethan . .	040	00	00
Dalzell . . .	040	00	00
Bothwell . . .	300	00	00
Munkland . . .	066	13	04
The Town of Rutherglen .	010	00	00

			Lib.	s.	d.
LANERK.	Aikenheid	.	010	00	00
—	Crawfuirds fermo	.	010	00	00
	Coutts	.	005	00	00
	Cassiltoun	.	013	06	08
	Carmunnock	.	013	06	08
	Catchkin [Cathkin]	.	013	06	08
	Cambuslang	.	040	00	00
	Blantyre	.	040	00	00
	Hamiltoun	.	090	00	00
	Machanshire	.	040	00	00
	Kilbryd and Glassfuird	.	200	00	00
	Avandale	.	160	00	00
	Stanehous	.	040	00	00
	Lesmahagow	.	200	00	00

THE OVER WARD OF CLIDSDALE.

		Lib.	s.	d.
Douglas	.	200	00	00
Crawfuird Douglas	.	200	00	00
Lamyntoun	.	040	00	00
Wistoun	.	040	00	00
Symontoun	.	040	00	00
Robertoun	.	040	00	00
Cowter [Culter]	.	040	00	00
Pittenane	.	040	00	00
Carnwath	.	200	00	00
Jerviswood and Broomlie		010	00	00
Cleghorne	.	020	00	00
The Lye	.	020	00	00
The Breadwood	.	020	00	00
Maulslie	.	050	00	00
Crawfurdjohn	.	066	13	04
Bonytoun	.	020	00	00
Carphyn [sic]	.	013	06	08
Stevenstoun	.	002	00	00
		2393	13	04

THE TAXT ROLL OF THE SHERIFEDOM OF RENFREW.

	Lib.	s.	d.
The Lordship of Eglisham pertaining to Lord Montgomery	066	13	04
The Mernis pertaining to Lord Maxwell	160	00	00
Eastwood pertaining to Lord Montgomery	020	00	00
Cathcart	040	00	00
Cruixse and Inchenane	100	00	00
Lie Cuningham heid	007	00	00
Cardonald and Easter Hendriestoun	011	00	00
Wester Hendriestoun	005	00	00
Lord Ross, Halkheid and Ralystoun	032	00	00
Saserhill and Hunterhill	002	00	00
Raislogan [Logan-Rais]	010	00	00
Raisstewart	001	03	04
Blackhall, Argownie, Auchingown and Fermock	020	00	00
Ramforlie, Knox & Griffiscastell	018	13	04
Selviland	001	00	00
Griffiscastell Monfyde	003	06	08
Houstoun	040	00	00
Barochan	020	00	00
Boighall	010	00	00
Fulwood Birkenheid	007	00	00
The Lordship of Erskine	066	13	04
Barscub	005	00	00
Donermuir [?]	005	00	00
Finlaystoun, Maxwell	002	10	00
The Lordship of Douthquhell [sic]	047	00	00
Craigbett, Tar and Threiplie	005	00	00
Ladmure	001	00	00
Greenoch and Fynnart	026	13	04
Greenoch Stewart	026	13	04
Spangoks	012	00	00
Dunrod	010	00	00
Kellie Bannatyne	005	00	00
Lundrisland	001	04	00
The town of Renfrew	010	00	00
Thorniclie, Blair	005	13	04
Stantlie and Thorniclie part of Kitchland	012	15	06
Ellerslie	005	00	00
Fowar [Foullar]	003	00	00

X

		Lib.	s.	d.
RENFREW.	Leichland, Ross and Leichland, Knox	002	04	04
—	Auchingrewt	003	06	08
	Craiginfcouch Chambers	003	06	08
	Laidtoun	005	00	00
	Knockmaid and Caldwell Easter . . .	008	06	08
	Caldwell Wester	003	06	08
	Authinbothic Sempill	003	06	08
	Authinbothie Wallace and Neather Johnstoun . .	009	06	08
	Girvane and Risk	008	00	00
	The lordship of Sempill propertie and tenandrie .	080	13	04
	Easter Cochran	006	13	04
	Wester Cochran	003	06	08
	Cauldershauch	005	00	00
	Auchnemes	013	06	08
	Over Johnstoun	002	10	00
	Lauchliebosyde	008	00	00
	Artherlie	003	06	08
	Porterfield	002	00	00
	Ramforlie, Coningham, Waterstoun and Finlaystoun .	061	06	08

THE KIRKLANDS OF THE SHIRE OF RENFREW.

	Lib.	s.	d.
The Lordship of Paisley, Glen and Auldhouss . .	109	06	08
The Lordship of Govane and the lands of Glasgow .	040	00	00
The Deanfield and the Chanon lands of Glasgow .	004	00	00
The Lyon cross of the Abbot land of Kilwining .	006	13	04

THE TEMPLE LANDS.

	Lib.	s.	d.
The chapel Rig	006	13	04
The two Freelands	005	00	00

THE KINGS PROPER LANDS—VIZ.:

	Lib.	s.	d.
The Blawhill, Zoker, and Kings meadow	010	00	00
	1239	00	06

TAXT ROLL OF THE SHIRE OF AIR.

(CALLED KINGS KYLE.)

	Lib.	s.	d.
Dalrymple	032	00	00
Martnan	080	00	00
Sundrum	040	00	00
Gaitgith	040	00	00
Ochiltree	066	13	04
Cumnoch	108	13	04
Langlands	010	00	00
Carnistoun	005	00	00
Drumdow	002	13	04
Wrighthill	002	13	04
Duchrays	005	06	08
Stair Montgomery	014	00	00
Stairquhite	006	00	00
Drongane	016	00	00
Polquhairne	010	08	04
Knokgulrimes	003	06	08
Monyhagane	005	06	08
Lochinssie	008	00	00
Shankistoun	004	00	00
Glasnock	005	06	08
Dalmelingtoun	033	06	08
	498	15	00

TAXT ROLL OF THE BALYIERE OF KYLE STEWART.

	Lib.	s.	d.
The Sornbeg	008	00	00
The Galstorn	020	00	00
Denholme, Achinruglen, Sornehill, Sorne and Milrig	010	00	00
The Bar and Galsholmes	036	00	00
The barony of Craigie and Riccartoun	133	06	08
Cappringtoun	020	00	00
Ardneill	002	13	04
Dreghorne	012	00	00

		Lib.	*s.*	*d.*
Sowaltoun	. . . . . .	005	00	00
Clavence	. . . . . .	005	00	00
Corrayt	. . . . . .	005	00	08
Corsbie and Craigistane	. . . .	025	00	00
The Mares and Gallis	. . . .	004	00	00
The Trone	. . . . .	002	00	00
The Fullartoun	. . . . .	002	00	00
Adamestoun	. . . . .	020	00	00
Barneill, Hamiltoun, and Barneill, Herries	. .	082	00	00
The barony of Auchinleck	. . .	033	06	08
Glenmuir	. . . . .	020	00	00
Auchintruiffs [Auchineruive]	. . . .	015	00	00
Giffen and Wrighthill	. . . .	066	13	04
Previck	. . . . . .	012	00	00
Bruntwood Campbell	. . . . .	002	00	00
The Laird of Sanquhar his lands in the Laich of Kyle by and attour the barony of Barneill-Hamiltoun & Barneill-Herries		041	06	08
Colynane	. . . . . .	005	00	00
Hilhous and Holmes	. . . . .	005	00	00
Helhies and Haly	. . . . .	010	00	00
Cesnock	. . . . . .	040	00	00
Dundonald being the Kings lands	. . .	020	00	00
Torboltoun	. . . . .	100	00	00
The 20 merk land called Meikle Dreghorn lying in Cuningham and annext to bailyerie of Kyle Stewart	. . .	...		
The Hayning	. . . . . .	020	00	00
Camieslane	. . . . . .	006	13	04
		789	**00**	**08**

Left margin: KYLE STEWART.

THE RETOURS OF THE FREEHOLDERS OF CUNYNHAME.

Loudoun	. . . . . .	100	00	00
Grugor	. . . . . .	040	00	00
Robertoun pertaining to Earl of Eglintoun	. .	040	00	00
Kilmaures, Stevingstoun and Corsbie	. . .	100	00	00
Rowallan	. . . . . .	066	13	04
Kilmarnoch and Dawry [Dalry]	. . .	100	00	00
Powkellie	. . . . . .	020	00	00
Cunynghamcheid	. . . . .	010	00	00
Peirstoun, Barklay	. . . . .	010	00	00
Stane	. . . . . .	010	00	00

	Lib.	s.	d.	
Knochintibber and Bushbie	011	13	04	KYLE
Colinskeith [sic]	010	00	00	STEWART.
Eglintoun	020	00	00	
Fairle-Crevoch	006	13	04	
Meikle Dreghorne	013	06	08	
Dunlop	013	06	08	
Aikit	001	13	04	
Glengarnoch	026	00	00	
Laird of Langshaw	020	00	00	
Fairley	010	00	00	
Ladyland	013	06	08	
Laird of Robertland	017	06	08	
Kilburny	033	06	08	
Pitcon	004	13	04	
Lochrig	005	00	00	
Brumelands	005	00	00	
Kelburn	005	00	00	
Giffertland	013	06	08	
Ardrossane	100	00	00	
Blair	053	06	08	
Rysholme	007	06	08	
Southenane	013	06	08	
Tarbet	013	06	08	
Monfoid	010	00	00	
Hunterstoun	006	13	04	
Aradill and Portincross . . .	006	13	04	
Montgrenan	006	13	04	
Largis bishoptoun . . .	005	06	08	
Knock	010	00	00	
Kelsoland	010	00	00	
Lord Casills lands of Stewartoun, Irvine, and Dunlop .	022	00	00	
	991	00	00	

THE TAXT ROLL OF CARRICK.

	Lib.	s.	d.
The barony of Cassills, propertie and tenendrie	148	00	00
The barony of Dunure and Cairnleck . .	036	13	04
The barony of Culzean . . .	020	00	00
The barony of Bargany . . .	026	13	04
The barony of Ardsher [sic] . . .	050	00	00
The barony of Kirkoswell . . .	012	00	00

		Lib.	s.	d.
CARRICK. The barony of Glenassil, Daltippand, and Newark	. .	054	13	04
The Laird of Blairquhane	. . . . .	055	00	00
The Laird of Knockdolian	. . . . .	066	13	04
The Laird of Carltoun	. . . . .	066	13	04
The barony of Glenstincher and Mt. Cumyne	. . .	020	00	00
The Laird of Dalquharran	. . . .	006	00	00
The Laird of Drumelland	. . . . .	012	06	08
The Laird of Balmaclonchan	. . . .	020	00	00
The Laird of Trochrig	. . . . .	010	00	00
The Laird of Girvanmaynes	. . . .	010	00	00
Montgomerystoun	. . . . .	002	06	08
The Balloch	. . . . .	004	10	00
The lands of Prymont	. . . .	003	13	04
The lands of Kirkpatrick Glenassill	. . .	005	00	00
The lands of Trolorg	. . . . .	002	10	00
The Laird of Dundas	. . . . .	021	00	00
The Laird of Keires	. . . . .	015	00	00
The Laird of Kirkmichaell	. . . .	013	06	08
The lands of Cumray	. . . . .	010	00	00
The lands of Brochlach	. . . .	008	00	00
Lands of Machriemore, Balinleuch, Burnfitt and Lochspallander		008	00	00
The Laird of Kelwood	. . . . .	014	00	00
The Laird of Corverbae	. . . .	016	00	00
The Laird of Craigcaffie	. . . .	002	00	00
The lands of Callochwreich	. . . .	010	00	00
The Laird of Barneill, Maclane	. . .	004	00	00
The Laird of Barneill, MacCrymill	. . .	004	00	00
The Lands of Garfoir	. . . . .	001	06	08
The Laird of Midle Auchindryne	. . .	003	06	08
The Laird of Bridgend	. . . .	003	06	08
The lands of Auchinflor	. . . .	002	13	04
The Laird of Kilquhenzie	. . . .	007	00	00
The Laird of Grumet	. . . . .	008	06	08
The Laird of Benan	. . . . .	004	06	08
The Laird of Carslo	. . . . .	004	00	00
The Laird of Conclad [Cloncaid]	. . .	003	06	08
The Laird of Kerss	. . . . .	010	00	00
The lands of Dalquhand	. . . .	003	06	08
The lands of Gass	. . . . .	003	06	08
The Laird of Camragan	. . . .	005	00	00
The Laird of Corsays	. . . . .	002	06	08
		819	13	04

THE TAXT ROLL OF THE SHERIFEDOM OF WIGTOWN.

	Lib.	s.	d.
The Laird of Corswells lands	038	06	00
Bonchtrig [sic]	006	13	04
Laird of Garthlands	026	00	00
Laird of Kinhilts lands	021	13	04
Laird of Freuchs lands	015	06	08
Laird of Stronrawers lands	003	06	08
Laird of Knockincross	001	13	04
Laird of Lesmuir	010	00	00
Laird of Portincross	020	00	00
Laird of Craigcassie	008	00	00
Laird of Craich	002	06	08
Laird of Craichlaw, M'Kee	016	13	04
Laird of Mochrum Park	053	06	08
Laird of Mochrum Loche	050	13	04
Laird of Merton, M'Culloch	053	06	08
Laird of Glassartoun	025	00	00
Laird of Fersigill	003	06	00
Laird of Polmallart	003	06	08
Laird of Coutts	005	00	00
Laird of Brochtoun	010	00	00
Laird of Egerns [?] and Balcur . . .	008	13	04
Laird of Sorbie	023	06	08
Laird of Clouch	005	00	00
Laird of Rennistoun	043	06	08
Laird of Libreck	006	13	04
Laird of Barnbarroch	013	06	08
Laird of Capanoch	003	10	00
Laird of Clugestoun	025	13	04
Laird of Curhous, M'Culloch . . .	007	06	08
Laird of Curhous, M'Kee	002	13	04
Laird of Curhous, Mure	004	00	00
Laird of Drumquhat alias Coatland . . .	004	00	00
Laird of Barrawer [sic]	007	13	04
Laird of Auchlown	006	13	04
Laird of Glenturk	004	13	04
The Laird of Kilcreach	039	00	00
Sheriffe of Wigtouns lands	013	06	08
Laird of Logan	025	06	08

		Lib.	s.	d.
WIGTOWN.	Laird of Creichlaw Gordon	031	13	04
—	The Laird of Cairnefield	003	06	08
	The Laird of Muireth	020	00	00
	Laird of Mertoun's heirs	025	13	04
		698	15	04

THE TAXT ROLL OF STEWARTRIE OF KIRKCUDBRIGHT.

KIRKCUD-
BRIGHT.

	Lib.	s.	d.
The Laird of Garleys lands	051	00	00
Kenmure and Lagan	012	13	04
Balmaclellan and Park	013	06	08
Torskrothand and Dalbato	010	00	00
Dunrod Sannik	003	06	08
Glenshyreburne & Over Pollerie	022	13	04
Ewingstoun, Blackcraig & Knocknow	002	13	04
Harlands and Moneboy	004	00	00
Nether Polereo and Creoch	004	13	04
Catbullie	010	00	00
Laird of Camlodan, Murdoch	010	00	00
Laird of Larg	014	00	00
Laird of Camlodan, M'Lurg	010	00	00
Laird of Mathrimoire	003	06	08
Laird of Cockpool	030	00	00
James M'Culloch of Barholme	003	06	08
Laird of Nisbet of that Ilk	007	00	00
Laird of Cuiltoun, Pittillo	007	00	00
John Gordon of Holme	004	00	00
Laird of Craigo-Gordon	005	00	00
Laird of Craigo-M'Eligan	005	00	00
Alec Gordon of Hardlands	001	00	00
Laird of M'Kittrick for Callathie	003	00	00
Laird of Gaitgirth for Fintilloch	017	06	08
Laird of Gailstoun	042	00	00
Laird of Brochtoun	040	13	04
Laird of Cardineis	062	13	04
Laird of Bombie	070	00	00
Laird of Apilgirth	016	00	00
Thomas M'Lellan of Auchlene	002	00	00
Laird of Lag	012	13	04

	Lib.	s.	d.
Duchra	010	00	00
Laird of Livingstoun for Little Ardes	020	00	00
The Aires Portioners of Blaithet	009	06	08
The Laird of Spotts	012	13	04
The Laird of Ochartoun	015	00	00
The laird of Kirkdale	008	00	00
Laird of Calie for Calie Kirkenan Ballochan, Blackbullie & Maynes	041	06	08
Laird of Fairgirth	014	13	04
Laird of Barscob	003	06	08
Laird of Blairquhan	050	00	00
Laird of Lag for Drumhoward	037	06	08
Laird of Lauchop for Balgreddan	006	13	04
Laird of Dalbatie for Barkarrow	003	06	08
James Gordon for Gaidzell	005	00	00
" " for Barnbarrow & Barnhowrie	004	00	00
Laird of Kirkconnell	013	06	08
Laird of Kilquhanadie	006	13	04
Lachinquhing [sic]	003	06	08
Brown of Carsluth	012	13	04
Littletoun	002	00	00
Laird of Drumconcren for Coklex, etc.	002	13	04
Laird Sipeland [?]	006	13	04
Midlethryd	006	13	04
Herries of Maidenpapes	006	00	00
Laird of Partoun	040	00	00
Laird of Balmaghie	020	00	00
M'Torrie in Keltone	008	13	04
Maxwell of Hillis	012	00	00
Laird Garro	005	00	00
Daltoune, Castlemady & Kelmoney [sic]	006	13	04
Laird Troquhane	005	06	08
Laird of Killerne	002	00	00
Castramen and Dirregoun	003	06	08
Culcreoch and Grobdaill	005	00	00
Gordon of Auchinreoch	003	06	08
Laird of Barnsoul	003	06	08
Gordonston	026	13	04
Earlestoun	026	13	04
Grenan	014	00	00
Kirkpatrick Irnegray	020	00	00
Borgis	020	00	00

KIRKCUD-
BRIGHT.

						Lib.	s.	d.
KIRKCUD-BRIGHT.	Barnbathie	.	.	.	.	006	00	00
	Chapmanleyes	.	.	.		000	13	04
	Prestoune	.	.	.		040	00	00
	Kirkguinzeane	.	.			040	00	00
	Half barony of Urherries [*sic*]		.			053	06	08
						1163	00	00

TAXT ROLL OF THE SHIRE OF DUNFREIS.

Carlaverock	.	.	.	.	053	06	08
Carneshalloch and Duriesqueens	.	.	.	014	13	04
Tynwald	.	.	.	.	020	00	00
Dunow [Duncow]	.	.	.		020	00	00
Millheid within Kirkmacho	.	.	.	002	00	00
Lord Maxwell's land within Dunfreis	.	.	005	00	00
Haliwood barony	.	.	.	.	120	00	00
Terriglis	.	.	.	.	066	13	04
Kirkinizeane	.	.	.	.	040	00	00
Torthorwald	.	.	.	.	053	06	08
Dalswinton	.	.	.	.	041	00	00
Keltoun Maxwell	.	.	.	008	00	00
Kelwood Charters and Lowrie lands	.	.	010	00	00
Glencorss	.	.	.	.	002	10	00
Auldgirth	.	.	.	.	002	00	00
Kelwoodcraiggs	.	.	.	010	00	00
Barony of Sanquhar	.	.	.	120	00	00
Crawfuirdtoun	.	.	.	028	00	00
Kirkpatrick of the Gait	.	.	.	006	13	04
Barony of Glencarn	.	.	.	120	00	00
Auldgirth Dunduff	.	.	.	003	06	08
Monkland	.	.	.	.	040	00	00
Clossburn	.	.	.	.	048	00	00
Brigburgh	.	.	.	.	010	00	00
Aleisland	.	.	.	.	002	00	00
Assleck Sundrum and Layne	.	.	.	009	06	08
Kirkland of Dalgarno	.	.	.	005	00	00
The Ross	.	.	.	.	048	00	00
Drumlanrig	.	.	.	.	120	00	00
Tibbers	.	.	.	.	093	06	08

	Lib.	s.	d.
Dalgarnock	006	13	04	DUNFREIS.
Over Glencorss	002	00	00
Mortoun	040	00	00
Halydayhill	002	00	00
Knocke [Enoche]	020	00	00
Carzell and Kirktoun	010	00	00
Windichills, Charteris	002	00	00
John M'Brears lands within the territorie of Dunfreis .	002	00	00
Conhaitrig	003	06	08
Lag	004	13	04
Aird	014	00	00
Dalgarno holme	013	00	00
Windichills Greirson	005	00	00
Collyne	008	00	00
Tibbers called Messengers land . . .	006	13	04
Dunraggan and Bardony	005	00	00
Laird of Kirkmichaels lands	030	00	00
Durrisdeir	031	13	04
Hempisfield	040	00	00
Snaid	020	00	00
Ealis [sic, Eccles?]	020	00	00
	1408	03	04

TAXT ROLL OF THE SHIRE OF PEEBLES.

PEEBLES.

Caverstoun	.	005	00	00
Purveshill	.	005	00	00
Pyrn	.	005	00	00
Bold	.	016	00	00
Traquair . . .	.	020	00	00
Erleischortchert [Earle-orchard]	.	002	00	00
Glen	.	016	00	00
Grestoun . . .	.	012	00	00
Gillieshauch . . .	.	002	13	04
Cardron	..	010	00	00
Hopkello . . .	.	010	00	00
Henderstoun . . .	.	010	00	00
Hornehuntersland . .	.	005	00	00
Ormestoun Easter . .	.	010	00	00

		Lib.	s.	d.
PEEBLES.	Horsburgh	010	00	00
	Lermondshauch	000	13	04
	Smithfield	002	00	00
	Corscuningfeild	004	00	00
	Hutchingfield	001	05	00
	Melvingland	001	13	04
	Winkiestoun	002	10	00
	Fullage	003	06	08
	Blackbarony	040	00	00
	Kidston and Wormestoun	010	00	00
	Stewartoun	007	00	00
	Curhoip	002	00	00
	Dean Easter	004	00	00
	Romanno and quarter of Curhoip	007	13	04
	Bogend	004	00	00
	Holmyre	008	00	00
	Two Acre fields	000	06	08
	Kingsland	003	06	08
	Bonyngtoun	005	00	00
	Cruikstoun	005	00	00
	The barony of Halycards	010	00	00
	Maner pertaining to the Lowis and Hopringle	010	00	00
	Posso	010	00	00
	Glenrath	010	00	00
	Henderland	010	00	00
	Dawick	020	00	00
	Drumelzior	020	00	00
	Glenbrack	006	13	04
	Glenvinfuird	005	06	08
	Halkshaw	015	00	00
	Earlshauch	004	00	00
	Glencraig	004	00	00
	Langlandhill	002	00	00
	Baron of Bruchtoun	040	00	00
	Stoikfield	004	00	00
	Skirling	040	00	00
	Kircurd, Ladyurde	040	00	00
	Glenholme	030	00	00
	Swynhoip	010	00	00
	Burrowfield	000	10	00
	Eddarstoun [sic]	008	00	00
	Jedburghfield	002	00	00

	Lib.	s.	d.
Lynhoprews and Meggart	020	00	00	PEEBLES
Oliver Castle .	013	06	08	—
Esthells	020	00	00
Lintoun and Newlands	040	00	00
Kilbocho	066	13	04
	711	18	04

THE TAXT ROLL OF THE SHERIFEDOM OF SELKIRK.   SELKIRK.

	Lib.	s.	d.
The lands of Craig	013	06	08
The lands of Robertoun and Howcleuch . .	006	00	00
The lands of Borthwickbrae and Slake . .	010	00	00
The lands of Greenwood and Lyne . . .	005	00	00
The lands of Almure	010	00	00
The lands of Todrig	010	00	00
The lands of Hoistcoitts	002	00	00
The lands of Whitslands	006	13	04
The lands of Philhope	010	00	00
The lands of Bellendean and Buccleuch . .	020	00	00
The lands of Southsyntoun	010	00	00
Sonderland and Sonderlandhill . . .	010	00	00
The lands of Philiphauch	010	00	00
The lands of Holldane	005	00	00
The lands of Hadderslie and Baits . . .	005	00	00
The lands of the Lordship of Selkirk . . .	010	13	04
	143	13	04

TAXT ROLL OF THE SHERIFDOM OF ROXBURGH.   ROXBURGH.

	Lib.	s.	d.
The Laird of Cessfurd's lands . .	180	00	00
The Laird of Buccleuch's lands . .	063	13	04
The Laird of Fernihirst's lands . .	007	00	00
The Laird of Cranstoun's lands . .	077	08	04
The Laird of Mow's lands . .	010	00	00
Laird of Minto's lands . .	020	00	00
Laird of Hunthills lands . .	020	00	00
The Laird of Mackerstouns lands . .	060	00	00

		Lib.	s.	d.
ROXBURGH.	The Laird of Gladstanes lands	010	00	00
—	The Laird of Newtouns lands	008	00	00
	Laird of Riddell's lands	020	00	00
	The Laird of Langlands	010	00	00
	The Laird of Lochinvar's lands	040	00	00
	The Laird of Coldingknow's lands	010	00	00
	The lands of Clistoun in the hands of Drumelezor; the goodman of Torwoodlie; David Happringle of Hownand Walter Pringle in Clistoun and Pringle of Ashetrees . .	040	00	00
	The Laird of Overtoun	010	00	00
	The lands of Bedrewle	018	00	00
	The lands of Over and Nether Newhall : . .	004	00	00
	The Laird of Fulmashe's lands	010	00	00
	The Goodman of Gallowsheill's lands . . .	020	00	00
	The Laird of Midleshcills lands	010	00	00
	The Sheriff of Twedale's lands	020	00	00
	The Laird of Hadden's lands	010	00	00
	The Laird of Edmistoun's lands	020	00	00
	The Laird of Hundyke's lands [sic, also Lumleye's] . .	040	00	00
	The Laird of Edzartoun's lands	020	00	00
	The Lord Mortoun's lands of Longnewton . . .	013	06	08
	The Laird of Drumlenrig's lands	113	06	08
	The Laird of Clock's lands	005	00	00
	The Laird of Rayknow's lands	020	00	00
	The Laird of Harwood's lands	010	00	00
	The Laird of Litledeans lands	030	00	00
	The Laird of Bonjetburt's lands [Bonjeddars] . . .	020	00	00
	The Laird of Greenhead's lands	011	00	00
	Laird of Wauchops lands	010	00	00
	The Laird of Dowcates lands	006	13	04
		997	08	04

LAWDER-DALE.   ## TAXT ROLL OF THE BAILYARIE OF LAWDERDALE.

	Lib.	s.	d.
Tulloushill	005	00	00
Barony of Blyth	005	00	00
Thirlestane	005	00	00
Eastmaynis, Westmaynis, and Woodencleuch . .	005	00	00
Egrop	002	00	00

	Lib.	s.	d.	
Nenetharne	010	00	00	LAWDER-
Litle Newtouns	003	06	08	DALE.
Laird of Wachtouns lands	003	06	06	
Laird of Haygitsyde's lands	003	06	08	
Lands of Dalcove pertaining to Thomas Ker of the Shaw .	005	00	00	
Six husbandlands of Robert Lauder of that Ilk . .	002	00	00	
Andro Ker of the Scheird's lands	003	00	00	
For his lands in Myretoun	005	00	00	
Lands of Myretoun, Boutcher; Coitt and Lochflatt, Henry Halliburton	010	00	00	
Lands of Bemersyde	010	00	00	
Whyterig and Brotherstanes	002	00	00	
Forrest of Lauther	005	00	00	
Ladiepart	002	00	00	
Whytlaw pertaining to Laird of Haltoun . . .	002	00	00	
Trabroun	005	00	00	
Pilmuir	005	00	00	
James Borthwick of Cocklaw	004	00	00	
Hartsyde	005	00	00	
Kirktounhill	002	00	00	
Greingilt	004	00	00	
Haitshaw	002	00	00	
Carfray	010	00	00	
Adinstoun	010	00	00	
Lord Saltouns lands in Ugstoun	002	00	00	
His lands of Quholiplaw	005	00	00	
His lands of Eylistoun [Lylestoun]	004	00	00	
John Cranstoun of Burncastle	002	00	00	
Newbigging	005	00	00	
	152	19	10	

RETOUR OF THE SHIRE OF BERWICK.   BERWICK.

West Nisbet . . .	015	00	00
Wedderburn . .	017	00	00
Balcadder and Hatoun	017	00	00
Aytoun . .	020	00	00
Ershell . .	005	00	00
Cockburn . .	005	00	00

		Lib.	s.	d.
DERWICK.	Cumlego	001	10	00
—	Lethington	005	00	00
	Foulden	010	00	00
	Hornden and Half Hartoun	007	00	00
	Edmesdains	002	00	00
	Hoprigs and the sheills	005	00	00
	Ellein [Ellem]	005	00	00
	Cranshaws	004	00	00
	Longformachouse	004	00	00
	Ryslaw	010	00	00
	Messingtoun [Mersington]	005	00	00
	The west quarter of Whystoun	003	10	00
	Riccartouns, Hopburn	010	00	00
	Growelldyks	002	10	00
	Bassinden	003	00	00
	Meikle Harlaw	002	00	00
	Ranburn	004	00	00
	Reidpath	002	00	00
	Burnhouss	002	00	00
	Easter Winsheills	000	10	00
	Barony of Bonclo	030	00	00
	Langtoun	020	00	00
	Lord Home's, lands	050	00	00
	Coldenknows	009	00	00
	Purves of Purveshauch	002	00	00
	Laird of Touch	004	00	00
	Spottiswood	005	00	00
	Thornedykes	005	00	00
	Woderlie	005	00	00
	Mellestanes	007	00	00
	Hopringle for Faroms [?]	001	10	00
	Legertwood	005	00	00
	Birkinsyde	004	00	00
	The barony of Boune	012	00	00
	The barony of Haliburtoun	005	00	00
	The Laird of Greenlaw	005	00	00
	The Laird of Reidbraes & Polwart	007	00	00
	Brentoun, Welsitland [sic] & Quickwood	004	10	00
	Laird of Bowmaker	003	00	00
	West Borthwick	001	00	00
	Butterdane	003	00	00
	Blackburne	003	00	00

	Lib.	s.	d.	
Darchester and Graden .	003	00	00	BERWICK.
Whytsounlaws . .	005	00	00	
Prandergeist . . .	012	00	00	
Wyliecleuch . . .	002	10	00	
Easter Borthwick . .	001	00	00	
Labroshiell [?] . .	001	00	00	
John Skeith of Overburn .	001	00	00	
Belchester . . .	002	00	00	
Richard Edgar for Bassindane	002	00	00	
	387	10	00	

THE TAXT ROLL OF CONSTABULARIE OF HADDINGTOUN.

	Lib.	s.	d.
The Laird of Bass	030	00	00
The Laird of Wachtoun	030	00	00
The Laird of Hermistoun	030	00	00
Eistcraig	001	10	00
Fentoun Tellor	002	00	00
Laird of Neather Sydsersse	002	00	00
Cokairis now Home in Pincartoun . . .	002	00	00
Blanss	002	00	00
Staniepeth	003	00	00
Innerweik	020	00	00
Gilkerstoun	001	00	00
Petkoks Thornedyks	001	00	00
Whytelaw	004	00	00
Spott	013	00	00
Gamesheills	002	10	00
Routhlaw	005	00	00
Newton	010	00	00
Hoprig and Penstoun	006	13	04
Alderstoun	004	00	00
Ormestoun	010	00	00
Laird of Colliston	006	13	04
Laird of Leuchie	001	00	00
Letham	010	00	00
Hartriewood	005	00	00
Easter Gairmtoun	010	00	00
Thuristoun	020	00	00

z

		Lib.	s.	d.
HADDING-TOUN.	Humbie	001	00	00
	Spotsheill	001	00	00
	Coldenstanes	000	06	00
	Wait in Belheaven	000	03	00
	Aitkin in Dunbar	000	13	04
	Earle of Bothwell	066	13	04
	Lord Yester	040	00	00
	Lord Seatoun	040	00	00
	Lord Dirletoun	040	00	00
	Lord Lindsay	030	00	00
	Lord Saltoun	020	00	00
	Lord Keith	020	00	00
	Lord Home of Thornetoun	020	00	00
	Lord Home of Douglas	010	00	00
	The Earle of Angus for Thometallon	010	00	00
	Lord Oliphant for Hedderwick	006	13	04
	Lord of Leithingtoun	010	00	00
	Boltoun	005	13	04
	Stevingstoun	005	00	00
	Laird of Whittinghame	006	03	04
		565	12	04

TAXT ROLL OF THE SHERIFFDOM OF EDINBURGH.

The barony of Borthwick	040	00	00
The lands of Lord Creichtoun	030	00	00
The lands of Cranstoundow	005	00	00
The lands of Cranstoun-Riddell, Murray	005	00	00
The Laird of Dalhousies lands	020	00	00
Laird of Roslings	040	00	00
The barony of Pennicuick	010	00	00
The lands of Newhall	003	06	08
The lands of Halbous	001	00	00
The lands of Gilmertoun pertaining to the Laird of Whythill	001	00	00
Whythill pertaining to the Laird of Cambusnethem	005	00	00
Lands of Gilmertoun pertaining to the Laird of Niddrie Marshall	005	00	00
Lands of Gilbertoun	003	00	00
Lands of Niddrie-Mershal, Wachope	010	00	00
Lands of Niddrie-Mershal, Edmistoun	005	00	00
Laird of Craigmillar's lands	040	00	00

	Lib.	s.	d.
Lands of Straitoun and Southouss belong to Laird of Straitoun	004	00	00 EDINBURGH.
Lands of Straitoun pertaining to the heirs of George Henderson of Fordell	005	00	00
Lands of Over Libertoun pertaining to John Carkettle . .	001	00	00
The barony of Glencross	010	00	00
Lands of Over Libertoun pertaining to Dalmahoy . .	005	00	00
The lands of Fulfuird	002	00	00
The lands of Priestfield	002	00	00
The lands of St Gely Grange	002	00	00
The barony of Dalmahoy	010	00	00
The barony of Maule	015	00	00
The Earle of Mortoun's lands	040	00	00
The lands of Cousland	010	00	00
Lands of Balarno and Newtoun . . .	010	00	00
The Laird of Calder's lands	040	00	00
Lands of Bonyntoun and Piltoun pertaining to Earle of Eglington	005	00	00
The Laird of Haltoun's lands	020	00	00
Warristoun and Spittellstoun	006	00	00
Lands of Malcolmstoun	007	00	00
Lands of Ratho, Marjoribanks	004	00	00
The barony of Currie and Longhirdmestoun . . .	005	00	00
Lands of Currie and Longhirdmestoun pertaining to James Mossman	002	10	00
Lands of Reidhous	002	00	00
Lands of Riccartoun	004	00	00
Lands of Hill	002	00	00
Lands of Whytelaw	001	00	00
Lands of Kilbawbertoun	000	10	00
Lands of Malleny	001	00	00
The barony of Collington	017	00	00
The lands of Redhall pertaining to John Morburn .	001	00	00
The lands of Woodhall and Bonaly . . .	008	00	00
Lands of Colmaston	003	00	00
Auchingane belonging to the Laird of Craigmiller .	001	00	00
Lands of Craiglockart	003	00	00
Lands of Gorgy	004	00	00
The lands of Merchiston	010	00	00
The lands of Wrights houss	004	00	00
The barony of Braid	010	00	00
The Laird of Corstorphin's lands . . .	040	00	00
The lands of Leny, Houstoun and Borthwich . .	010	00	00
The Laird of Innerleith's lands . . .	020	00	00
The Laird of Restalrigs lands	040	00	00

		Lib.	s.	d.
EDINBURGH.	The lands of Craighous	001	00	00
	The lands of Lawriestoun	005	00	00
	The lands of Muirhous	003	00	00
	Grantoun lands	003	00	00
	Balvillaw and Over Barntoun	005	00	00
	Lands of Lugtoun-Douglas	004	00	00
	Lands of Lugtoun-Creichtoun	002	00	00
	Land of Lockerworth and Middleton pertaining to Lord Yester	002	00	00
	Keitherd lands pertaining to Murray	002	00	00
	Lands of Harlaw, Crosbie and Adamestoun	002	00	00
	Lands of Cramond Regis, Adamesone	002	00	00
	Cramond Regis pertaining to Laird of Carmok	001	00	00
	Giffertlands in Cramond	000	10	00
	Douglas lands there	000	10	00
	Edwards lands there	000	10	00
	Clistoun and Clistoun hall pertaining to Laird of Pumphrastoun	004	00	00
	The lands of the Dean pertaining to Lord Lindsay	004	00	00
		651	16	08

TAXT ROLL OF THE SHERIFDOM OF LINLYTHGOW.

LINLYTH-
GOW.

	Lib.	s.	d.
The barony of Kinneill with tenents and tenendries	100	00	00
The barony of Carriden with tenents and tenendries	018	06	08
The barony of Dalmeny with do.	040	00	00
Tortraven	013	06	08
Prestoun	005	00	00
Waterstoun	005	00	00
Carriber	005	00	00
Portersyde	020	00	00
Dechmont	020	00	00
Muirhouse	020	00	00
Grugfut	005	00	00
The barony of Abercorn, with tenents and tenendries	061	00	00
The barony of Winchburgh with tenents and tenendries	038	00	00
Strabrock	040	00	00
The barony of Kinpont	015	00	00
Eleistoun	005	00	00
Little Kettilstoun	010	00	00
The barony of Levingstoun	020	00	00
Blackburn and Whytburn	010	00	00

				Lib.	*s.*	*d.*	
Polkennet	.	.	.	005	00	00	LINLYTH-
Binnings	.	.	.	007	00	00	GOW.
Bormey	.	.	.	005	00	00	
Bonsyde	.	.	.	001	00	00	
Bathgate	.	.	.	010	00	00	
Lochtullo	.	.	.	010	00	00	
Meikle-Blaikburn	.	.	.	010	00	00	
Bancreife	.	.	.	020	00	00	
Riccartoun	.	.	.	010	00	00	
Litle Parklie	.	.	.	001	00	00	
Hiltlie	.	.	.	001	00	00	
Hilhous	.	.	.	003	00	00	
Ethling	.	.	.	010	00	00	

KIRKLANDS IN LINLYTHGOW.

Kirklistoun with tenents and tenendries . .	024	00 00
Ecclesmachan.	026	13 04
Killeith	020	00 00
Queensferry	006	13 04
The barony of Ogilface in propertie and set in feu .	033	06 08
In tenendrie Cockburn's part . . .	005	00 00
Westcraigs	004	00 00
Eastcraigs	002	00 00
Baldlormy	004	00 00
The barony of Ketlestoun	014	13 04
Torphichin	066	13 04
Meikle Parkley	006	00 00
The Kirklands of Strabrock	001	06 08
The Kirkland of Abercorne	002	00 00
Kirkhill	006	13 04
Kinglass	003	00 00
Lochhous	006	13 04
The Grange	010	00 00
Part of Bynnings	005	00 00

THE KINGS PROPERTIE—*VIZ.*:

Bonyntoun	003	06 08
Blackness	004	00 00
Maynes of Abercorn, Morton and Mill	013	06 08
Kingcavil and the park . .	006	13 04
The Weard	002	00 00

		Lib.	*s.*	*d.*
LINLYTH- GOW.	Kingsfield .	000	10	00
	Houstoun .	010	00	00
	Drumcorse .	006	13	04
		837	16	08

THE ISLES.

RENTAL OF THE ISLES.

SHERIFFDOM OF AIR.

The Land of Kintyre is	480 merk land
of the which 240 merk land pertains to the Lord of the Isles' own house; and the other 240 given be him to James Kaynoch [*sic*] and his forebears	
Islay is	360 merk land
whereof 20 lib. land portanes to Macleane holden of the Lord of the Isles, and 40 merk land pertanes to James Kaynoch and 10 lib. land to Mackayne of Ardmorthyn [Ardnamurchan] and the remanent to the Lords own house	
The Isles of Teray is	140 merk land
The Lahararsis [*sic*] in the Isle of Mull . . .	20 lib. land
The Morargne	80 merk land
Swonartis	20 lib. land
Summa 1100 merk land of auld extent	

SHERIFFDOM OF INVERNESS.

Lands of Lochaber is	300 merk land
pertaining to the Lord of the Isles, Mamore and Garisdavock	
The Isle of Ouiss is	160 merk land
Slaite is	20 lib. land
Trotirness is	81 merk land
Summa of the haill Isles is .	1590 merk land

Item, the Lieutenandrie of the south and north Isles of Scotland, with the Lieutenandrie of the north side of the water of Spey; Commission to hold justice aires and courts of justiciarie with the execution and punishment of rebells both be fire and sword that contemneth our sovereign lord, his regiment, and authority, with the escheates of the barons and rebells that shall happen to be forfaulted and speciallie those who hold land of said lord of the Isles within the bounds of the Lieutenandrie foirsaid.

II.

GENERAL TAX ROLL OF 1633

(SHERIFFDOMS, STEWARTRIES, KING'S PROPERTY, BENEFICES, AND BURROWS)

SHERIFFDOMS, STEWARTRIES, ETC. (TERMLY).

Inverness	£2269	0 0
Caithness	514	0 3
Cromarty	73	11 2
Nairn	182	0 0
Elgin & Forres	310	0 0
Aberdeen	2732	3 6
Banff	799	0 0
Kincardine	570	0 0
Forfar	1649	6 0
Perth	2306	5 0
Strathern Stewartry	344	18 0
Menteith	129	13 6
Fife	1476	0 0
Kinross	101	10 0
Clackmanan	213	0 0
Stirling	1062	0 0
Lanark	3129	10 0
Renfrew	1581	11 0
Dunbarton	937	5 0
Argyle and Lorn	1233	5 0
Bute	103	0 0
Arran	150	0 0
Ayr	703	10 0
Kylestewart Bailiary	1106	10 0
Cuningham	1590	14 0
Carrick	1244	6 6
Wigtown	1059	0 0
Kirkcudbright	1714	10 0
Dumfriess, Eskdale & Wauchopdale	2354	5 0
Annandale Stewartry	2385	0 0
Liddesdale Lordship	400	0 0

Linlithgow	£742 0 0
Edinburgh	931 10 0
Haddington	850 13 6
Berwick	1567 13 9
Lauderdale Bailiary	215 10 0
Roxburgh	3133 2 6
Selkirk	183 10 0
Peebles	1089 15 0
	£43,138 8 8

THE KINGS PROPERTY (TERMLY).

Earldom of Orkney and Lordship of Zetland . . .	£900 0 0
Earldom of Ross	363 0 0
Lordship of Ardmanoch	140 0 0
Petty Braichlie, Strathnern and Cullaird . . .	90 0 0
Beaufort	7 10 0
Earldom of Murray	240 0 0
Abernethy	15 0 0
Urquhart, Glencarnie, Glenmoriston & Ballindalloch . .	80 0 0
Pittendreich, Sheriffston, Levenhauch, and Darclene . .	6 0 0
Lands of Duffus	30 0 0
One hundred merk lands of Braemar . . .	100 0 0
Garioch and Kintore	81 0 0
Lands of Wards	15 0 0
Lands of Warthill	3 0 0
Six-pound lands of Ruthven	9 0 0
The lands of Coull	3 15 0
The lands of Kincardine-Oneill . . .	5 0 0
Brechin and Navar	66 0 0
Kinclevin	152 0 0
Lordship of Dissoir and Toyer . . .	52 0 0
Lordship of Strathern	169 0 0
Thanedom of Fettercairn	28 16 0
Tilling-Campbell	15 0 0
Polgavie	12 0 0
Monteith	221 17 0
Stewartrie of Fyffe	196 0 0
Lordship of Stirling	150 0 0
Castle of Dumbarton	80 0 0

Howcleuch £6 land	£9	0	0
Hormangill, Whitegill and Southwood	20	0	0
Zoker (5-merk land)	5	0	0
Blavathill (Blawhill) (5-merk land)	5	0	0
Kings meadows	5	0	0
Cowal and Roseneath	27	0	0
Isle of Bute	200	0	0
Little Cumbray (5-merk land)	5	0	0
Dundonald (£20 land)	30	0	0
Stewartoun (40-merk land)	40	0	0
Trabench and Tarinzean (£40)	60	0	0
Thomastown (£10 land)	15	0	0
Glenhead (£10 land)	15	0	0
Carrick, Leswalt and Monebrigs	127	10	0
Lordship of Galloway	683	5	0
Duncow £20 land	30	0	0
Lordship of Linlithgow	96	15	0
Lordship of Balincreiff	52	10	0
Dunbar and Colbranpath	150	0	0
Earldom of March	334	18	0
Lordship of Ettrick Forrest	1000	0	0
Henderland (£5 lands)	7	10	0
Lordship of Kintyre	361	0	0
Isle of Jura	13	2	0
Trotterness (80-merk land)	80	0	0
Slate £20 land	30	0	0
North Uist, etc. (78 : 13 : 4 land)	118	0	0
Isle of Islay	236	12	0
Tyrie and Arros in Mull & Morven	258	2	0
Colonsay	21	5	0
Isle of Swonart	29	15	0
Ardnamurchan	73	10	0
Summa of Kings Propertie	£7370	13	0

PRELACIES AND SMALL BENEFICES (TERMLY).

ORKNEY.   ORKNEY.

Bishopric of Orkney .	.	£344 8 10
Archdeacon of Zetland	.	27 10 4

CAITHNESS.   CAITHNESS.

Bishopric	. . . . .	344 8 10
Deanery	. . . .	20 13 4
Chantorie	. . .	27 10 4
Chancellor } of Caithness	. . .	20 13 4
Archdeanry	. . . .	41 6 8
Treasurer	. . . .	30 0 0
Prebendary of Dunett	. . .	14 12 1
Parsonage of Kirkmichael	. . .	25 0 0

ROSS.   ROSS.

Bishopric of Ross	.	413 6 8
Abbacy of Fern	.	137 15 6
Priory of Beauly	.	103 6 8
Dean	.	41 6 8
Chantor	.	39 8 10
Chancellor	.	41 6 8
Treasurer } of Ross	.	41 6 8
Sub-dean	.	62 0 0
Sub-chantor	.	20 13 4
Arch-dean	.	41 6 8
Parsonage of—		
Rosken .	.	41 6 8
Kiltearn .	.	27 10 4
Logie Easter	.	27 10 4
Kirkmichael	.	31 0 0
Vicarage of Kilmuir .	.	20 13 4
Provostry of Tain	.	20 13 4

MORAY.   MORAY.

Bishopric of Moray	. . .	688 17 9
Lordship of Kinloss	. . .	447 12 7
Priory of Pluscarden .	. . .	275 10 10

Dean	£109 17 6	MORAY.
Chantor	113 6 8	
Chancellor	51 13 4	
Treasurer of Moray	82 13 4	
Archdean	51 13 4	
Sub-dean	20 13 4	
Sub-chantor	51 13 4	
Parsonage of—		
Dipple	27 10 4	
Duffus	51 13 4	
Spynie	35 5 6	
Moy	25 16 8	
Botarie	20 13 4	
Kinnoir	20 13 4	
Aberlour	20 13 4	
Rothes	20 13 4	
Vicarage of—		
Duthil	20 13 4	
Inverness	25 16 8	

ABERDEEN.

		ABERDEEN.
Bishopric of Aberdeen	688 17 9	
Priory of—		
Fyvie	68 17 9	
Monymusk	68 17 9	
Lordship of Deer	344 8 10	
Parsonage of—		
Philorth	27 10 4	
Kinkell	206 13 4	
Kincardine O'Neil	137 15 6	
Urie	41 6 8	
Banchorie	49 10 0	
Lunmey	20 13 4	
Belhelvie	49 10 0	
Coldstane	·20 13 4	
Clatt	27 10 4	
Invernochtie	35 5 6	
Cruden	41 6 8	
Tureff	103 6 8	
Metlick	35 5 6	
Aberdeen	41 6 8	
Tullinessil	20 13 4	

ABERDEEN. Parsonage of—

		£	s.	d.
Ruthven	. . . . .	£82	13	4
Murthlak	. . . . .	49	10	0
Fetteresso	. . . . .	103	6	8
Arbuthnot	. . . . .	68	17	6
Fottercairn	. . . . .	68	17	6
Conveth	. . . . .	68	17	6
Durris .	. . . . .	25	16	8
Fordoun	. . . . .	27	10	4

Vicarage of—

Piterugie	. . . . .	25	16	8
Longley .	. . . . .	20	13	4
Aberchirder	. . . . .	27	10	4
Inverurie	. . . . .	20	13	4
Tarves .	. . . . .	35	6	6
Logie durno	. . . . .	20	13	4
Coul	. . . . .	20	13	4
Aboyne .	. . . . .	20	13	4
Benholme	. . . . .	51	13	4
Dean	. . . . . .	122	6	8
Chantor	. . . . . .	41	6	8
Chancellor	. . . . .	47	18	9
Treasurer	. . . . . .,	41	6	8
Archdean	. . . . .	68	17	9

Common Kirks of Aberdeen (viz., Fordyce, Logie buchan, Rathin, Glenbucket, Logie-mar, Kildrumie and Drumeth) . 139 6 1

BRECHIN.

BRECHIN.

		£	s.	d.
Bishopric ⎫	. . . .	344	8	10
Dean ⎪	. . . .	55	0	8
Chantor ⎪	. . . .	27	10	4
Chancellor ⎬ of Brechin	. . . .	27	10	4
Treasurer ⎪	. . . .	20	13	4
Archdean ⎪	. . . .	34	7	1
Vicar ⎭	. . . .	34	7	1

Parsonage of—

Finaven	. . . .	34	7	1
Glenbervie	. . . .	34	7	1
Lethnot	. . . .	51	13	4
Dundee .	. . . .	68	17	6
Nevay .	. . . .	20	13	4

Parsonage of—

Esse	.	.	.	.	.	£27 10 4
Kinettles	.	.	.	.		34 7 1
Inverarity	.	.	.	.		41 6 8
Tannadies	.	.	.	.		68 17 6
Dunloppie	.	.	.	.		20 13 4
Logie Montrose	.	.	.	.		41 6 8
Inchbrek	.	.	.	.		68 17 6
Edvie	.	.	.	.		41 6 8
Kinneil	.	.	.	.		41 6 8
Edzell	.	.	.	.		34 7 1
Dumbarnie	.	.	.	.		62 0 0
Kinnoull	.	.	.	.		55 8 0
Forteviot	.	.	.	.		62 0 0
Cults	.	.	.	.		34 7 1

Vicarage of—

Dundee	.	.	.	.	.	68 17 6
Panbride	.	.	.	.	.	21 13 4
Lintrathen	.	.	.	.	.	20 13 4
Glamis	.	.	.	.	.	28 6 8
Kerriemuir	.	.	.	.	.	34 7 1
Longforgund	.	.	.	.	.	20 13 4

Lordship of—

Scone	.	.	861 2 2
Arbroath		.	2066 13 4
Coupar	.	.	861 2 2

Priory of—

Restennet	.	.	275 10 10
Charterhouse	.	.	334 8 10
Elcho	.	.	103 6 8

Provostry of Methven | . | 82 13 4

DUNKELD.

Bishopric of Dunkeld	.	.	.	1033 6 8
Abbey of St Colme	.	.	.	234 16 8
Priory of Straphillan	.	.	.	35 5 6
Chantor	.	.	.	27 10 4
Chancellor	.	.	.	35 5 6
Treasurer	.	.	.	35 5 6
Dean	of Dunkeld	.	.	.	123 16 8
Archdean	.	.	.	52 2 6
Sub-chantor	.	.	.	34 10 0

DUNKELD.	Parsonage of—					
	Menmuir	.	.	£51	13	4
	Monydie	.	.	27	10	4
	Mucharsie	.	.	27	10	4
	Fern .	.	.	27	10	4
	Lundiff .	.	.	23	5	0
	Crieff .	.	.	62	0	0
	Weems .	.	.	20	13	4
	Strowan .	.	.	20	13	4
	Blair .	.	.	20	13	4
	Vicarage of—					
	Strogaith	.	.	20	13	4
	Tibbermuir	.	.	20	13	4
	Logierait	.	.	20	13	4
	Don .	.	.	40	5	7
	Cargill .	.	.	20	13	4
	Prebendary of—					
	Fongorth	.	.	27	10	4
	Forguendenie	.	.	23	5	0
	Alveth .	.	.	20	13	4
	Common Kirks of Dunkeld—					
	Auchterhouse	.	.	41	6	8
	Meigil .	.	.	41	6	8
	Sawling .	.	.	26	1	2
	Fothergill	.	.	34	10	2

DUNBLANE.

Bishopric of Dunblane	.	334	8	10
Lordship of—				
Inchaffray	.	16	13	4
Inchmahome	.	275	10	10
Culross .	.	334	8	10
Dean ⎫		27	10	4
Archdean ⎬ of Dunblane	.	51	13	4
Chancellor ⎭	.	27	10	4
Provost of Abernethy	.	27	10	4
Parsonage of—				
Tullieallan		20	13	4
St Madoes		23	6	8
Vicarage of—				
Aberfoyle	.	20	13	4
Abernethie	.	20	13	4

ST ANDREWS.

		£	s.	d.
Archbishopric of St Andrews .	.	1722	4	6
Priory of—				
St Andrews	. .	1722	4	6
Portmook	. .	55	8	0
Pittenweem	. .	206	13	4
Eccles .	. .	172	4	5
Coldstream	. .	172	4	5
North-berwick .	.	516	13	4
Haddington	. .	516	13	4
Manuell	. .	55	5	8
Lordship of—				
Dunfermline	.	1722	4	6
Lindores	.	861	2	2
Balmerino	.	275	10	10
Holyroodhouse .	.	877	15	6
Newbottle	.	516	13	4
Kelso .	.	1377	15	6
Coldingham	.	688	17	9
Dryburgh	.	688	17	9
Barony of Brughton .	.	500	0	0
Ministry of—				
Scotlandwell		48	11	4
Peebles .		103	6	8
Archdean of—				
St Andrews	.	165	16	8
Lothian .	.	103	6	8
Provost of—				
Craill .	.	41	6	8
Kirkeuch	.	82	13	4
Corstorphin	.	27	10	4
St Giles .	.	82	13	4
Trinity College .		62	0	0
Crighton	.	51	13	4
Dalkeith	.	16	5	0
Bothans .	.	34	7	1
Dunglas .	.	27	10	4
Parsonage of—				
Tarbet .	.	27	10	4
Kemback	.	27	10	4
Dunno .	.	37	7	0

2 B

ST ANDREWS. Parsonage of—

	£	s.	d.
Flisk	51	13	4
Dysart	66	17	6
Cuilt	34	7	1
Auchterarder	51	13	4
Balingrie	41	6	8
Muckhart	34	7	1
Slamanan	20	13	4
Strabrock	51	13	4
Inchmachan	34	7	1
Caldercoats	55	0	8
Kirknewton	27	10	4
Gogar	27	10	4
Pentland	27	10	4
Pennicook	41	6	8
Leswalt	103	6	8
Melville	20	13	4
Restalrig	103	6	8
Carrington	27	10	4
Keithmarshal	20	13	4
Linton	103	6	8
Oldhamstocks	62	9	0
Dunbar	34	7	1
Moran	20	13	4
Pitcoks	34	7	1
Belcome	20	13	4
Spott	27	10	4
Upsetlington	20	13	4
Whitstone	34	7	1
Dunse	51	13	4
Ednam	27	10	4
Polwarth	26	13	4
Chirnside	20	13	4
Fowlden	20	13	4
Minto	20	13	4
Ashkirk	26	5	0
Auldroxburgh	62	0	0
Newbottle	55	0	8
Ancrum	37	7	1
Hawick	82	13	4
Wilton	27	10	4
Lempetlaw	20	13	4
Sudrum	20	13	4

Parsonage of—

Lintown	.	.	£20	13	4
Stobo .	.	.	134	8	10
Kilbucho	.	.	20	13	4
Stenton .	.	.	34	7	1
Kirkard .	.	.	27	10	1
Bedrule .	.	.	20	13	4
Newlands	.	.	82	13	4
Lyn .	.	.	34	7	1

Vicarage of—

Kilrynnie	.	.	.	.	.	20	13	4
Kinneuchar	.	.	.	.	.	41	6	8
Largo .	.	.	.	.	.	20	13	4
Sconny .	.	.	.	.	.	20	13	4
Kenair .	.	.	.	.	.	10	15	0
St Andrews	.	.	.	.	.	68	17	6
Leuchard	.	.	.	.	.	34	7	1
Coupar .	.	.	.	.	.	27	10	4
Markinch	.	.	.	.	.	27	10	4
Kirkcaldie	.	.	.	.	.	27	10	4
Kinghorn	.	.	.	.	.	34	7	1
Lathrisk	.	.	.	.	.	20	13	4
Stirling .	.	.	.	.	.	20	13	4
Falkirk .	.	.	.	.	.	62	0	0
St Cuthberts	.	.	.	.	.	27	10	4
Crimond	.	.	.	.	.	20	13	4
Linlithgow	.	.	.	.	.	32	5	7
Aberlady	.	.	.	.	.	20	13	4
Tranent .	.	.	.	.	.	20	13	4
Tinningham	.	.	.	.	.	55	0	8
Gulane .	.	.	.	.	.	20	13	4
Pencaithland	.	.	.	.	.	17	17	0
Haddington	.	.	.	.	.	27	10	4
Musselburgh	.	.	.	.	.	27	10	4
Earlston	.	.	.	.	.	27	10	4
Lindean	.	.	.	.	.	20	13	4
Castletown	.	.	.	.	.	20	13	4
Ettleston	.	.	.	.	.	68	17	6
Peebles .	.	.	.	.	.	27	10	4
Inverleithen	.	.	.	.	.	34	7	1
Linton .	.	.	.	.	.	27	10	1
Stobo .	.	.	.	.	.	34	7	1
Sacrist of Cleish	.	.	.	.	.	68	17	6

ST ANDREWS. Abbey of—

	£	s	d
Cambuskenneth	861	2	2
Jedburgh	516	13	4
Melrose	1124	0	0

Preceptory of—

Torphichen	516	13	4
St Anthony's	34	7	0
Archpriestry of Dunbar	41	6	8

Prebendary of—

Pincarton	27	10	4
Falaw	34	7	1
Dean of Dunbar	68	17	6
Kirk of Houston	41	6	8

GLASGOW.

GLASGOW.

Archbishopric of Glasgow	1033	6	8

Lordship of—

Paisley	1387	16	6
Kilwinning	688	17	10

Abbey of—

Corsrugall	275	10	10
Holiwod	239	16	8
New Abbey	344	8	10

Dean	138	6	8
Chantor	82	13	4
Chancellre of Glasgow	82	13	4
Treasurer	82	13	4
Archdean	138	6	8
Subdean	138	6	8
Ministry of Faill	175	5	4

Priory of—

Blantyre	20	13	4
Cannabie	20	13	4

Parsonage of—

Glasgow	138	6	8
Air	138	6	8
Renfrew	55	0	8
Govan	55	0	8
Carstairs	20	13	4
Cardross	34	7	1
Eaglesham	55	0	8
Kilrennie	55	0	8

Parsonage of—   GLASGOW.

Douglas	.	£55 0 8
Cambuslang	.	27 10 4
Torbolton	.	82 13 4
Cumnock	.	82 13 4
Luss .	.	82 13 4
Sanquhar	.	51 13 4
Kirkmaho	.	94 10 0
Durisdeer	.	41 6 8
Stanhouse	.	51 15 0
Strathaven	.	86 5 0
Glasford	.	34 7 1
Crawford-john	.	50 0 0
Culter .	.	41 6 8
Biggar .	.	35 5 6
Hartsyde	.	35 5 6
Lamington	.	35 5 6
Carmichaél	.	20 13 4
Liberton	.	51 13 4
Covington	.	20 13 4
Dolphington	.	20 13 4
Thankerton	.	20 13 4
Colyquhen	.	30 0 0
Inchalleoch	.	47 10 0
Monieabroch ·	.	27 10 4
Southwick	.	27 10 4
Kirkquhian	.	41 6 8
Kirkpatrick Irongray	.	27 10 4
Tynwald	.	34 7 1
Kirkmichael	.	20 13 4
Garvald .	.	20 13 4
Kilpatrick Juxta	.	20 13 4
Apilgeirth	.	27 10 4
Lochmaben	.	27 10 4
Ruthwill	.	20 13 4

Vicarage of—

Glasgow	27 10 4
Moffat .	51 13 4
Erskine .	40 9 0
Barlandrig	41 6 8
Mearns .	20 13 4
Eastwood	20 13 4
Kilbarchan	20 13 4

GLASGOW. Vicarage of—

Kilmacolm	.	.	.	.	£27 10 4
Innerkip		.	.	.	20 13 4
Erskine	.	.	.	.	20 13 4
Calder & Monkland		.	.	.	27 10 4
Kilcalton	.	.	.	.	27 10 4
Kilpatrick	.	.	.	.	47 10 0
Dalry	.	.	.	.	35 5 6
Dunlop	.	.	.	.	27 10 4
Kilmaurs	.	.	.	.	20 13 4
Kilburn	.	.	.	.	20 13 4
Gawston	.	.	.	.	20 13 4
Dreghorn	.	.	.	.	20 13 4
Dundonald	.	.	.	.	27 10 4
Stewarton	.	.	.	.	20 13 4
Mayboll	.	.	.	.	27 10 4
Kirkbean	.	.	.	.	51 13 4
Ure	.	.	.	.	27 10 4
Dumfriess	.	.	.	.	28 13 4
Penpont	.	.	.	.	27 10 4
Dunscor	.	.	.	.	20 13 4
Kirkbrid	.	.	.	.	34 7 1
Kirkconnell	.	.	.	.	27 10 4

Provostry of—

Bothwell	.	.	.		103 6 8
Hamilton	.	.	.		20 13 4
Dumbarton	.	.	.		165 0 0
Lincudden	.	.	.		206 13 4
Common Kirks of Glasgow	.		.		138 6 8

GALLOWAY.

Bishopric of Galloway	.	.		.	344 8 10

Abbey of—

Thongland		.	206 13 4
Dundrennan		.	516 13 4
Glenluce		.	344 8 10
Saulset	.	.	138 8 6

Priory of—

Whithorn	.	.	1033 6 8
St Mary's Isle	.	.	103 6 0
Archdean of Galloway		.	82 13 4

Parsonage of—

Kirkeanor	. £4138	6	8
Wigtown	. 68	17	6
Dalry .	. 55	8	0
Partown .	. 27	10	4
Kirkcrist	. 27	10	4
Kellis .	. 32	0	0
Balmaclellan	. 27	10	4

Vicarage of—

Moniegaff	25	16	8
Anwith .	20	13	4

THE ISLES.

Bishopric of the Isles .	. 206	13	4
Abbey of Inchcolmkill	. 344	8	10

ARGYLE.

Bishopric of Argyle . .	. 172	4	5
Prior of Ardchattan . .	. 103	6	8
Archdean of Argyle . .	. 27	10	4
Parsonage of Glassiter .	. 27	10	4
	£48,342	8	7

BURROWS (TERMLY).

Edinburgh . .	. £4791	9	0
Perth . .	. 917	0	0
Dundee . .	. 1555	16	0
Aberdeen . .	. 1333	6	8
Glasgow . .	. 916	13	4
St Andrews . .	. 500	0	0
Dysart . .	. 250	0	0
Stirling . .	. 300	0	0
Lithgow . .	. 250	0	0
Ayr . . .	. 344	8	10
Haddington . .	. 300	0	0
Kirkaldie . .	. 388	17	9

			£	s.	d.
Montroso	.	. . .	£444	2	2
Coupar	.	. . .	200	0	0
Anstruther East		. . .	258	6	8
Dumfries	.	. . .	366	13	4
Inverness	.	. . .	333	6	8
Brechin	.	. . .	116	13	4
Irvine	.	. . .	191	13	4
Elgin	.	. . .	166	13	4
Jedburgh	.	. . .	150	10	0
Kirkcudbright		. . .	166	13	0
Wigton	.	. . .	125	0	0
Pittenweem	.	. . .	125	0	0
Dunfermline	.	. . .	100	0	0
Dunbarton	.	. . .	100	0	0
Renfrew		. . .	83	6	8
Lanark		. . .	133	6	8
Arbroth	.	. . .	83	6	8
Burntisland	.	. . .	138	17	8
Peebles	.	. . .	83	6	8
Cryle [sic, Crail]		. . .	200	0	0
Kinghorn	.	. . .	122	0	0
Tayne	.	. . .	100	0	0
Anstruther W.	.	. . .	55	11	1
Selkirk	.	. . .	83	6	8
Culross	.	. . .	100	0	0
Dunbar	.	. . .	100	0	0
Banff	.	. . .	66	13	4
Whithorn	.	. . .	41	13	4
Forfar	.	. . .	55	11	1
Rothsay	.	. . .	41	13	4
Forres	.	. . .	50	0	0
Rutherglen	.	. . .	41	13	4
North berwick		. . .	33	6	8
Cullen	.	. . .	33	6	8
Nairn	.	. . .	33	6	8
Lauder	.	. . .	41	13	4
Inverkeithing		. . .	83	6	8
Kilrennie		. . .	25	15	6
Lochmaben	.	. . .	27	15	6
Sanquhar	.	. . .	27	15	6
Annan		. . .	27	15	6
New Galloway		. . .	8	6	8
			£16,613	18	7

INDEX.

2 c

www.ingramcontent.com/pod-product-compliance
Lightning Source LLC
Chambersburg PA
CBHW020847270326
41928CB00006B/590